The shifting worlds of Kiran Nagarkar's fiction

The shifting worlds of Kiran Nagarkar's fiction

Edited by
Yasmeen Lukmani

INDIALOG PUBLICATIONS PVT. LTD.

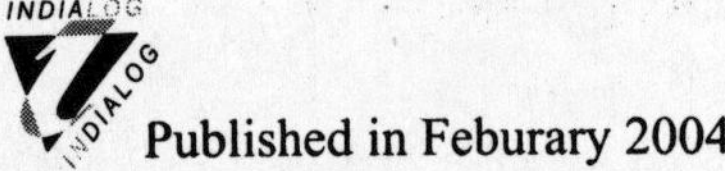

Published in Feburary 2004

Indialog Publications Pvt. Ltd.
O - 22, Lajpat Nagar II
New Delhi - 110024
Ph.: 91-11-29839936/29830504
Fax: 91-11-29834798
www.indialogpublications.com
www.onepageclassic.com

Printed at Chaman Offset Printers, Darya Ganj, New Delhi.

ISBN 81-87981-59-8

Contents

Introduction

I would like to begin with a quotation from Makarand Paranjape's review of *Cuckold* in *The Pioneer* (April 5, 1997):

> Kiran Nagarkar's *Cuckold* is a most extraordinary novel. Alas, I doubt whether we have the means and the ability to appreciate it, applaud it, and promote it in a fitting manner. Our book industry or culture of reading is just not equipped to recognize what a splendid achievement it is.

It is surprising how often the press, critics and readers point out that Kiran Nagarkar's *Cuckold* is one of the most under-rated and overlooked books in the canon of post-independence literature. This is somewhat difficult to explain since Nagarkar's works are not just engaging but veritable page-turners.

It is partly to redress this situation that this volume has been undertaken. It is an attempt to look at Nagarkar's fictional oeuvre, place it in the perspective of current writing in English in India, consider the enormous variety that exists in the three novels he has written, and examine the range of values, cultural milieus and fictional techniques that he presents.

How does one explain why *Cuckold* is not far better known, both in India and abroad? Why has it not attracted the kind of interest and readership that it richly deserves in spite of being so highly rated by literary connoisseurs, and in spite of having won the Sahitya Akademi Award, India's highest literary award? I would like to propose two sets of answers, one for India and another for the West.

However unconsciously, recognition by the West is crucial for the Indian reader when it comes to Indian novels written in English. The work must be published there to be taken seriously here in India, and if in addition, it gets a large monetary award, its standing is assured. In fact, the question of how much money was advanced by the foreign publisher, or what the earnings were is considered crucial in India in determining the prestige of a writer: Pankaj Mishra's *The Romantics* netted 250,000 pounds sterling abroad; Arundhati Roy got a million dollar advance.

We have so liberally imbibed the "Orientalist" doctrine that we see ourselves only through the eyes of the West. We are painted in the colours they choose for us, giving rise to the anomalous situation of appreciating fiction when it is directed at the foreign, not the Indian reader, titillating him/her with strange and unusual customs. *Cuckold* is based on quintessentially Indian themes: Rajput India in the 16th century, the first encounter with the Moghuls, the life of Meerabai and her husband, the Crown Prince of Mewar. It raises a host of questions about the nature of the godhead, about love, honour, friendship, the conduct of warfare, the meaning of rationality, adherence to social and spiritual ideals, mainstream and deviant behaviour.

Recognition in the West comes easier when a work is aimed at a Western audience, or if it is at least brought out by a Western publisher. *Cuckold* was published in India by an Indian subsidiary of a foreign publisher (HarperCollins) and it is unashamedly aimed at an Indian audience, taking for granted their knowledge of Indian history and cultural traditions. The fact that many Western readers have found it to be a great work (and I use the word "great" advisedly) indicates that it has universal elements which transcend the local. This is the subject of one of the essays in this volume, "The local and universal in *Cuckold*" by two American writers, George Dardess and Peggy Rosenthal.

I turn to a statement from Jacquelin Singh in the *Indian Review of Books* (16 June, 1997):

> ... a word about Nagarkar's language. He employs a distinctive yet unobtrusive narrative voice which comes as a welcome relief from recent novels whose styles call attention to themselves and trivialize the material in the process, whose relentless quirkiness soon becomes a bore. Likewise we have to thank him for the absence of magical realism, a device that has been flogged to death by every writer aspiring to be another Marquez or Rushdie.

Most people consider the publication of Salman Rushdie's *Midnight's Children* in 1981 as the date when contemporary Indian literature broke with the past and came into its own. But the first third of *Seven Sixes are Forty-Three* was published much earlier, in a literary magazine in Marathi, *Abhiruchi*, in 1967 and the full novel in 1974.

Seven Sixes is a strange and powerful novel unlike anything written in India till that time, frankly, even to date. Its narrative technique, fragmentary and cinematic, its gallows humour, the huge risks it takes with language and plot construction, the aloofness of its tone, and its compassion in the face of human futility and helplessness make it quite out of the ordinary. But it was not recognised as the starting point of the new Indian novel perhaps because it was written in a vernacular language and, also perhaps, because it was impossible to copycat it in the way many writers have attempted to take over Rushdie's style.

A brief comparative analysis of the two novelists may throw an interesting light on their methods and their preoccupations. Rushdie leaves an indelible and unmistakable mark on each of his novels. The wonderful, exuberant wordplay and the pot pourri or hotch potch plot, which are trademark Rushdie, occur again and again. The problem with Nagarkar or rather the essence of his work is exactly the reverse: if it was not for his name on the jacket and the title-page, it would be impossible to tell that it was the same author who had written *Seven Sixes*,

Ravan and Eddie and *Cuckold*. Unlike Rushdie, Nagarkar makes use of entirely different content, themes and techniques in all his works.

Barring the rare exception, the characters Rushdie creates are not memorable. One is not expected to build up a relationship with them. They are occasions, opportunities and showpieces for displaying Rushdie's playful mastery over language and his flamboyant imagination and for whatever is encompassed by the rather vague and capacious term "magic realism." Nagarkar hardly ever opts for the flash and mad roller-coasting pyrotechnics of an irrepressible blend of English and Hindi/Urdu phraseology.

Even in *Ravan and Eddie*, his most witty and polemical novel to date, where the turn of phrase is ebullient and energetic, the focus remains on character. Perhaps this is an area where Nagarkar is really old-fashioned: he makes the reader have a stake in his characters. You worry about those two kids, Ravan and Eddie, and how they are going to make out way after the novel is over. You do not just root for the minor characters, you grieve for them: as you do for Shobhan, the young woman with the club foot who buys kites for Ravan, and hangs herself in the end. As for the Maharaj Kumar, the protagonist of *Cuckold*, he is one of the most memorable characters in 20th century literature. The end of Rushdie's novels is his stunning virtuosity. The end of Nagarkar's novels seems to be the fate of his characters and the fate of humankind.

Few authors in India or anywhere else have been able to deal with such a range of characters and from such a variety of social strata. Nagarkar seems to write from the inside whether it is about the genteel and suffocating middleclass, the very poor, or princes and kings. Moreover, as the "asides" and "meditations" in Ravan and Eddie show, he has a fierce sympathy for the poor and the have-nots. He is, at times, a feisty polemicist, but always a pithy and racy one.

Nagarkar is constantly trying out new techniques and

fictional experiments, but in a very low key. He is not obsessed with virtuosity. He goes back to an earlier novelistic technique, not much in evidence today, namely the use of digressions. He brings in digressions on a variety of topics, on the Indian obsession with white skin, the loss of human dignity suffered by people in chawls, ruminations on language, and these are all introduced in the texture and body of the narrative itself. In *Cuckold* the experimentation is of a very different order. It is an epic novel, a novel of action, intrigue and war. One would hardly think it possible to weave introspection into a book of this kind. And yet, Nagarkar makes *Cuckold* a veritable philosophical meditation on the human condition, while still making it read as if it were a thriller.

One major aspect that separates Nagarkar from Rushdie and many of the bright Indian novelists in English is sex. Rushdie seems acutely uncomfortable with the subject while Nagarkar deals with it head on, harking back to an ancient Indian tradition. Western sociologists, historians and art critics in general isolate the erotic elements in the sculpture of Khajuraho and other Indian temples and almost obliterate the presence of everything else. Sex is indeed an integral and important element of Indian temple sculpture but it's just a small percentage of the life depicted. Following in this tradition, Nagarkar too is utterly unself-conscious when dealing with matters sexual and erotic, these being merely a fraction of the turbulent and engrossing portrait of the life he paints.

From the late eighties a whole new crop of writers has emerged. There has been a resurgence of tremendous energy coming out of India and some of the writers have done extremely interesting work. In particular, I would like to mention Amitav Ghosh. There are also many others like Vikram Seth, Shashi Tharoor, Arundhati Roy, Upamanyu Chatterjee. A point worth making is that these writers, however different they might be, have certain things in common. It was Rushdie who was the inspiration for many of them. Another aspect is that they write almost exclusively about the middle class. In contrast, Nagarkar has consistently forged his own quite different path.

Nagarkar's two novels prior to *Cuckold* are also very different in theme, nature of characters, style and plot construction. *Seven Sixes are Forty-Three*, the first, was published in Marathi in 1974 by Mouj Prakashan and then translated into English by Shubha Slee and published by Queensland University Press, Australia, in 1978, reprinted by Vikas India. It was published again in 1995 by Heinemann in its Asian Writers Series, and recently by Katha. When it first came out it won a number of awards in Marathi, including the Maharashtra State Award for the best first novel. The story of a highly sensitive young man's life, his interactions with others, his several varied romantic encounters, his coming to grips with himself as an individual, it is tragic and uproariously funny by turns. Following his growth to adulthood in Mumbai in the 1960s and the shaping of his highly individual identity, which nevertheless represents the identity problems of Indian youth, torn between westernised norms and Indian cultural moorings, the book raises many issues – a characteristic of all Nagarkar's novels – issues relating to love, honour, pain, suffering and death, rationality and its limits.

Ravan and Eddie, the next in line, was published by Penguin Books, India in 1995. A screenplay called *Ravan and Eddie: The Grown-Up Years* written in 1979, deals with the characters as young adults, whereas in the novel (written later) they are much younger. The novel deals with two young boys, one Hindu, the other Christian, living in a poor tenement building, but inhabiting entirely different worlds. It is a rollickingly funny book, but with a tragic undertone and the analytical comments on life characteristic of Nagarkar.

Cuckold, the last to date of the novels, is Nagarkar's masterpiece. It represents the fine honing of a rich sensibility and presents an engaging story operating on many levels. It is a mosaic of different personalities (some of them bearing some resemblance to legendary figures), of different value systems and patterns of life. The youthful vitality of *Seven Sixes* and the exuberance of *Ravan & Eddie* give way to a mature vision of life, with many currents and upheavals disturbing the peace, but withal a tone of quiet confidence and control.

In contrast to the rest of his work, Nagarkar's latest novel allows us the luxury of identification with the central character. His earlier work was characterised by a sense of alienation, achieved in *Seven Sixes* by the use of disjointed narrative and a plethora of characters, none of whom, while striking and complete in himself/herself, was clearly focal to the novel, not even the protagonist. In *Ravan & Eddie,* the effect of alienation was achieved using central characters to whom one could only react in an ambivalent fashion. However, in Cuckold, there is no alienation, and a very deep involvement is set up with the main character, the Maharaj Kumar.

All the novels are modernist in parts and post-modernist in others. The narrative technique, again, is always highly innovative. *Seven Sixes* in Marathi has large chunks of Hindi and English, indicating the cultural plurality of the city of Bombay, but this aspect is unfortunately lost in the translation. It follows no known method of plot construction, being neither picaresque nor following a narrative line dictated by cause and effect. It leaps backwards and forwards in time; it zooms to a close-up and pans over large vistas. The events in themselves are loosely connected around the central figure of the protagonist, nevertheless, there is a tautness to the events which seem to be linked through a logic internal to his world. There is also, constantly, the juxtaposition of the farcical and the tragic, of the sensitive and the more robust. It is one of the earliest examples of black humour in Indian writing.

This volume of essays deals with diverse aspects of *Cuckold* and *Ravan and Eddie*, with some mention of *Seven Sixes*. The genesis of the volume was a seminar on Kiran Nagarkar's fiction organised by the Department of English, University of Mumbai, in February 2000 in honour of the Sahitya Akademi Award that he had recently received. Some of the essays are revised versions of papers delivered there, while others were written specifically for the volume.

The volume takes no account of Nagarkar's work for the stage, the best known of which are the two plays, both written in Marathi, *Bedtime Story* and *Kabirache Kay Karaiche. Bedtime Story* has had a chequered career. Considered an onslaught on the revered figures of the *Mahabharata* and on the divinity of Krishna, it has never been allowed to be published, though it has been translated into English and Hindi. It was extra-legally banned for years and even now is rarely performed publicly in India. It has not been produced commercially, the public performances being in two experimental theatres: the National Centre for the Performing Arts (NCPA) Experimental Theatre and Chhabildas School, both locations being in Mumbai. There have, however, been a number of readings to invited groups in India and abroad, and it has recently been performed at the Pembroke New Cellars, Cambridge University and at the Edinburgh Fringe Festival, 2003. Nagarkar continues to be a bilingual writer, and *Kabirache Kay Karaiche,* born out of the anguish of the communal riots in Mumbai and elsewhere, presents an analysis and visual representation of the situation. This has had several public performances.

The essays by Makarand Paranjape and Meenakshi Mukherjee place Kiran Nagarkar in the perspective of Indian writing in English. Paranjape feels that the reason *Cuckold* is not better known is that public culture is inadequately prepared for a work as serious and complex as this novel. This leads him to ask what determines the literary tradition in Indian English writing. He finds that it is a literature of minorities of one kind or another, and it is in this sense that he considers Nagarkar to be an unMaharashtrian Indian English novelist. To arrive at Nagarkar's place in Indian English fiction, Paranjape sets out to analyse the Indian literary canon and how it is constituted, one way of doing which was to turn to the list of Sahitya Akademi award recipients. He finds that Nagarkar, who, it appears, is the only Maharashtrian to get the award for English fiction, does so perhaps because there are no specifically Maharashtrian elements in his writing. All his protagonists are Outsiders, the Maharaj Kumar in *Cuckold* even more so, because he does not even belong to this century. In his article, Paranjape talks about Nagarkar's Brahmo Samaj background, where the point of departure from accepted Hinduism was a monotheistic faith drawing its sustenance from Upanishadic commentaries. However, oddly enough, Nagarkar himself seems to be continually tantalised by the polytheism practised by his brethren and one of the gods who recurs time and again in his writings is Krishna.

Meenakshi Mukherjee focuses on the relationship between the novel *Cuckold* and its historical content. The novel deals with a past – 16th century Mewar – which is still historically fascinating, yet it is not a historical novel. Meera is a legendary figure with a continuing hold on the popular imagination. Her husband is a shadowy figure both in history and folklore. Nagarkar foregrounds this anti-hero but not as victim and not *only* as a husband. He is presented as a thinking human being of many dimensions, who recognises his role in history, is conscious of his princely duties, who initiates innovative measures in public health and warfare. Nagarkar's story, anchored in the specificity of history while located in the indeterminacy of myth, revels in the imaginative space thus provided. Creative writers who use history, do not highlight the historicity of their work, pleading freedom of the imagination. Tagore believed that the primary function of a historical novel was not to record facts but to evoke the life of the times.

A hundred years later, she finds that we have a historical novel with a hero who is not larger than life, and who is interesting not for his actions but for the quality of his introspection. Nagarkar focuses on the Maharaj Kumar's loneliness, his self-critical brooding nature, at odds with the Rajput heroic code. Nagarkar questions the paradigm of hyper-masculinity valorised by Rajputs and generations of readers fascinated by narratives of heroism and bravery. The essay suggests that this fascination was partly the result of the propagating of the myth of the effeminacy of Indian men by the British rulers in order to help establish their own superiority and right to rule. Women, correspondingly, were seen as weak and defenceless. Mukherjee finds that it is perhaps inevitable that novels of a century later will destabilise these gender assumptions, but Nagarkar's Rajput novel does so with a truly startling subversion in his portrayal of the Maharaj Kumar. Conversely there are in the novel strong women like Kausalya, Karmavati and the Princess. Gender expectations are deliberately overturned.

Janet Giltrow applies Bakhtin's ideas of "dialogism" to an analysis of *Cuckold*. Bakhtin opposes epic and poetry to novel, privileging the latter. These opposing forms, however can fraternise in Nagarkar's novel, as the speaking subject, the Maharaj Kumar, occupies epic locales in a spirit of novelistic resistance. According to Bakhtin, epic and poetry both turn away from the contemporary reality and its accompanying speech diversity. The epic form imposes a sealed past on a living present forfeiting new possibilities in observing antique glory. Poetry according to Bakhtin isolates the individual voice, as self-sufficient and uninvolved in the unfolding voice of the other. Novelistic style, on the other hand, invites "dialogic" heteroglossia. For Bakhtin this is the zone of democratic possibility.

In *Cuckold* Nagarkar, using "an easy colloquial currency of language," a "contemporary idiom" subject to the availability in the 16th century of concepts we use today, invites the free traffic of words across contexts which Bakhtin sees as dialogic. For example, to speak of budgets, memos, cost estimates and job interviews in the context of 16th century Mewar is to bring epochs into dialogic contact with one another, producing unforeseeable meanings.

Bakhtin locates novelistic intention to the arrangement of "languages" or "voices" in relation to one another, the interanimation of voices, to which, in the truly dialogic novel plot is subordinated. This intentionality is not revealed through authorial expression, but through the arrangement of distance between the representing consciousness (or distal consciousness, which is intangible, and all indications of subjectivity are assigned to the third person) and the represented consciousness (or proximal consciousness in the Princess chapters, when readers are in the custody of an unacknowledged self as narrator). Giltrow further applies, to her analysis of *Cuckold*, Wallace Chafe's more technical account of the relation between representing and represented consciousness in narrative, examining the use of tense, modality, indexicality, presupposition, reported speech.

Yasmeen Lukmani deals with narrative technique in the novels, particularly with the aspect of voice – that of the novelist, the narrator and the protagonist. This brings in differences in perspective and in points of view, and along with the handling of space and time, she finds that these help to illuminate the life of the Maharaj Kumar and the presentation of Mewar history in the 16th century. She analyses in depth the use of the first, third, and on occasion, the second person pronoun in achieving this difference in perspective, relating to each of the three novels. The contrast between the events and perceptions that can be dealt with through the voice of the protagonist and of the third person narrator is brought out, as also, the degrees of fusion between the protagonist's and narrator's voices. She also considers the use of digression, song, epigraph, stories of the past, and aspects of cinematic technique in colouring the texture of the narrative, and the perception of reality that emerges.

Hira Steven looks at the co-existence in Nagarkar's *Cuckold* of the old and the new primarily in two areas: that of the moral values and codes of conduct presented within the novel, and that of form and technique in the construction of the novel. In the first case the 16th century Rajput ethos and codes of conduct are seen through the essentially modern sensibility of the Maharaj Kumar. The result is a fascinating study of a highly complex character and his inevitable conflicts – internal and external – which spring from the fact that he is a man before his time. In the handling of the novelistic form, *Cuckold* seems in many ways to go against current literary fashion. It is a historic novel on an epic scale essentially in the realistic novel tradition, in that the text is transparent, not drawing attention to itself and taking for granted a shareable reality. But *Cuckold* also contains a number of experimental elements: the modern, often colloquial English of the narration, the switches between first and third person narrative, the figure of Bhootani Mata (is she real or imagined?), the ending/s, among other things. Ultimately *Cuckold* is a multilayered, multifaceted work of great complexity.

Anirudh Deshpande concentrates on the aspect of warfare and military strategy in *Cuckold*. He finds Nagarkar's research regarding the battle between the Rajputs and Babur, when placed against authentic historical accounts, impeccable. In fact, his scholarship is so exemplary that in certain places, where historical records are lacking, the insightful conjectures Nagarkar offers as part of the depiction of battle in the novel, can be considered as plausible attempts at historical reconstruction. The paper deals with the nature of military strategy in Europe and India in the medieval period, tracing back Indian military strategies to the time of Alexander, bringing in Central Asian warfare techniques, and even those used in China.

He finds by dispassionately considering the past that, right through history, Indians have done nothing but lose in battle.

The Rajputs, with their overweening sense of honour, have been particularly prodigal in sacrificing human life for no observable gain. In spite of being numerically stronger, the Indian armies, irrespective of whether they were led by Ibrahim Lodi, the Marathas, or the Rajputs, were usually technologically much weaker than the foreign armies which attacked them. Instead of being invincible, elephants proved to be a handicap and an easy target when the enemy introduced firearms and cannons. The armies were further impeded by a disproportionately large number of camp followers. In addition, Indian military strategy had not evolved for centuries and lacked any flexible concept of strategic planning or direction for the functioning of an army: they allowed it to move as one phalanx, with no outflanking contingents, no focal areas of thrust. Above all, there was a complete absence of contingency plans for orderly retreat. In *Cuckold* this crucial lack makes Rana Sanga's defeat at the hands of Babur (with much smaller though technologically advanced forces) a disastrous rout.

Manjula Padmanabhan considers *Cuckold* in another light, that of the Maharaj Kumar's personal life. She argues that Kiran Nagarkar presents a different ideal of romantic love – different from the familiar Western ideal of monogamous love, where one man can only love one woman, no arguments. The romantic ideal of the One True Love in the West is linked to the religious ideal of the One True God. The romantic devotion that is idealised in Western books and films echoes the theme of monotheism: that there is only One truth, whether it is in the form of one God or one lover/beloved. By contrast, she finds that Nagarkar presents the possibility of multiple loves: a "Krishnaic" ideal, without guilt and without betrayal, because in order to betray, one has to believe in the notion of single-pointed fidelity to begin with. She feels that while Nagarkar leans towards the Krishnaic ideal in his other books, in *Cuckold*, it emerges as the dominant theme.

Various thematic aspects of *Cuckold* are also dealt with.

George Dardess and Peggy Rosenthal look at the three novels from a perspective which claims that all human cultures require violence in the form of scapegoating in order to channel and sacralise the imitative desire that otherwise threatens to tear these cultures apart (Rene Girard). "Imitative desire" is a desire aroused and inflamed by rivalry alone. Violence, focused and exhausted upon an appropriate victim, is thus a precondition for culture to continue to exist. The authors look at *Seven Sixes* as dealing with domestic violence (opening page), at *Ravan & Eddie* as dealing with the conflict between two opposing generations and communities, and then move on to analysing *Cuckold* where a possibility of escape from this endemic violence is held out. But this escape is no bail out. It involves mortal risks and painful moral effort and an infinite love of play. It involves Krishna himself, whoever Krishna is, whoever he is not. This is an extremely interesting and different analysis of the philosophical underpinnings of the book, looking at parallels between the Christ figure and the Krishna figure, and provides an approach for analysing a novel about 16th century Rajput society.

Jacquelin Singh considers *Cuckold* as an exploration of the meaning of loss and redemption. She feels that the term "cuckold" applies not only in the context of the Maharaj Kumar's relationship with his wife who has Krishna as her lover, that is, at the personal level. It applies at a larger, public level of the Maharaj Kumar being made to give up something that was rightfully his own – the kingdom of Mewar. Loss and betrayal are, thus involved. But the possibility of redemption is held out by the novelist. Jacquelin Singh feels that here finally, we have a protagonist whose inner light enables him to redeem his dignity – even as all is lost. He makes it possible for us to recognise the potential in ourselves to overcome the destructive power of loss through the redemptive power of self-knowledge.

Usha Hemmady also focuses on ethical dilemmas in *Cuckold* and Maria Luisa Parra the opposition between realism and the non-rational in *Cuckold.* Other dimensions are added by V. Padma who deals with historically revisionary readings of women characters in *Cuckold*, and C. T. Indra and Shobha Viswanath who both discuss the treatment of humour in *Cuckold.* While Indra brings in issues concerning hagiography versus history, Vishwanath examines aspects of introspection and the human condition in Nagarkar's fiction as a whole. I have gone into detail about some of the essays because they assume a certain familiarity with technical concepts. There is less need to deal in depth with the other articles because they speak for themselves.

I end this brief introduction to the volume by recording my gratitude to several persons whose help was invaluable. I must first thank the contributors, some of whom worked under great pressure to finish their essays. I do not know how I could have done without the active support of Hira Steven, whose help in editorial work was crucial. I must also mention Perveen Mahoney, whose involvement at the initial stages of conceptualisation and editing helped clarify issues. Thanks are also due to Adrian Steven for his help in computer-related difficulties. Lastly, I owe special thanks to the publishers, Chandana Dutta and her team, for their forbearance in awaiting the manuscript, and for their cooperation and support.

Kiran Nagarkar and the Tradition of the Indian English Novel[1]

Makarand Paranjape

My purpose in this essay is to locate Kiran Nagarkar in the tradition of Indian English writing. I wish to approach my task in a somewhat unorthodox way. I would like to begin, if I may, on what might seem both a personal and a parochial note. Let me say, first of all, how delighted I am personally to be part of this volume to honour Kiran Nagarkar and to celebrate his getting this year's Sahitya Akaḍemi award for the best book in English by an Indian author. There are few living Indian writers whom I admire as much as Kiran Nagarkar and, perhaps, none that I'm as fond of. That is why I'm particularly thrilled that Kiran has got this award – though it comes not a day too soon.

My second reason to be delighted might seem somewhat more parochial, even chauvinistic. Nagarkar is the first Maharashtrian to get this award for English and what is certain is that he's not only the first Maharashtrian to get the award for English *fiction*, but also the first Chitpavan Brahmin to be so recognised. However, any attempt to capitalise on or emphasise Kiran's Chitpavan-ness, in an

---

[1] This revised transcript of the Keynote talk I gave at a conference on Kiran Nagarkar at the Department of English, University of Mumbai, on 7th March 2001, retains, I hope, the flavour and the tone of the original.

attempt to place him in a larger body of writers or a tradition of writing, comes up against this rather curious, if obvious obstacle: there are no Chitpavans to speak of in Kiran's books! *Cuckold* is set in 16th century Mewar, with non-Marathi protagonists and even *Ravan and Eddie* shows greater familiarity with Goan Christians and lower-caste Ghatis in a suburban Bombay chawl rather than with the Konkanastha Brahmins of present times. However, what seems to attract Nagarkar, what inspires him is not identity but *Otherness*. He is most at ease writing about people who seem least like his own supposed community and group.

All the same, Nagarkar is not so unusual in the difficulty he presents in fitting into a suitable location in the body of Indian English writing. In "Minority and Ethnicity in Indian English Literature" I have argued that Indian English writing is particularly amenable to what we might call minority voices – whether these are religious minorities, women, or homosexuals. It is Christians, Parsis, Sikhs, Muslims, and even Jews (who are a microscopic minority of the Indian population), who have distinguished themselves in Indian English writing in much greater proportion to their actual numbers, than their Hindu counterparts. And even among those writers from the so-called Hindu communities or dominant language families, it is usually those who are outsiders in those communities that have become major Indian English writers. I could give you several examples. From the earliest generation of writers, consider Mulk Raj Anand. He cannot be thought of as a "typical" member of a lower-caste agrarian Punjabi community (his father was from the coppersmith caste and served as a subaltern in the British Indian army). He moved out, not only to study in England, but also to take a very critical look at his own community, its own caste structures, and other social problems in India. In fact, his novels interrogate Hindu traditions and customs such as untouchability and the oppression of women. Take another example, Anita Desai. The daughter of a Hindu Bengali father and a German mother, educated in Delhi, she married a Gujarati executive, lived in Bombay and Delhi for several years, and for the last ten years or so, has lived in the US. In another paper, I called the dominant group of major Indian English novelists, "debrahminised brahmins," in that sense thrice born (see "Caste of the Indian English Novel" in *Towards a Poetics of the Indian English Novel*).

In other words, I am suggesting that not only is Indian English especially hospitable to "outsiders" but the "insiders" also function, at times, as "outsiders." I mean Anglicised Hindus also display signs of minoritarianism by being aliens, for one reason or the other, to their own communities. To elaborate upon this point, let me invoke a famous, early 20th century Bengali novel by one of India's greatest writers. I am referring to Rabindranath Tagore's *Gora* (1908), more specifically to the Brahmo-Hindu conflict in it. Being a Brahmo, the novel shows, was a very significant break away from mainstream Hinduism, especially upper-caste Hinduism, in the 19th century. Being a Brahmo meant being ostracised and excommunicated from your caste, which had very far-reaching implications in those days, including the denial of commensality and endogamy. It meant losing your identity, also, in some cases, losing your livelihood. No one would marry your children, no one would attend your weddings and feasts or funerals: your social life was killed. In a word, at least till you found another identity, another community to belong to, you were a *persona non grata*.

I have deliberately brought up *Gora*, with its theme of the Brahmo-Brahmin conflict, because it has a special resonance to Nagarkar's own story. His grandfather started as an orthodox Chitpavan Brahmin, but later became a Brahmo, for which he was ostracised from the community. Actually, it wouldn't be entirely accurate to call him a

Brahmo because in Western India, a similar reformist sect of Hinduism was set up as the Prarthana Samaj. Nagarkar's grandfather married a second time to someone totally outside the community – to a Jewess. From his mother's side, Nagarkar has Bengali and UP Brahmin blood. The Brahmos were, of course, monothesistic and against idol worship. The rest of the Hindus considered them very Westernised. Nagarkar's father was not only English-literate, but Anglicised. Kiran Nagarkar's earliest years were spent in the heart of a genteel lower middle-class Maharashtrian locality called Hindu Colony in Dadar. In his own career, he tried his hand at teaching but was fired for failing too many students! He later became a copywriter and creative director of an advertising agency. And his first novel, in Marathi, *Saat Sakkam Trechalis*, earned him only Rs. 120 and was, besides, panned by the hidebound Marathi literary establishment!

I mention these biographical details to suggest that Nagarkar, both by his family background and in his own individual life is very clearly an outsider, not just to the more narrowly defined community of Chitpavans, but to Hindu society itself. Temple worship and the piety of conventional religion were alien to the Brahmos, but they substituted this by a somewhat dull and insipid form of worship, which relied on sermons and a dignified but not terribly lively music. Nagarkar is averse to both these – the dark and cavernous Hindu temple with its suffocating smells (in one of his interviews he alludes to his aversion to smelly dhotis), and this "bowdlerized" form of Brahmo worship. The fact that Nagarkar is an outsider to both these is related not only to the creation of his own idiom and world-view as a writer but also to the special kind of literary modernism that I shall discuss later. This is the modernism which is rebellious without rejecting tradition totally, irreverent without necessarily being totally impious. Nagarkar's work, thus, is typical of many other Indian English texts in that it is the product of a cultural outsider, but it is, at the same time, different in that it reflects not just a bilingual sensibility, but one that is deeply grounded in Indian traditions. It is the sort of heterodoxy of the critical insider more than that of a rank outsider.

In other words, I wish to offer a counter-argument to my own parochial applauding and appropriation of him as the first Chitpavan novelist to win the Sahitya Akademi award in English. Instead, I would say Kiran Nagarkar is a part of this larger tradition of Indian English Literature in which not so much insiders and majorities, but outsiders and minorities have found voices. In fact now it is proven that the first Indian English writer was not Henry Derozio, who incidentally, was actually another minority person, but a man called Dean Mahomed (1759-1851). Michael Fisher has written a book on him entitled *The First Indian Author in English* (1996). Mohamed, whose father served the British army in India, started life being kidnapped during a villagers' raid, then found patronage under an Irish army cadet, toured India with him, went to England, married an Englishwoman, and eventually became a "shampooing surgeon" in Brighton. His novel, for which he raised money with subscriptions, is in the form of thirty-eight letters addressed to an unidentified recipient. It details Indian life in the late 18th century and also has some observations on Mohamed's stay in England and Ireland. But more to our point, writers like Mohamed, Derozio, and later Toru Dutt, all were outsiders to mainstream "Hindu" traditions. I shall give you just one more example. Jayanta Mahapatra, who is often read, unlike most other modernists, as a writer whose work is deeply rooted in his community, that is in Cuttack and its environs, and in the Oriya ethos, is actually revealed to be an uncompromising critic of that community and culture. The rootedness is deceptive because the society he writes about is portrayed as traditional, static, almost atavistic and pervasively cruel. In a way, that is his attitude to "traditional Hindu India"; it is certainly neither a nostalgic celebration nor a sentimental appreciation. Again, we must not forget that Mahapatra is Christian and his grandfather was a convert, a "rice Christian," as Mahapatra himself puts it, that is someone persuaded to convert during a famine with the inducement of food. A careful reading of Mahapatra thus shows a sustained critique of the *status-quo*, of traditional, hierarchical, and unjust Oriya society. I think Kiran Nagarkar shares in this tradition. It is therefore not surprising to notice his proclivity to write not about "average" Maharashtrians but about "others."

I would therefore suggest that the first step in trying to locate Nagarkar in the tradition of Indian (English) writing would be to see him as an "outsider" in his own community, though a "critical insider" to the larger tradition of modern, secular India. I therefore see him as a member of a literary avant-garde, in fact, as one of the progenitors and inaugurators of literary modernism in Marathi and English. It may seem that I have quite suddenly introduced this claim, inserting the idea of modernism without sufficient preparation. I shall talk about this later at greater length, but right now I will only say that he was already recognised as a modernist pioneer in Marathi before he turned to writing in English. It is this avant-garde tendency that he also brings into his English writing. I will also add that this aspect of his work cannot be viewed in isolation but must be seen in conjunction with the work of other important Marathi bilingual writers like Arun Kolatkar, Dilip Chitre and Vilas Sarang. What we have here is a quartet of modernists who write in both Marathi and English, and who are very different from other Indian English modernist writers like Nissim Ezekiel or Keki Daruwalla on the one hand, and neo-traditionalist Marathi writers like Shri Mahanur on the other.

There is a third way in which I would like to talk of Nagarkar's writing, and I propose to do so by problematising the very idea of a tradition of Indian English literature. This is a rather contentious and as yet unresolved issue. It has been asked if Indian English literature has a tradition at all, and if it does, should it be divorced from and considered separately from the larger tradition of Indian literature written in its many languages? One of the best discussions of this question is in Aijaz Ahmad's *In Theory*. The earliest scholars to write about Indian English literature, such as K. R. Srinivasa Iyengar and M. K. Naik have argued that there is, indeed, a tradition of Indian English literature. However, focusing for the time being on poetry, a number of modernist writers actually say there is no tradition. They contend that their poetry has nothing in common with that of earlier writers like Sarojini Naidu, Sri Aurobindo, and Rabindranath Tagore. These modern poets and anthologists believe that the tradition of Indian English poetry begins, paradoxically, after independence, in the 1950s, with Nissim Ezekiel. This view has been repeated again and again by most of the major modernist poet anthologists such as R. Parthasarathy, Keki Daruwalla, Vilas Sarang and Arvind Krishna Mehrotra. They imply in the introductions to their anthologies that the earlier poets are practically worthless. In effect, what they imply is that there is actually hardly any tradition of Indian English literature – there is no tradition but there is only a contemporaneity. The argument is that there are no literary continuities but only a major discontinuity between the writers of the 19th century and the writers of the 20th century.

We can ask the same question of fiction: is there a tradition of Indian English fiction? Again, we find a rather common view that Indian English fiction begins in the 1930s with the Big Three – Mulk Raj Anand, R. K. Narayan and Raja Rao. In recent years, more and more works are being unearthed to push the tradition back. But the question of the relationship between the earlier writers and the more recent ones remains undecided as does the worth of these earlier writers. Whether we go back to Bankim Chandra Chatterjee's abortive attempt to write in English – *Rajmohan's Wife* published in 1864, which is a sort of half completed novel or hurriedly completed novel, after which he stopped writing in English altogether – or *Bianca,* which is another incomplete work by Toru Dutt, we find that the Indian English novel has very tenuous and tentative beginnings. The form remains less frequently practiced than poetry and produces few examples of what might be called a stable or satisfying novel. Even works such as *Govinda Samanta* (1874) by Lal Behari Day or an earlier work, "A journal of forty-eight hours of the year 1945," which was published in *The Calcutta Literary Gazette* of June 6, 1835 and long considered the first Indian English short story, can hardly be considered well-developed examples of the genre. But what is important about these early texts is that they show a desire for experimentation with the various *types* of narrative, only a few of which survive and stabilise into the 20th century. In this regard, we should recall some novels of the early decades of the 20th century where we see an attempt to write historical fiction. I can think of two examples: Sirdar Jogendra Singh and Aiylam Subrahmanier Panchapakesa Aiyar. Singh went on to write novels like *Kamla* (London: Selwyn and Blount, 1925), *Nasrin: An Indian Medley* (London: James Nisbet, 1911), but his first book was a historical novel, *Nurjahan: The Romance of an Indian Queen* (London: James Nisbet, 1909). Aiyar's works include *Baladitya: A Historical Romance of Ancient India* (Bombay: Taraporevala, 1930). Now, we must remember that historical novels were very popular in languages like Bangla and Marathi, but failed in English. I mention this genre especially because

Nagarkar's *Cuckold* may be considered a very special example of it.

But the one kind of novel which did hold the most promise in the early years of Indian English fiction was represented by the social realism of K. S. Venkatramani. In *Murugan, the Tiller* (London: Simpkin, Marshall, Hamilton, Kent, 1927) and *Kandan, the Patriot* (Madras: Svetaranya Ashrama, 1934) one sees, for the first time a socially responsible realism linked to the freedom struggle. After the first glimmers of Indian English fiction in the early 19th century, it took nearly a hundred years for such a novel to be written. It is this type of novel that attains the greatest prestige in later years with practitioners like Mulk Raj Anand, Raja Rao, Bhabani Bhattacharya, and others, right down to Vikram Seth's *A Suitable Boy*. In *Towards a Poetics of the Indian English Novel*, I have tried to show how in the 19th century some types of writing emerged which were then developed or practiced later. That is why, going back to the 19th is important. The later novels were predicted by these earlier efforts. Even in *Rajmohan's Wife*, you see elements which are developed in later writings. That is why I consider it is possible to talk of a "tradition" of Indian English fiction.

There is another kind of critique of this notion of a tradition of Indian English writing that is more persuasive than the merely narcissistic obsession with one's own generation of writers. According to this other argument you cannot constitute a tradition of Indian *English* writing at all; you have to constitute a tradition of Indian writing or Indian fiction, which takes into account the literary productions in all the major Indian languages. That is to say that monolingualism is a colonial imposition; to carry it forward to this date would be to reify a colonial legacy. The cultural complexity that is India will not respond to such an imposition of a monolingual literary tradition. The argument here is that because Indian English creativity is a kind of bilingual creativity in the first place, you cannot consider Indian English literature in isolation. There is no Indian English tradition as such but traditions which talk to works written in other Indian languages. In other words, if you want to read let's say Kiran Nagarkar then you must also read say Bhalchandra Nemade in Marathi, or you must read Nirmal Verma in Hindi, or you must read O. V. Vijayan in Malayalam. Only then will you see something emerging of what might be called the tradition of modern Indian fiction. Only when you read across these linguistic borders can you see, for example, how there are narratives of the nation in the early 20th century in all major Indian languages; works by Tagore and Sarat Chandra in Bengali, Kuvempu in Kannada, Viswanatha Satyanarayana in Telugu, Fakir Mohan Senapati in Oriya, and indeed similar works in every major Indian language. These are large books with a very big social sweep. Later on, after independence, in the 1960s, you have more fragmentary books, where this kind of nationalist paradigm, indeed where the nation itself, is being deconstructed, as happens in *Midnight's Children,* much later.

To talk of a tradition of Indian *English* writing is therefore considered unsatisfactory. What is required is to talk of a tradition of Indian writing. May I admit that by and large, I think such a view has much going for it? A productive way of reading Nagarkar's works would thus be to place them in the larger context of Indian fiction. I cannot do this in any great detail here, but perhaps, I might suggest a few beginnings.

First of all, let us consider *Ravan and Eddie.* Though the book was actually published as late as 1995, it was begun many years earlier as a screenplay. I would argue that *Ravan and Eddie* is an example not so much of the sort of national narrative that I mentioned earlier, but a local one which, though fragmentary, does serve to redefine our concept of the nation. I could of course use the word "postmodern" to describe *Ravan and Eddie*. All I will say is that *Ravan and Eddie* clearly shows certain features and formal characteristics of what might be called postmodernism. It is fragmentary in style, with discursive intrusions in the narrative. It has, moreover, all kinds of effects, for example, "doubling," and the supernatural gifts of Ravan. One might be tempted to compare it with *Midnight's Children* but, as far as I know, the book was started in Marathi much before *Midnight's Children* was published. This makes one think about and question the accepted notion of how literary movements begin. There is an idea that they start in one particular place. For example literary modernism is assumed to have started with Eliot and Pound in England. I believe, however, that literary movements start simultaneously in a number of different places. So, for example, postmodernism seems appropriately decentered, with Marquez, Gunter Grass and O. V. Vijayan all writing at the same time and doing similar things not because they are reading each other's work but because something is happening all over the world. We need to see these literary movements as decentred and multiple in their elaboration, with cross currents and multilateral exchanges of influence, even if these are not deliberate. We need not believe, for instance, that things start in the West and then find their echoes in India. Rather, we might begin to see them as having multiple centres of origin and dissemination. Thus what Rushdie was doing in *Midnight's Children*, Nagarkar, independently of him, was already doing to an extent in *Ravan and Eddie*.

In *Ravan and Eddie* you have two boys, in this case one Goan Catholic, one Hindu, who appear as doubles, if not twins. This is similar to the kind of doubling that you have in *Midnight's Children*. You also have the supernatural gifts, the change of names, inter-religious dialectics, criticism of communalism, and the use of cinema. This last is very important. Here, allow me an aside to suggest, as I hinted earlier, that Nagarkar differs from monolingual writers. For example, just as Arundhati Roy, uses *The Sound of Music* as an important inter-text in *The God of Small Things,* Nagarkar uses *Rock Around the Clock* in *Ravan and Eddie.* But unlike Roy, Nagarkar has not just *Rock Around the Clock* but also *Dil De Ke Dekho*, thus bringing in a different kind of cultural mix which you do not find in the work of writers who are exclusively Indian English in their consciousness. I shall come back to this right at the end of my essay.

Let me finally turn to *Cuckold*. When we talk about the tradition of Indian English writing we very soon find that *Cuckold* does not fit anywhere. You might say *Ravan and Eddie* does fit in, in that you can call it a post modernist novel. But what do you do with *Cuckold* when Indian English writing lacks a well developed tradition or body of work which deals with history. There are no major historical Indian novels in English, discounting the few examples I mentioned from the earlier period and more recent works such as Bhagawan Gidwani's *The Sword of Tipu*. On the other hand, Bankimchandra Chatterjee wrote several historical novels, and in Marathi there is a finely developed tradition of historical novels. One might argue then, that Nagarkar needs to be placed in that wider tradition as I had suggested earlier. However, what Nagarkar does is totally different.

In fact, this is what Bhalachandra Nemade says of the Marathi historical novels. He calls them the *Mochangad* trend and for him they represent "the tendency to create an illusion of a non-existent reality." He adds, "the *Mochangad* trend was a combined product of Romanticism, Nativist revivalism and the Marathi tradition of the stylized retelling of the *Ramayana* and the *Mahabharata*. The characteristics of this trend are a fixation for a glorious past, suspense, fantasy and horror. This trend then is deliberately and self consciously anti-realistic." I have mentioned Nemade here also because he has written an important essay about the spectrum of the Marathi novel, in which he talks about three basic idealised types. Of course the actual novels do not precisely confirm or conform to these types. These abstractions are only a way of trying to organise large bodies of work. The three types are *kriti*, *pratikriti* and *riti*. I have modified and redeployed them myself in *Towards a Poetics of the Indian English Novels*. These three types, in fact, correspond to what Scholes and Kellogg, Lodge and others have talked about in trying to analyse British and American novels. The *kriti* is a realistic novel; *kriti* suggests action, it suggests work, it also suggests a composition. It is, hence, a novel which goes towards society, engages with society, is a part of that society. *Pratikriti* is the counter to that because it goes into fantasy and fabulism, moving away from reality. It is true, of course that magic realism is not something that does not engage with society. One should not therefore take Nemade's rigid categories at face value, because such novels though anti-realistic on the surface actually demonstrate a very strong engagement with contemporary reality. Nemade's third type is formalism, *riti* where the aesthetics of the form, the language, the experimentation with style are important, rather than content and theme.

For Nemade it is the *kriti* which is very important; that is, a socially engaged novel which can actually intervene in and change society. To that extent, Nemade is following a very powerful Marxian strand of criticism represented by critics such as Lukacs, for whom the novel is the literary form *par excellence*, which can actually promote working class consciousness or can at least foreground issues of class conflict. A novel thus, is a form which is designed – unlike the allegory which is a feudal form, unlike the epic which is a classical form – as a work of art reflecting the dominance of the bourgeois consciousness. To that extent, it is best suited to challenge the *status quo* and therefore to engage with the "real" history of a society.

In my own book, mentioned above, I argue that the Indian English novel hardly ever does this. Because of a disjuncture between the language and social experience, because the text is written about people and events in a language which is not the language of those people, the natural tendency of an Indian English writer is to move away from society instead of toward it. There is an exception to this alienating clash between the medium and the culture when and if you write only about the people who speak in English in India. But if you did that you would be confined to writing about a very small section of people. If, however, one is writing about Meera, or about the Maharaj Kumar as in this case, or if one is writing about a variety of characters from different social strata, all of whom don't normally speak in English, then there is this problem, this emotional distance which has been noticed right from the beginning. It is a part of the discourse of Indian English criticism right from Paul Verghese and Meenakshi Mukherjee to Tabish Khair's recent book, *Babu Fictions.* The point then is that except for a brief period during the freedom movement when a number of Indian English novelists actually wrote about socially relevant issues, the Indian English novel has by and large been a novel of retreat from social engagement, either into personal, psychological reality as in Anita Desai or Arun Joshi; or it is formalistic, with verbal experimentation, virtuosity and display of skill in the manner of presentation as in Rushdie or Roy. So the Indian English novel, I have argued, is not usually a *kriti*, is not an artistic act of engagement, but rather *riti*, an aesthetic act which is distant from its social milieu.

Can we say that *Cuckold*, like the other historical novels that Nemade classifies as *pratikriti*, tends towards the anti-realistic? But, if so, why hasn't Indian English literature despite all its other efforts at fantasy produced historical novels? Well, that's a different question. Let's focus on *Cuckold* to ask if it too is a part of this anti-realistic trend. How does one place this novel? I would say that what makes *Cuckold* so unique as a cultural product is that it is working at once in two contradictory ways and at two levels.

At one level you have the historical events and action – the wars, the invasion of Babur, the Battle of Khanua, battles against the Gujarat forces, as well as the various intrigues, politics, statecraft. But there is also the psychological level, the interior landscape as it were. And the most important manifestation of this is the ongoing battle between the Maharaj Kumar and Meera, on the one hand, and the Maharaj Kumar and his rival Krishna, on the other. The novel thus works simultaneously in the public and in the private domains. It *is* historical, yes, but its historicity works in a completely different way because it is also a completely contemporary novel. You can draw up lists of words, phrases, and practices that are totally contemporary, but which Nagarkar injects into the narrative of history. In a totally "normal" way, the Maharaj Kumar writes in his journal that he went home "after office hours." We can prove, in fact, how the whole vocabulary of modernity has been injected into a historical setting. This is what makes the novel a unique experiment; not its recreation of the past, but its *interpellation* of the present into the past. But it is not enough to say that. What makes it very special is that you have a medieval setting with a modern protagonist, a protagonist with a modern consciousness; a feudal social order and its cultural productions with a bourgeois protagonist. When I say "bourgeois," I mean a character with a specific kind of historical consciousness that is linked to a particular mode of production. The Maharaj Kumar, in other words, is modern because he represents the *values* not of the feudal order to which he belongs but those of the modern bourgeoisie.

The Maharaj Kumar wants to modernise statecraft. He wants to set up systems which will function independently of the people who run them. He wants to professionalise the functioning of the State. What is more, he wants to strengthen civil society. He promotes town planning and sanitation. The Maharaj Kumar is the first one to recognise that the engine of history is driven by technology and not by ideology. This is a very modern idea. That is why he sets up an Institute of Defence Studies, like our own contemporary National Defence Academy. He is also interested in new forms of weaponry. More specifically, he wants, for example, to move away from the Rajput code of honour and conduct warfare in a more pragmatic fashion. His, in other words, is a real protestant intervention, like that in Ingmar Bergman's *The Seventh Seal*, where you have a questioning, skeptical protagonist in an age of faith. In *Cuckold* you have all the trappings of the feudal order which is about to collapse and a modern protagonist who, among other things, wants to create a secular polity. Look at the way he is trying to balance the religious claims of the different groups; look at his notion of economics; his idea of statecraft, among other things. Consider, also, all the modern, even Freudian psychological elements in this novel, the use of dreams for example, or the idea of the Oedipal complex. These are modern elements, injected into that historical milieu, which make the novel a fascinating work. This combination of a feudal context and a bourgeois consciousness is a peculiar graft and also a peculiar craft that Nagarkar pulls off. You have modernity hybridised with medievalism, somewhat reminiscent of Girish Karnad's *Tughlaq*, creating a situation in which you have two contending forms of consciousness, which can only be contained, if not reconciled in the *form* of the novel. It is this that provides *Cuckold* with its peculiar *tension*.

But as I said if we look at these two plot lines, the historical and the secular on the one hand, and then the personal and mystical, then you have a continuous tension being played out. The novel then is constantly functioning at two levels and the chapters alternate between the first person narrative and the third person narrative. It would be interesting to ask how the third person narrative can do things the first person narrative cannot. Introspective as the Maharaj Kumar is, which is also a modern trait – he is clearly the *most* introspective character in the novel always asking who he is, trying to define himself and his existential quest, – he cannot deal with or reveal or confront certain things about himself. And it is in the third person narrative that these features of his personality emerge. As I had said earlier the novel has a Freudian element. We find this in the Maharaj Kumar's Oedipal relationship with Kausalya, who is his *dai* or wet nurse as well as his lover, the person who initiates him into sex. Interestingly, there is also an Electra complex seen in the feeling that Leelawati, Adinathji's daughter, has for him. The novel thus has an epic sweep dealing with external events of great import *and* an introspective voice providing a constant play between two fictional modes. All this makes *Cuckold* a very special type of historical novel.

Before I end, I want to ask one question and it has to do with Meera or "Greeneyes," as the Maharaj Kumar sometimes calls her. I think it is interesting that Nagarkar did not put Meera at the centre of this narrative. The character who appealed to him more was the Maharaj Kumar because he was a historical blank and Nagarkar could recreate him any way he liked. In a way he is recreated as a classic modern outsider, almost a Camus figure; a person who is doubted by his father, intrigued against by his stepmother, opposed and betrayed by a younger brother who wants to usurp the throne. All this is on the public front. On the private front he cannot have sex with his wife who constantly resists him, and what is worse, is obsessively in love with her. So there is this constant anxiety in his life, an intolerable *pressure,* if you will. He is a wounded person with a wounded psyche, and the healing never quite happens, except perhaps at the end in a masterly reversal. What Nagarkar pulls off at the end is utterly stunning. According to well-known legend, Meera disappears into the statue of Krishna. Here you have the Maharaj Kumar disappearing into the statue of Krishna! It is he who has become the ultimate *bhakta*, the devotee – he who had always been so *vibhakta*, so divided, both internally and externally. It is he who finds that absolution of ultimate identification with that God who is both his rival and his refuge. Instead of taking the original version of Meera as the *bhakta*, as the devotee *par excellence*, Nagarkar makes the Maharaj Kumar the exemplar. What an astonishing and brilliant way of rejecting the effete, cliché-ridden, tamed and neutralised traditional stereotype of the saintly singer in white, eyes downcast, strumming on her *ektara,* and substituting it with a modern character, an outsider, a "sinner" with all his psychological traumas, as an emblematic representation of the struggle of the soul, the spirit and the body. Meera, the saint, seems to have been a very boring, flat, one-dimensional character to Kiran Nagarkar, with his modernist perspective. He is reacting against the manner in which saints are constructed, the way their hagiographers make them out to be perfect, that the people who worship them are satisfied. That is why he puts a modern figure like Maharaj Kumar at the spiritual centre of the text. It is he who becomes the *bhakta*, who is struggling with Krishna, who tries to impersonate Krishna, who starts playing the flute, who colours his body indigo, who in the end *becomes* Krishna by embracing the idol.

Centering the novel on the Maharaj Kumar makes the novel fictionally much more interesting. With Meera as the protagonist it would have been very difficult for the writer to get inside her consciousness. This, however, gives rise to a problem. Meera continues to be seen from the outside as a somewhat inexplicable character whose motivations seem contradictory. On the one hand, she greets the Maharaj Kumar after his victory over the Gujarat armies and saves the day when there is an orchestrated movement to call him a traitor, with black flags being waved. On the other hand, whenever the relationship becomes comfortable something happens to drive them apart. There is a constant tussle between her and the Maharaj Kumar. Hence, the Maharaj Kumar can get close to Krishna as a very reluctant *bhakta*, who is almost dragged by his feet because he is blocked spiritually to begin with. But worse, his spiritual advancement is forced because of another kind of block: his natural avenues of fulfilment in coming close to the woman he loves are barred. That is why there is a kind of mandatory sublimation or transformation that he goes through. That this is extremely painful is well-documented in the novel. But in the process, Meera, in my opinion, remains unrealised, remains a character who is rather unconvincing because she is always seen from the outside, in *relation* to the Maharaj Kumar. Because she is seen as somebody whom the Maharaj Kumar cannot understand – whether she is dancing or singing or absorbed in devotion – she is rendered so to us too. Weird, crazy, inscrutable. In other words, Meera is an object in the novel, never attaining the maturity of a true subject. While other characters seen from the outside by the protagonist-narrator attain a sense of subjectivity and self-hood, Meera alone remains inscrutable and implausible.

There is an additional problem with all the scribblings of Meera in the novel. Yes, Nagarkar makes her a writer, in addition to being a singer. And his renderings of what we know of Meera's compositions are very unconvincing. It is an aggravated example of the Ramanujan problem of rendering in a modern idiom a sensibility which is essentially not just non-modern, but unavailable and unrecoverable to modernity. If you hear Meera's bhajans, even as they have been sung today, and compare them with Nagarkar's versions, we see a great gap, a gulf that cannot be bridged. Even though they are not intended as translations, they don't fit in with the figure of Meera. This is the one area where I believe the novel has a major problem. While we might argue that the novel shows Meera as writer, singer and dancer and that Nagarkar has not attempted to translate Meera's bhajans, or provide another version of them, the fact that "Greeneyes" or "Little Saint" is very different from the Meera of tradition cannot be wished away. In the Maharaj Kumar, Nagarkar comes up with a credible historical character; in him, history is illuminated by fiction. In Meera, on the other hand, we see a veiling of history in a character who bears little resemblance to the popular idea of Meera. Nagarkar's Meera neither resembles the popular hagiographical image of her, nor to modern methods of reconstructing the lives of female saints and mystics as exemplified, say, in *Manushi.*

Before I conclude, let me return to the question that I had raised at the start of my specific discussion of *Ravan and Eddie* and *Cuckold*. This was the question about how to locate or situate these two texts in the spectrum of the Indian (English) novel and was the third way in which I wished to discuss Kiran Nagarkar's work and the tradition of Indian (English) fiction. Are these two texts in the *riti* or formalistic mould or should we say that *Ravan and Eddie* is of the *riti* type and *Cuckold* the *pratikriti*, the anti-"realistic" novel type that Nemade spoke of? Well, let me say quite clearly that I wouldn't think of either *Ravan and Eddie* or

Cuckold as being entirely in the *riti* mode. They are both experimental and experimentation implies *riti,* and not necessarily social engagement. But there are important ways in which both these novels do engage with society. *Ravan and Eddie*'s discussion of the Hindu-Christian question is almost prophetic in the manner in which religious intolerance has been manipulated in the last few years. The novel not only opposes such intolerance, but demonstrates how ridiculous and unfounded it is. It shows that identities are not just hybrid and complex, but susceptible to cross-overs and interchanges. It shows that communities that live next to each other not only display compatibility and co-existence, but actually interpenetrate and become the *other*. The *other* and the *self* – this dialectic is very important in *Ravan and Eddie*. Eddie himself, to become his self's other, becomes his other's self – he joins the RSS, becoming one of its staunchest members! This move is of course shown in a comic and parodic fashion. This is to say that all these identities are very flexible and interchangeable, not rigid and essentialised.

Again, in *Cuckold* there is an engagement with the manner in which India has been shaped and formed. Nagarkar underscores the claim that it is the Battle of Khanua, where Babar defeated Rana Kumbha, rather than the Battle of Panipat in which Babur defeated Ibrahim Lodhi, that is more important to the rest of Indian history. If *Ravan and Eddie* is about Hindu-Christian relations, *Cuckold* is about the Hindu-Muslim contact. Again, Nagarkar resists simplistic notions either of difference or identity, weaving instead a complex narrative of how both individuals and collectives function denominationally. He invites us not to simplify history, but to re-engage with it imaginatively. *Cuckold* is an experiment on how to participate in our past; indeed, memory and its workings constitutes one of the important themes of the novel. How do a people construct and preserve their past? How do they narrativise it? The novel asks us to think through such questions. In the figure of Sajani Bai, Nagarkar, perhaps, portrays a character who functions as a writer such as himself might, someone who sings and immortalises our past, not necessarily in the way it happened, but its essence, its mood, its feel, its inner quality, so that we don't forget. If this is not social engagement, I don't know what is.

At the end of my article, I would like to return to what I said about the special kind of literary modernism that Nagarkar helps to engender. It is here that I think we can place his contribution most accurately *vis a vis* the tradition of recent Indian fiction. The best way to do this would be comparative, to place him alongside the other members of the quartet of contemporary bilingual modernists of Maharashtra. It is the study of this quartet, Chitre, Kolatkar, Nagarkar, and Sarang that will give us some idea of the special kind of literary modernism that was produced in Bombay. All these writers are cosmopolitan, experimental, irreverent, even visionary, but in ways that are substantially different from the Anglicist modernists. The latter debunk their own traditions, deriving their styles and content from Western sources. Unlike them, the Bombay quartet, mines Indian sources and therefore creates a modernism that is neither alienating, nor derivative. They are Indian *and* modern in an unusual and interesting way. This also makes them different from several vernacular modernists, who have been shown to be derivative too, even though they write in Indian languages. So, I would say that the most useful way of exploring Kiran Nagarkar and the tradition of Indian (English) fiction would be to have a study, a Ph.D. dissertation or a book, perhaps, on these four writers who are all bilingual – Kolatkar, Chitre, two poets, and Nagarkar and Sarang, two novelists. (Of course Sarang is also a poet.) It would be fascinating to see exactly how the Marathi and the English combine, coalesce, collude, conflict and clash.

I would like to end by pointing out that much still needs to be done before we can do justice to a writer of Kiran Nagarkar's calibre and stature. A serious writer may spend seven or eight years writing a book like *Cuckold*. How can we hope to be fair to it in the space of a few pages? Often, we're ill-prepared for such a work. Indeed, I wonder how many people have read this book seriously, the way it deserves to be read and savoured. Perhaps, a hundred? Perhaps, even less. What is more, in my own essay, I have not even looked at the first novel, *Saat Sakkam Trechalis* or its translation, *Seven Sixes are Forty-Three*, let alone his other works, prominently, *Bedtime Story.* I therefore feel a sense of inadequacy. What I have offered here, then, is merely the beginning of what I hope is a more sustained engagement with Nagarkar's oeuvre, – Nagarkar, who is clearly, the most under-rated Indian writer alive.

Works Cited

Fisher, Michael. *The First Indian Author in English*. Delhi: Oxford UP, 1996.

Khair, Tabish. *Babu Fictions: Alienation in Contemporary Indian English Novels*. Delhi: Oxford UP, 2000.

Kishwar, Madhu, ed. "Women Bhakta Poets." *Manushi* 50-52, January-June 1989.

Lodge, David. *The Modes of Modern Writing: Metaphor, Metonymy, and The Typology Of Modern Literature.* Ithaca, New York: Cornell UP, 1977.

Nagarkar, Kiran. *Cuckold*. Delhi: HarperCollins India, 1997.

———. *Ravan and Eddie*. New Delhi: Penguin, 1995.

———. *Saat Sakkam Trechalis*. Mumbai: Mauj Prakashan, 1974.

———. *Seven Sixes are Forty-Three*. Trans. Shubha Slee. St. Lucia: U of Queensland P, 1980.

Nemade, Bhalchandra. "Kadambari." Trans. G. N. Devy. *Setu: Journal of Indian Literature in Translation* 2 (1986): 29-71.

Paranjape, Makarand. "Minority and Ethnicity in Indian English literature." Presented at the 10th Triennial ACLALS Conference, Colombo, Sri Lanka, 17 August 1995; an abridged version was published in *New Straits Times*.

———. *Towards a Poetics of the Indian English Novel*. Shimla: Indian Institute of Advanced Study, 2000.

Scholes, Robert E., and Robert Kellogg. *The Nature of Narrative*. 1966. London and New York: Oxford UP, 1990.

Celebrating Cuckold[1]

Meenakshi Mukherjee

Kiran Nagarkar is a writer who deserves to be known, read and discussed far more widely than has happened so far. Writing about him is not easy because Kiran Nagarkar is not one person but several persons rolled into one. I had a hard time deciding which of the various Kiran Nagarkars I should focus on – the trendsetting novelist in Marathi who stopped writing after a brilliant debut, the playwright whose work has been performed several times in Mumbai, the actor whose brief role in a recent film *Split Wide Open* attracted critical attention, or the novelist in English whose two books, *Ravan and Eddie* and *Cuckold* are so vastly different from each other that they cannot easily be brought together within a single frame of discussion.

I decided finally to concentrate on his novel *Cuckold*, not because it has recently won the Sahitya Akademi Award, but because it is his most substantial achievement, a major Indian novel dealing with a past that still remains historically fascinating to many of us. Yet, it is not what one generally understands as a historical novel. The book is written in a racy contemporary idiom, with humour, vivacity and

[1] Revised version of a paper presented at the Nehru Centre, Mumbai on March 4, 2001.

immediacy, making us engage with the story at a human level, yet incorporating in it certain larger questions about ethics and statecraft, religious faith and personal loyalty, love and desire that are relevant to us even now. I was amazed, specially when I read the novel again very recently – with renewed pleasure – at the range of issues that are woven together in this compelling and complex novel.

But before I go on to the novel, please permit me the indulgence of a few minutes of reminiscences. It is a joy for me to recall a brief and rich period of my youth – rich in terms of the friends I made then and the literary contacts that were initiated at that time – when Kiran and I both lived in Pune in the late '60s. A retired editor and critic called Prabhakar Padhye had founded an informal group where writers and literary people met and often had lively discussions. I met Kiran for the first time at one of those sessions. Padhye had an enviable talent for bringing people together and getting them to talk. Some of the young writers I met in that forum have subsequently gone on to become well-known literary figures – for example, U. R. Ananthamurthy, Dilip Chitre, Ashok Vajpeyi. Among the Pune people who came to these meetings often were Ashok Kelkar and Gauri Deshpande. Kiran had at that time finished writing his Marathi novel, *Saat Sakkam Trechalis* – though I believe it was still unpublished. My Marathi was not good enough to form any opinion of the work on my own, but Dilip Chitre's long paper on the novel which he presented at one of the meetings made us sit up and take notice of a truly path-breaking talent, work which was changing the idea of the novel in Marathi by ignoring all existing conventions, and creating a narrative that was discontinuous yet absorbing, darkly humorous, bawdy and disturbing.

Some years later when I had the opportunity to read *Saat Sakkam* in an English translation, I could see that Dilip Chitre's assessment was by no means over-enthusiastic. It was indeed a landmark novel, and retrospectively I feel quite proud that we were able to publish a chapter from this translation in the English journal *Vagartha* which I edited from Delhi for a good part of the seventies. This came out even before the book got known to a larger non-Marathi reading public through the published version of the English translation (superbly done by Shubha Slee) – *Seven Sixes are Forty-three* – first brought out by Queensland University Press, followed by an Indian reprint.

We left Pune in 1970 and lost touch with Kiran. Many years later while in Delhi I vaguely heard of his English novel with the intriguing title, *Ravan and Eddie* (1995) but somehow never got around to reading it. Two years later *Cuckold* was published. I must confess I was mildly surprised that a writer who was so powerful in Marathi should now choose to write in English. Also *Cuckold* seemed to me an oddly Shakespearean title for a contemporary novel – the word has such an old-world coyness about it.

When I did get round to reading *Ravan and Eddie* and *Cuckold*, these two books not only gave me much pleasure but have also given me a lot to think about. These novels, which I enjoyed for quite different reasons, made me aware that the language of a novel does not necessarily affect the world it creates. I also began to realise that the use of English does not automatically give a writer a global readership. Nagarkar's novels are so intensely and unselfconsciouly located in their milieu – in one, it is a Mumbai chawl in all its raw liveliness, and in the other, Rajput life in 16th century Mewar – that for readers entirely outside the cultural context of India, it may not be easy to respond to the humour in one, or decode the allusions and references woven into the texture of the other. Predictably enough, neither of these two novels were picked up by multinational publishing houses abroad or received critical attention outside our country. And indeed, even within the country not enough attention was paid to the novels because, unfortunately much of our literary judgment is shaped by how the western press reacts to a book. Questions of location, perspective, target audience and reception – are these important in talking about literature? These used to be issues ancillary to literary criticism, but cannot be shut out altogether today, when we begin to discuss books written in a global language, in a world driven by market economy.

The uproariously funny *Ravan and Eddie* plays with the nuances of differences among the norms of two religious and regional communities with their various political allegiances, who live in close proximity in a *chawl*, creating a local brand of humour that may not have export potential. The totally dissimilar second book, *Cuckold,* ambitious in scope, based on substantial research and replete with music, dance, military campaigns and the resplendent colours of Rajasthan, takes for granted a collective memory where history and legend overlap and a mere reference to the name of a river or fort, a colour or a flower, or a phrase from a song can strike a chord or evoke a mood. It is an intricate tale of love and war set in the early 16th century when Rana Sanga of Mewar is busy fighting the King of Gujarat, leaving his crown prince in Chittor in charge of the kingdom. This conspicuously unnamed prince, the Maharaj Kumar, is the protagonist of the novel; and his equally unnamed wife, who we gradually recognise to be the legendary Meerabai herself, emerges as the obsessive centre of his life, both in his longing and loathing, whether he is busy dispensing justice, fighting battles or performing stately rituals. This errant and elusive wife declares herself to be the betrothed of another – and the Prince confronts an enemy who defies all earthly prowess. The Blue God with whom the Maharaj Kumar had identified as a child now looms as the adversary. "We were finally face to face. Two mortal enemies. Correction. One mortal, the other divine and immortal" (171).

Cuckolded by the invincible Krishna, the Maharaj Kumar faces public humiliation for not being able to control a wife who sings and dances in public view, in the temple. His rival for the throne, Prince Vikramaditya, loses no chance to jeer at the "spineless prince whose wife is a common *nautanki* girl" and advises him in front of the court elders: "Look after your own affairs, heir aspirant, instead of pretending to look after the business of the state. I have a suggestion for you. That wife of yours, the city knows, dances for free. Why not become her pimp?" These insults hurt the Prince at a superficial level but it is the unarticulated conflict within the Prince's own mind that gives the novel its depth and poignancy. His intimate enemy – the icon of the Flautist – at fleeting moments seems to be his own mirror image.

Meera has been a well-known figure for us through the centuries; her songs are sung to this day not only in Rajasthan and Gujarat where the language of her lyrics is known to the people, but in other parts of the country as well, and M. S. Subbulakshmi's rendering of Meera's bhajans is perhaps one of the most influential confluences of Hindustani and Carnatic music. As Susie Tharu and K. Lalitha point out in their meticulously researched work *Women Writing in India* (vol. I), in the century-long history of Indian cinema no less than ten films have been made on Meera's life, a sure measure of her continuing hold on the popular imagination. But Meera's husband has never been more than a shadowy figure – often a negative abstraction of the authority who tried to subdue her rebellion. Neither literature nor folklore nor film has ever tried to individualise the anguish of this spurned man. Nagarkar foregrounds this anti-hero in his novel, but *not* as a victim figure and not *only* as a husband. The Princess and her songs recede to the background for hundreds of pages at a time while other characters and events crowd into the Prince's life. The Maharaj Kumar is represented as a thinking human being of many dimensions – one who recognises his role in history, who is conscious of his princely duty to keep Mewar secure from enemies on all sides, who initiates innovative measures in public health, who risks certain strategic actions for the long term good of the State and is acutely aware of his responsibility to the people in times of pestilence and other crises. Several chapters of the first half of the novel dwell on his unusual decision to give shelter to the enemy's son, Shehzada Bahadur, for diplomatic reasons, and how he saved his life twice by risking his own. A certain irony is added to these events when we know from the Historical Note appended to the novel and from larger chronicles of history that this same Bahadur in later years would attack and vanquish Chittor. Historians tell us that Chittor was sacked three times: once by Alauddin Khilji in 1303, when the women of the fort committed *johar*, an event to which mention is made in the novel, then by Bahadur Shah of Gujarat in 1534 and finally by Akbar in 1658.

Thus, Kiran Nagarkar's story is anchored in the specificity of history while being located in the indeterminacy of myth. The central characters have been cleverly chosen to provide the author this freedom. History has never provided a record of Meerabai's husband. Colonel James Tod's *Annals and Antiquities of Rajasthan* (1829 and 1831) claims that Rana Kumbha's wife was a famous poet-devotee and singer, but Tod's work whatever be its value as the repository of the lores of genealogy and tales of heroism collected from the bards – the wandering *charans* and *bhats* of Rajputana – by a young British officer in the early 19th century, is not an archive to which one goes back for accuracy of facts and dates. Nagarkar refers to Kumbha as the great grandfather of his protagonist who built Kumbhalgarh and was still remembered with pride and awe as a great builder of forts and temples. Whether Meera was a historical figure or not is also shrouded in some ambiguity. The only agreed knowledge about her is that her natal home was in Merta and she was married into the powerful Rajput royal family of Chittor. And that she gave up the life of a wife and a queen to dedicate herself to the worship of Krishna. The relationship, as recorded in her songs, is intense and erotic. In several songs she describes herself as mad – *baawari* ("*log kahe Meera bhayee baawari*") and her religious experience is one of ecstasy and abandon. No one is sure how many, if any, of these fourteen hundred compositions attributed to her – and which carry her signature line at the end, were actually hers. The novel thus straddles the interstices of fiction and fable, chronicle and legend, myth and history, and Nagarkar revels in the imaginative space that opens out to him in the process. A gifted story-teller, he flaunts the fictiveness of the narrative in the Afterword: "The last thing I wanted to do was to write a book of historical veracity. I was writing a novel, not a history." Yet he acknowledges certain signposts of Mewar history that act as pegs to tether his tale. "So much for the facts," he concludes, "As for the rest, novelists are liars. We all know that."

Kiran Nagarkar is in good company. Hosts of well-known writers who used history as the backdrop of their fiction from Walter Scott to Bankimchandra Chatterjee have disavowed the label "historical novel." Critics love neat categories – we all know of the work done by Georg Lukacs more than half a century ago in a volume called *The Historical Novel* – so influential in the discourse on the novel – but creative writers have never felt at home in these restrictive slots. There was a time in India – in the late 19th and early 20th centuries – when past-based novels became very popular in different Indian languages (one can off hand recall the names of Bankimchandra Chatterjee and Romeshchandra Dutt in Bangla, Hari Narain Apte in Marathi, C. V. Ramana Pillai in Malayalam) but most of them, despite the considerable research undertaken by them while writing their novels, never actually highlighted the historicity of their work. In 1883, Bankimchandra wrote in an Introduction, "I shall be much obliged if my readers do not consider *Anandamath* and *Devichaudhurani* as historical novels," in spite of the fact that we know he had taken some of the incidents from Hunter's *Statistical Report of Bengal*. Elsewhere he says, "The Sanyasi Rebellion is a historical fact, but I do not see any reason to inform the readers about it." Kishorilal Goswami, an extremely popular Hindi novelist of the late 19th century disarms the reader by admitting in the introduction to his novel *Tara,* which uses as its background the court of Shah Jahan, how he has relied primarily on his imagination "and history has been made secondary. At places imagination has only saluted history from a distance." Even in the heyday of the novels which drew their material directly or indirectly from history, there was some uncertainty and disagreement about what exactly constituted a historical novel.

One of the best essays that I have read on the theoretical debate around these issues was written more than a hundred years ago. The title of the Bangla essay is "Aitihasik Upanyas" or, "The Historical Novel" and it was written by Rabindranath Tagore in 1898. Rabindranath emphasises that the primary purpose of historical fiction is not the accurate recording of facts, but the evocation of an atmosphere larger than our ordinary daily life, making audible to us echoes of the magnificent rhythm of the chariot of time. He says – I will try to summarise a long argument in an inept and abridged translation –

> The joys and sorrows of ordinary men are enough for them – enough to cast in shadow the larger events of the world. But once in a while a few individuals appear whose joys and sorrows are linked with a larger cycle – the rise and fall of kingdoms. Their private loves and

> feuds merge with the great orchestra, that like the roaring of oceans swells and subsides according to the remote working of *mahakal*.... In order to see such men ... as part of history, we have to stand back, place them in time, so that we can see them along with the enormous stage on which they were protagonists.... This distancing from our ordinary lives is important. While we are spending our days in routine jobs, in laughter and tears, in eating and sleeping, in the broad thoroughfares of the world, the chariot of time is being driven by men larger than us. This realisation gives us a momentary release from our circumscribed existence. This is the true aesthetic experience of history.

A hundred years later, we are now reading a novel where this aesthetic experience is deliberately subverted by the choice of a hero who is not larger than life, who becomes interesting to us not because of his actions but because of the quality of his introspection. It will not be quite right to say that he plays no part at all in the shaping of history, because by the time the novel ends, momentous changes are happening in India. Pages from the diary of Babur drift into our story and are accurately construed by the protagonist whose unconventional gameplan, if it had been executed, might have prevented Ibrahim Lodi's defeat at the hands of the Moghul invader. Vasco da Gama is mentioned when Portuguese traders visit the Chittor court and the astute Prince can read in their eyes territorial ambition overriding mere commercial interests. But Nagarkar focuses more on the Maharaj Kumar's loneliness, his inward-looking, self-critical brooding nature which are at odds with the Rajput's heroic code of honour. A Rajput prince who worries about wanton blood-letting and shrinks from motiveless violence cannot gain the respect of his people. Nagarkar deliberately interrogates the paradigm of hyper-masculinity that was valorised by the Rajputs themselves and endorsed with admiration by generations of readers who were fascinated by these narratives of heroism and bravery.

At the time I first read *Cuckold* I was working on a research project that required me to go into the reasons why in colonial India the popular imagination responded so enthusiastically to two themes from the Indian past – the glory of the Rajputs and the valour of the Marathas. Numerous novelists drew from Tod's accounts and Grant Duff's *History of the Marathas,* to write about the prowess of the Hindu people against their Muslim adversaries, when in actual reality, the enemies at that time were not the Muslims but the British. I shall not inflict on you my findings and speculations on the subject except to briefly touch upon the question of masculinity. I found numerous examples to demonstrate that the British rulers had done much to propagate the myth of effeminacy as far as Indian men were concerned. This helped them to establish their own manliness and therefore "natural" superiority and the right to rule. (These examples range from James Mill, Thomas B. Macaulay, Robert Orme, Maud Diver to Rudyard Kipling.) Ashis Nandy has argued that the British dismissal of the Hindu male as weak and unmanly had resulted in a reflex reaction which invoked *kshatriyahood* as the only desirable masculine model, erasing in the process the inclusive androgyny of certain Hindu concepts. The assertion of this aggressive patriotism for which the Rajputs provided excellent paradigms, implies as its corollary the notion of women as defenceless, weak and vulnerable – the metaphoric embodiment of the country to be protected.

It is perhaps inevitable that novels written more than a century later will destabilise these gender assumptions. But Nagarkar's Rajput novel does so with a subversion that is truly startling. Not only does the protagonist, the Maharaj

Kumar not flaunt his machismo as a prince of Mewar is expected to, he performs without hesitation womanly tasks like nursing the sick and healing the wounded. Twice cuckolded, he does not seem particularly ashamed about his dishonour, and treats both his faithless wives on the whole, gently. Towards the end of the novel he almost revels in his condition, even on one occasion submitting to wearing women's clothes in his nightly play with the green-eyed Princess. Gender expectations are deliberately overturned – the trusted court eunuch, it turns out, can father a child, and women like Kausalya and Karmavati and the unnamed princess – the devotee of Krishna – emerge stronger and more resilient than most of the brittle men. Sexuality is very much foregrounded, but in ways that confuse conventional expectations – as in the Maharaj Kumar's erotic relationship with the woman who breast-fed him as a child. Some of the confusion is grounded in esoteric symbolism, as when the Princess expressed surprise that the highly renowned ascetic Swami Rupa Goswami was a man: "For if he was, what right did he have to enter Brindaban? Did the Goswami not know that there was but one male in the universe and that was the Blue One and all others, barring none, were women?" Echoes of this sexual ambiguity haunt us till the end of the novel specially at the miraculous finale when it is hinted that the Maharaj Kumar's body merges with that of his immortal rival.

Actually, there is not just one ending. I should have said, endings, because the author leaves the possibility open for a series of final alternatives. *Cuckold* is indeed that kind of the novel in which "what happened next" is very important. Whether or not you are interested in the subtler play between fact and fiction, realism and symbolism or pragmatism versus idealism, merely at the level of story it is a totally riveting read. There are passages of incandescent prose or incidental reflections on life where you might want to slow down the pace to prolong the moments of pleasure, but otherwise from page one to six hundred and two, it is a suspenseful and fast-paced journey. I will end by quoting two passages where I paused longer than I normally would. One is about music – the most difficult of experiences to render verbally. As the author himself admits, "To speak of music is to speak of intangibles. To attempt to catch its essence in words is foolhardy and doomed." Yet, the author indulges in this foolhardy act to reflect on the *alaap* when Sajani Bai sings on Janmastami night:

> It is an inward voyage, an odyssey into the unknown. You are alone, truly alone in the cosmos, no pakhawaj, no sarangi, just your voice feeling its way. It is wordless meditation, a rumination on matters that human thought cannot encompass ... Like all meditation, an aalap has the solitude and form of a prayer ... To plumb the depths you must leave the safety of the shallows, the easy sentiment and the company of the others. One's own frailties, mediocrity and the fear of the abyss – one must dare them all.... She struck a deep, low, majestic note and held it for an endless moment till it seemed to slip out of time, then almost imperceptibly shaded into another....

The other quotation contains a meandering reflection on language. It is truly incidental to the story – so incidental that the Maharaj Kumar has to remind himself of its irrelevance, "Am I talking rubbish?" His mind wanders while the priest is chanting Sanskrit hymns during his second marriage:

> The key to Sanskrit, the pundits never tire of telling us, is crystalline diction. They are right, absolutely right. What they forget to mention is that diction will make sense only if it is illuminated by understanding.... Who killed

> Sanskrit? It was not as if a cataclysm had wiped out the populace of the country or (it was decreed) one day that Arabic or Afghani would replace the mother of our languages. Was language like a woman from the zenana that we could abandon any time we felt like it? Would Sanskrit have survived if not just the brahmins and the court, but all castes had spoken it? Will the language of Mewar also die? Along with geography and religion, a mother tongue is the destiny of a people. I have the strange feeling that man created language but now it creates us. This is too big a question.

I will stop with this big question – which is actually quite marginal to the novel. But it is these digressions that make *Cuckold* so rich, illuminating the obscure recesses of the individual mind, while the central narrative gallops down the highway of history.

Works Cited

Chatterjee, Bankimchandra. *Bankim Rachanabali*. Ed. Jogeshchandra Bagal. Vol. I. Kolkata: Sansad, 1980.

Lukacs, Georg. *The Historical Novel*. Tr. Hannah and Stanley Mitchell. Boston: U of Nebraska P, 1963.

Tagore, Rabindranath. *Aitihasik Upanyas*. Rabindra Rachanabali. Vol. IV. 1898.

Tharu, Susie, & K. Lalita. *Women Writing in India*, Vol. 1, Delhi: Oxford University Press, 1991.

Tod, Colonel James. *Annals and Antiquities of Rajasthan*. London, 1829.

DEMOCRATIC INTENTION AND DIALOGIC INTELLIGENCE IN *CUCKOLD*

Janet Giltrow

Making distinctions now famous in literary-critical circles, Bakhtin opposes *epic* to *novel*, favouring the latter. Readers of Bakhtin also know that he opposes *poetry* to *novel*, again celebrating novelistic discourse. These terms and oppositions can fraternise in Kiran Nagarkar's *Cuckold.* As speaking subject, Maharaj Kumar himself occupies epic locales in a spirit of novelistic resistance – and he doesn't like poetry.

What does Bakhtin have against epic and poetry? As he characterises these forms, both turn a blind eye to contemporary eventuality, and a deaf ear to the surrounding currents of speech diversity. Epic instates the dominating word of the fathers, imposing a sealed past on a living present. Foreclosing the future, the deed of the ancestor forfeits possibility in favour of antique glories, *faits accomplis.*[1] Poetry (of the kind Bakhtin has in mind) isolates and indemnifies the individual voice as if self-sufficient and unimplicated in the unfolding voice of the other. Both epic

[1] See Giltrow and Stouck (2002) for an account of epic which recognises Bakhtin's complaints but suggests that epic expression can also contradict patriarchal and imperial hegemonies.

and poetry refuse the *historicity* of the word – its service to the epoch, "the day, even ... the hour" (263) – and its *sociality* – its rendering of groups, schools, generations, professions, and their positions and interests. For Bakhtin, the stylistic profiles of epic and poetry also project a philosophy of language and in turn a politics: centralised conceptions, unitary and unshakeable ideas, and uniform speech respectability. Novelistic style, on the other hand, incites "dialogic" heteroglossia, and the infinite calibrations of positions vis-à-vis the other's word. For Bakhtin, this is the zone of democratic possibility.

Cuckold, and Nagarkar's own statement of stylistic policy, can be read beside Bakhtin's commentaries. Nagarkar invites the kind of free traffic of words across contexts which Bakhtin imagines as dialogic: Nagarkar seeks, he says, "an easy colloquial currency of language," a "contemporary idiom" ratified by the availability in the 16th century of the "concepts we use today" (v). Yet, the correspondence of the ancient concept and the modern word can never be exact, or conclusive. According to Bakhtin, words are saturated with their sociohistorical uses – the practices and positions that accrue to them and to which they accrue. So, when the Maharaj Kumar mentions advances in military technology, his motives and attention can be analysed as indigenous to 16th century Mewar: historically contained and geographically plausible. But he cites himself speaking of these matters in 20th century wordings:

> Who has the expertise and who is selling it? Let's have competitive figures and last but not least, where can we hire experts and teachers to train our men?
>
> [...]
>
> I have set aside thirty thousand tankas from the defence budget for the project. I would like to have a preliminary report within two months

> and a detailed one in five months' time. I suggest that you treat this as top priority. (120)

The Maharaj Kumar's identity as the crown prince of a 16th century state engages with domains in which these words – *competitive figures, preliminary report, top priority* – perform 20th century domains of administration, corporate offices, transnational economies, and technological transfer. These wordings draw the Maharaj Kumar into, as Bakhtin says, their "orbits" (290) – in this case, cycles of interest and attention typifying the organisational ethos which in modernity manages not only the state but all the branches and procedures of what Foucault called "governmentality" (Burchell *et al.*, 1991). For example, matters of personnel are at once affairs of lineage, loyalty, alliance, and incumbency and, at the same time, images of modern selection:

> Father. Why do I feel like a greenhorn at his *first job interview*? Perhaps it's because he's behaving like a king and employer and has kept me waiting in the antechamber for the last fifteen minutes. (202, emphasis added)

Manoeuvring for the trust of Rao Viramdev, the Maharaj Kumar draws a conceit from the common experience of job seekers in modern labour economies:

> When a newcomer goes looking for a job, he's almost invariably told they are looking for a man with experience. To labour the obvious, how is he to get experience if no one gives him a job? (217)

In the governmentality of modern consciousness, wordings are transferred from expert disciplines to the everyday reasoning of ordinary people. (An example is the transfer, in North America at least, of the terms *dysfunctional family* and *co-dependency* from psychology to popular talk about troubled relationships.) His own language following such a path, the Maharaj Kumar, looking out over ancient Chittor and its population, notices its traditional colours ("Have you seen the reds and yellows and blues and greens...?" 49) and analyses the scene with a category provided by 20th century measurements of behaviour:

> Look at that woman rubbing charcoal powder mixed with a bit of opium into her gums. I can't see her features but that kind of slow, suffused pleasure in your waking moments can only come from *a borderline addiction* that's been inherited over generations. (49, emphasis added)

Later, profiling Kausalya's impressive intellectual resources, and remembering the days when she assigned him to read aloud to her Kautilya's *Arthashastra*, the Maharaj Kumar interprets her illiteracy in terms of a modern category from expert systems of assessment – including the public sympathies which accompany late 20th century programmes in adult education:

> Kausalya herself could neither read nor write. When she was a child she used to accompany princesses of her own age and shared their tutors. But she had *some learning disability* and was not able to master reading and writing. She was sensitive and proud and suffered because of the handicap. (137, emphasis added)

Borderline addiction, learning disability – these are terms produced by and for the operation of modern systems, and more especially the modern functions of surveillance of populations for their regularisation and normalisation. In a similar spirit, the Maharaj Kumar's civil-engineering project maps the city's terrain, to control its waste and purify its waters, for the health of its citizens. It is a typically modern project, one which gathers and catalogues information to manage the behaviour and circumstances of large numbers of people.

According to Anthony Giddens (1990), a symptomatic feature of modern systems is their capacity not only to monitor populations but also to monitor their own operation: this reflexivity improves systems' longevity, enabling them to react not only to changes in their field of activity but also to the conditions the systems themselves have produced. In *Cuckold*, the Maharaj Kumar's instinct for surveillance reaches its finale in plans for the last battle. At the meeting of the War Council he is "humoured" when, amidst traditional battle-planning, he announces an innovative strategy:

> The only battle plan we have is to soften the enemy under the feet of our thousand elephants and then to follow this up by getting the four seemingly monolithic blocks of our army to move forward and attack. We have no overall strategy, no way to monitor the progress of the war and to make continuous adjustments to exploit the weaknesses of the enemy and break his nerve or to rush help and reinforcements to wherever we are taking a beating. The first prerequisite for this is an overview where you can see the moment-to-moment developments taking place on the entire battlefield. You then have information to which people on the ground, both your own and the enemy's, are not privy. (575)

These are modern ambitions – the commanding overview from which no instances escape, the premium on centralised information, the sensitivity to unfolding pattern. But these ambitions are rendered in 16th century materials: a "mobile observation tower" (575), on wheels (576). The tower would be manned by an expert – "one who alone is fit to analyse and interpret the overview and decide what action needs to be taken" (576) – but this expert is embodied in 16th century authority, the king, the Maharaj Kumar's father. Across the tower project and the campaign for information two voices speak: the modern voice and the 16th century one.

For Bakhtin, it is in the oscillation of voices that we find the essence of *dialogism*: not so much the exchange of *dialogue*, where views and interests are contained in separate speaking subjects, and difference can be accounted as *debate*, but the infiltration of the single utterance by two voices. In Bakhtin's analyses, the occupation of the utterance by the alien word (usually but not strictly) occurs on the synchronic plane of contemporary social categories represented in wordings typical of recognisable groups. The result is a rendering in language of social stratification: an imaging, through language, of competing interests and world-views, a dynamics of typicality the outcome of which is never foreseeable, always experimental and unfinished as orders of social experience refract through one another, in step with or at odds with the author's *intention*, or somewhere in between the author's solidarity with and opposition to others' words.

In *Cuckold*, the plane of interlocution is not only synchronic but also diachronic, mobilising epochs and periods for dialogic "interanimation." This interanimation can occur across an episode, when for example, the tower project renders modern aspirations for central information and executive action in 16th century materials. It can also occur in smaller domains of utterance, where the refraction of epochs is more intimate or mundane but still unforeseeable in its outcomes and meanings. Returning from battle, approaching Chittor, the Maharaj Kumar measures the battalion's progress:

> We are galloping now, a little out of control. We have waited patiently for more than a year and a half for this moment. It doesn't make sense losing our heads when we are almost there. Whether you are *returning home from work at your office*, or from a long campaign, *it's in the last five minutes that most accidents occur*. (270, emphasis added)

Returning home from work at your office introduces into the tableau of the victorious army, mounted and triumphant, the trace of the modern-day commute, the mid-20th century masculine performance. This trace is impressed on the picture by a modern commonplace of statistical measurement and actuarials of traffic risk: *it's in the last five minutes that most accidents occur*.

Later, during a total solar eclipse, a most inauspicious time, the Maharaj Kumar records Chittor's response to the simultaneous news of Babur's imminent death in terms some of which are contemporary to the 16th century city and some to a 20th century prospect:

> Everything's come to a halt. There's a moratorium on war preparations. You would think we were celebrating Diwali in December. The clerks stopped writing in mid-sentence, the stable-master who had shod three of a horse's hoofs abandoned the fourth, the sword-makers have doused the smithy, tied up the forges and gone to the nautanki. Believe it or not they are distributing sweetmeats in some localities. Even the government offices and cabinet ministers who've been working overtime for three months running have taken the last two days off. The bells in the temples ring all day long and everybody including all our Muslim brothers are giving thanks. (555)

With *offices working overtime*, officials *taking two days off*, recognisably modern schedules cut across the astronomical calendar. At the same time, local terms – *the smithy, the forges, the bells in the temple* – stylistically presuppose readers' familiarity with these elements of life in Chittor, a shared ground which 20th century readers can temporarily occupy, like patrons of an interpretive centre at an historic site. *Working overtime* and *taking days off* indicate a 20th century transnational scope; simultaneously, readers can easily imagine a local history to support their reading of *smithy, forges, bells*. But Nagarkar's audience is not homogeneous, and for Western readers other terms are not so easily accommodated. The Maharaj Kumar's narrative projects a reader who can reckon the relevance of *Diwali in December* or *nautanki* as a destination or the [*distribution of*] *sweetmeats* in measuring this moment, its exceptionalism proportionate to the customary. Many – or most? – Western readers cannot know these measures: when is *Diwali* usually celebrated? when do people usually go to the *nautanki*? how rare or common is the distribution of sweetmeats? At these points, many Western readers (but how many? under these transnational orders of culture, how exact can the classification "Western" be?[2] become

[2] I am one of these "Western" readers, and it is from my own encounter with *Cuckold* that I estimate understandings and failures of understanding. At the same time, I am aware of the instability of the category "Western." For one thing, between early and later drafts of this essay, my own "Background Knowledge" (Sperber and Wilson 1995 [1986]) – my inventory of assumptions about the world – changed: from reading and travels, themselves characteristic of some late-modern Western customs, certain references in *Cuckold* resolved slightly or clarified a bit. In addition, reading *Cuckold* and finding deficits in my own understanding, I become aware of others in the audience too: not only readers in South Asia, but readers in the West, even in my own national community or my own circle of friends and colleagues, with South Asian connections and a richer inventory of assumptions on which to call in order to draw what Sperber and Wilson call "contextual implications." Under transnational orders of culture, the Common Ground (Clark 1992) on which language stakes its footing and positions its speakers and listeners is not terra firma. Disturbed by tremors and shifts, it calls language users' attention to what they take for granted. At the same time, it introduces at least into peripheral vision the multiple possibilities of reception. See Reed Way Dasenbrock (1987) for a non-technical account of the post-colonial politics of failures of understanding in "multi-cultural literature."

foreigners to the narrative, despite or in the midst of their familiarity with *overtime* and *days off*. At the same time, the "alien" word – which Bakhtin counts as endlessly inventive and eager in the space which surrounds its introduction – configures for Western readers alien speakers and populations, and immediately their own alienation. When we hear a word we do not know, we not only learn of the word's existence and a hint of its application: we also learn, sometimes with a shock of estrangement, of the concurrent discourses of other populations. Moreover, at these moments, for Western readers, the diachronic dialogism of the narrative – the engineered interlocutions between epochs – can upset, for Western readers may no longer know where to schedule *Diwali* or *nautanki*: to what Rajput consciousness are they contemporary? Are they dated and historical, or are they current traditions, survivors of the past?

When the Maharaj Kumar condemns the Princess's singing, and she excuses it, how do Western readers reckon the terms of their exchange? And, aware of other circles of reception, how do they reckon South-Asian readers' degrees of familiarity with these terms?

> "Do not sing. Is that understood? I will not have you sing under my roof."
> "Why?" she asked innocently or at least she did so with a fine imitation of innocence.
> "Because princesses don't sing for the public, at least not in this house. *Tawaifs* do."
> "It was only a *bhajan*."
> "Rasikabai ends every *mushaira* of hers with a *bhajan*. Like you she also gets an audience of a hundred or so to stand under the windows and balcony." (147-48, emphasis added)

Experiencing separation from other sectors of *Cuckold*'s audience Western readers might nevertheless adjust to these terms, inferring the relevance of *tawaifs, bhajan, mushaira*. But they will never get close to the precise calculation of trespass – or of perfections of observance, in other cases. When at his homecoming the Maharaj Kumar faces derision, the Princess moderates the hostility with items of ceremony:

> "You'll stop now," a soft voice spoke up. Slowly, very slowly the crowd froze. My wife, all five feet two inches of her, parted the people and walked towards me. She had a gold plate in her hands and in it were a lamp, kumkum and camphor. She did an arati, put the plate down and touched my feet.... She welcomed her uncle, Rao Viramdev, Rawal Udai Simha, Raja Puraji Kika and Tej and held out the plate for the men to pass their hands over the flames of the lamp. (272-73)

For Western readers, the calculation of these ceremonial values – *arati, plate* with *kumkum and camphor* – could soon collapse. These readers could be left with static typifications of the "foreign," the sedimentations of the "Orient" and its career of representation in the West. But they are not left to rest easy, for their positions are unstable: sometimes they are hospitably addressed in modern terms; sometimes they find themselves in less hospitable circumstances but they can accommodate[3] them; other times they must step to a periphery and only listen in, aware in

[3] Here and elsewhere in the essay, I use the term *accommodate* relatively technically, but in a sense which looks first to pragmatics rather than to sociolinguistics. In a pragmatic sense, language users *accommodate* presuppositions which inaccurately estimate their actual knowledge of the world. So, for example, a wedding guest might tell a friend about the festivities, saying, "The singer was fabulous, and the caviar!" Both the singer and the caviar may be in fact brand-new, unheard-of entities to the friend, but she can infer from their mentions their existence, and go on from there, without challenging the wedding guest with "what singer? what caviar?" The experience and effort of accommodation can impress a listener with a host of social, political and cultural conditions.

addition of an adjacent audience for whom indigenous terms may be historical or still contemporary or somewhere in between.

The *design*[4] of *Cuckold's* audience is complex, projecting positions for ratified participants, for overhearers, and for eavesdroppers. It arranges for a listening position from which readers can hear both 16th and 20th century voices, recognising modern experience even in the representation of an ancient setting. This position is partitioned, however, by those references which

---

[4] Focusing theoretically and empirically on the configuration of **audience** in contexts that are non-"literary" (110), that is, conversational contexts, Clark's *Arenas of Language Use* (1992) dismantles unitary notions of audience (which he shows to be the norm even in advanced work in linguistic pragmatics (205). Clark analyses *audience* as potentially comprising two categories
(1) *participants*
(2) *overhearers*
which are in turn subdivided into (1a) *addressees* (those from a whom a reply could be expected and who could be identified by a vocative); (1b) *side-participants* (those who are fully acknowledged as listeners, through hospitable assumptions of background knowledge, and could be at any time selected as addressees, and entitled to take a turn); (2a) *bystanders* (who are recognised by participants as within earshot but who will not be designated as participants); (2b) *eavesdroppers* (listeners of whom participants are unaware, and for whom no provisions can be made). Clark sees language itself as *designing audience*: in its capacity for registering speakers' estimates of listeners' background knowledge, through presupposing and non-presupposing expressions, language assigns audience positions. So, while, Kausalya listens, the Maharaj Kumar might say to Mangal, Where is the princess, Mangal? signalling Mangal's role as addressee not only with a vocative but also with a definite expression, which selects a listener who can identify the entity in question – i.e., someone who will not say "what princess?" If in his next utterance he turns to Kausalya, and says, "Do you know?" He makes her the addressee (with *you*) but also signals that she was a ratified participant in the first utterance, "Do you know?" being elliptical and depending on the previous utterance (addressed to Mangal) for its interpretation. Now, if a third person should be loitering in the vicinity, one who is not ratified as a participant – i.e., not eligible for vocative or second-person address – the Maharaj Kumar can *design* the audience position for that figure along one of two lines. He can estimate that person's knowledge of the referent as, say, incomplete and provide that the *overhearer* understand the reference – ... the princess, my wife ... – or he can ignore the overhearer's needs and leave them to infer the identity of "the princess." The final audience position is one that is out of the hands of the speaker: if the overhearer is concealed from the participants, then the speaker's language will bear no traces of the *eavesdropper's* presence.

entertain a South Asian experience of the world but shun a Western one. Acknowledged by some aspects of the narrative, Western readers can be moved by other aspects of it to the position of overhearer, or eavesdropper. But there is more to the design of *Cuckold's* audience than this array of listening posts. Some stylistic dimensions design a position for a more local reader, one fixed in a particular time and place. For example, presumably Western and South Asian readers alike must accommodate a reference in the Maharaj Kumar's account of sports events during a military campaign.

> There was a terrific festive air in the camp now. It was almost like *the annual competition* at Chittor. (219, emphasis added)

Such references may be geopolitically innocent, locating the speaker in a particular time and place now inaccessible to all modern readers, and designed for a reader whose experience is next-door to the Maharaj Kumar's. On the day of the solar eclipse, the Maharaj Kumar's inventory of the *givens*[5] of Chittor mirrors an indigenous, habituated recognition of locally familiar entities; just as the definite reference to 16th century Chittor's annual competition presupposes a local experience of the world, so too do these definite expressions:

---

[5] *Given* and *New* have long been categories of inquiry in linguistic pragmatics, and they are also bases for Clark's theories of audience design. Expressions which are designated as *given* are those whose form indicates that the listener/reader is taken by the speaker/writer to be able to identify the entity in question, either from co-text, as *the princess* and *the crowd* here – A princess stepped onto the balcony, observed by a large crowd. *The princess* began to sing, and *the crowd* drew closer – or from immediate physical context: a listener-speaker speaker pair are standing before a palace, aware of one another looking at the balcony, or from previous knowledge of the world, as in the example offered in footnote 1, Where is the princess, Mangal? See Ellen Prince. "Towards a taxonomy of give and new" for a careful analysis of the various conditions which trigger definite expressions and givenness.

> *The children* playing marbles and spinning tops in *the streets*; *the steady, hypnotic swing, and splash* of clothes at *the dhobi ghat on the river*; *the vegetable, fruit, pearl and precious-stone vendors* calling out and hectoring passers-by and *of course the continuous quarrying* of stone for Sahasmal's water and sewage system. (554, emphasis added)

Of course ("this is what you know as well as I") ties the circle of familiarity tighter. The circle is also sometimes explicitly indicated, coaxing from the congregation of readers a lightly-sketched but particular identity invoked for playful camaraderie –

> ... my clairvoyance is not yet foolproof. It had not taken into account a small twist of fate, or should I say foot. (As *you* can see I may criticize mediocre word play severely but catch me on a bad day and *you*'ll find me indulging in the foulest and most revolting of puns.) (284)

Or, for sober exposition:

> We Sisodias are, *as you know*, but regents of the supreme power of Shiva and that is the source of the authority vested in my family. (437, emphasis added)

When the eunuch Bruhannada retells a segment of the *Mahabharata*, the Maharaj Kumar describes him as "[choosing] Bhishma, the greatest celibate in the epic as the symbol of an abstemiousness that is not of one's choosing." The Maharaj Kumar's summary of Bruhannada's story addresses a reader who has a close familiarity with the tale:

> This is *of course* a bit of a grey area. *As you are well aware*, Bhishma's ageing father Shantanu fell in love with the beauteous Satyavati but she would not agree to the marriage unless her son

> and not Bhishma inherited the throne. (508, emphasis added)

These are careful preparations for an intended reader, someone in some way known to the Maharaj Kumar, who cannot be among those who come across the story in 1997, or 2004. This *you* makes us all overhearers – some entertained or acknowledged more readily than others but possibly each position in the audience of overhearers has its moments of ease, and familiarity, and its moments of accommodation.

The Maharaj Kumar's own scale of familiarity can also adjust according to his position. On the road, the ratio of newness to givenness rises, reminding us that it is not only the measure of the audience's experiences of the world which configures presupposing expressions but also the speaker's own experience of the world: when something is new to him, it is offered as novel to his reader as well. Riding out from Kumbhalgarh to Ranakpur, the Maharaj Kumar prepares for sightseeing –

> I woke everybody at one thirty.... I had not been to Ranakpur before and I wanted to see it in the first light at dawn. (361)

– and indefinite expressions (indicated below and elsewhere by italicising) configure the newness of the scene to him, his unfamiliarity with it:

> At the extreme corner of the building are *rounded bulwarks* as at any fort except that these are much shorter. Ranged across the entire plinth are *enclosure walls* that are really a series of miniature temples housing subsidiary luminaries from the Jain pantheon. *Four beautifully proportioned central gateways* interrupt the shrines on all four sides. (362, emphasis added)

In reports of travel, *newness* captures motion, in sync with the speaking subject's own movements, and with the limitation or dilation of his view, and his apprehension of his surroundings:

> It is impossible to gauge how stupendously large and complex the temple is until you get to the very heart of the edifice. And, yet, that is a limited and partial view for one has not yet climbed to the first and then the second story. (362)

In the venture into an unknown location, a world unfolds on the page according to and recording the momentum of the observing figure.

And across the pages of the memoir comes another traveller: Babur, the imminent conqueror, represented by his diaries and the Maharaj Kumar's reading of them. In his secret study of these documents, the Maharaj Kumar is particularly attracted by passages recording journeys and sightseeing along routes which are, as we will see, stylistically parallel to his own travel remarks. Babur was "constantly on the move, from Samarkand to Kabul to Kandahar to Samarkand and other places" (382). The diarist writes from this mobility, as new things appear, and/or are presented as new information:

> Farghana has *seven separate townships*, five on the south and two on the north of the Saihun river.
>
> Of those on the south, one is Andijan. It has a central position and is the capital of the Farghana country. It produces *much grain, fruits in abundance, excellent grapes and melons*. In the melon season it is customary to sell them out at the beds. Better than the Andijan nashpati, there is none. After Samarkand and Kesh, the fort of Andijan is the largest in Transoxiana. It has *three gates*. Its citadel is on

> its south side. Into it water goes by *nine channels*; out of it, it is strange that none comes at even a single place. Round the outer edge of the ditch runs *a gravelled highway*; the width of this highway divides the fort from the suburbs surrounding it. (380, emphasis added)

The Maharaj Kumar is absorbed by these passages, returning to them and their tangible renderings of an Other:

> It seems hard to believe that I am actually holding pages of matter written God-knows-where, Farghana, Samarkand, Kandahar or Kabul in my hands and that they are the words of a king whose ancestors hailed from the distant kingdom of Turkey.
>
> For some reason I keep going back to two passages, one about Andijan in Farghana and the other about his father. There is a quiet warmth in the tone of writing which could only come from someone who is deeply attached to his country. And yet it is devoid of the sentimentality that accompanies most writing about one's homeland, especially if one is an exile. It makes the reader want to go and explore the place for oneself. (388)

Why does the account of Andijan compel this reader – even move him to find the *place*? The Maharaj Kumar analyses his interest in terms of the writer's unsentimental attachment to his country – maybe something like a discretion, a kind of attentive reserve. But what are the materials of this attention? We have seen above that Andijan is reported in indefinite expressions which indicate newness *seven separate townships*, *three gates*, *a gravelled highway* – mixed with definite expressions indicating familiarity and expectedness – *its citadel*, *the suburbs*: in other words, a salient mix of Babur's immediate, fresh experience and his accumulated knowledge of the world. Although it is in "his country," Babur represents Andijan as a discovery, and finds aspects of it "strange," and unanswerable. So we might speculate that the Maharaj Kumar is compelled by the print of Babur's voice poised on the threshold of the new, each mention locating not only the object reported but also the consciousness of the reporter and its encounter with the unknown. Feeling an access to the diarist through these arrangements in language which signal the speaker's *position*, the Maharaj Kumar is ready to authenticate the documents he holds:

> I suspect that these words are true, and come from a man of great resolve and vision, a man whose sense of self is neither inflated nor modest, but matter-of-fact. (388)

This sense of authenticity triggers recognition – "I see myself in him" (383) – but also involves awareness of "unbridgeable differences between us" (383). The absolutism of Babur's faith alienates his clandestine reader:

> Diaries, at least those that are not written deviously with an ulterior motive and for public consumption, I'm convinced are far more revealing than a face-to-face encounter or even a long acquaintance with the person. One thing is certain the more I get to know Babur, the more I want to know him. Why must religion be such an unbridgeable divide? I would have liked to meet him, even be friends with him. (421)

Stylistically, the diary is also "unbridgeable." It comes in fragments – "scraps" (379), "bits and pieces" (378):

> "They don't always make sense," Mangal wrote, "but that's because our source picks up whatever he can and they are almost invariably out of context." (435)

We can expect these unbridgeables – perhaps like the religious ones – to index the writer's and reader's separateness, but in addition they also urge the Maharaj Kumar to imagine friendly intimacy with Babur:

> Sometimes I resolve to ask Babur himself for clarifications and annotations when we get together one of these days and are sitting outside his tent of an evening and drinking the wine which he so often talks of renouncing. (435)

With its patterns of assumed familiarity, and its projected contexts of understanding, language will always be a site both for affinity – a moment for recognition or for understandings so deeply shared as to be invisible – and for estrangement, when the sharing uncouples and collapses. But even then, when the overheard speech breaks into fragments, or on-going discourses move out of earshot – even then the estrangement can convert to affinity. So, just as the Maharaj Kumar eavesdrops on Babur (or, just as Western readers stand by as passages go on without them, or eavesdrop on passages that go on oblivious to them); just as the Maharaj Kumar finds the doubleness of identification and repudiation in his experience of reading the diaries, and then feels the sensation of friendly interrogation inspired by gaps and missing contexts, readers who are not the projected *you* of the Maharaj Kumar's narrative are in a ceaseless trepidation of understanding, seizing a moment of recognition, then jilted, each reversal portending the heterogeneous sectors of audience, and screening the elusive subject.

I

One aspect of Bakhtin's theories of dialogism that has been readily absorbed by rhetoricians but less thoroughly attended to by literary critics is his conception of *genre*. (At the same time, new-rhetorical[6] thought has been less attentive to dialogism *per se*.) For Bakhtin, genres are formations of discourse and lifeways in which language and interest are "knitted"[7] together. In fact, this knitting is what makes dialogism possible: words are impressed with *situation* – with the intentions, experiences, situations, values of the social groups which use them. Words are attracted into the "orbits" of these groups – and then detached for use in the dialogic contexts of novelistic discourse (and also for use in the ordinary give-and-take of heteroglossia, where wordings from different social strata come up against each other). From *Cuckold* itself, one example of the force of situation impressing language is the voice of the travel *genre* sounding in the narrative: its characteristic formation of indefinite expressions indicates the typical context of such utterance, the traveller's encounter with a mix of unfamiliar and familiar symbolised in the recognisable forms of travel narration, in this case the focus on architectural exteriors and layouts. Bakhtin sees the novel as a matrix of such genres[8] (for example,

---

[6] Broadly speaking, the "new" rhetoric distinguishes itself from, without rejecting, classical rhetoric by overriding classical distinctions amongst rhetorical, dialectic, and poetic language, and insisting, instead, on the "persuasiveness" of *all* language, including scientific language. Kenneth Burke's work can be identified as a watershed in the new-rhetorical conceptions of language.

[7] "Certain features of language (lexicological, semantic, syntactic) will knit together with the intentional aim, and with the overall accentual system inherent in one or another genre: oratorical, publicistic, newspaper and journalistic genres, the genres of low literature (penny dreadfuls, for example) or, finally, the various genres of high literature. Certain features of language take on the specific flavour of a given genre: they knit together with specific points of view, specific approaches, forms of thinking, nuances and accents characteristic of the given genre" (288-89). And woven into and through this generic stratification of language, substantively and practically, are the materials of "professional" stratification of language – the business, the interests, intentions, and conceptualisations of "the lawyer, the doctor, the businessman, the politician, the public education teacher and so forth ..." (289).

diaries, letters, memoranda, announcements, petitions), this matrix organising the author's vision of the concourse of the social order.

The Maharaj Kumar himself is aware of the precedents that compose the regularities of genres – and also aware of the implications they have for the identity of the speaking subject. For example, he hears Mangal through the genre which is dictated by their relative positions in the social order. Mangal's performance in the report/briefing genre fills out his executive position, his socio-political identity – yet, there is some residue, too, possibly, some aspect of being not entirely represented in this letter-perfect performance of an administrative genre:

> Is there any doubt that Mangal and I fed at the same breast after you've read his report? He may be more terse than I but that's because *the format of a briefing demands brevity, clarity, a conclusion and a line of action.* I doubt if I will ever have to rework a Mangal-report before presenting it to Father. (387, emphasis added)

Somewhere at heart, Mangal and the Maharaj Kumar are the same, but the brief-writing situation doesn't get quite to the heart.

The residual self, the identity not entirely fulfilled in the sociohistorical rendering, can also be a discrepancy – even a calculated one. So when Babur issues his *farman*, his proclamation renouncing wine, the Maharaj Kumar reads

---

[8] "The novel permits the incorporation of various genres, both artistic (inserted short stories, lyrical songs, poems, dramatic scenes, etc.) and extra-artistic (everyday, rhetorical, scholarly, religious genres and others). In principle, any genre could be included in the construction of the novel, and in fact it is difficult to find any genres that have not at some point been incorporated into a novel by someone. Such incorporated genres usually preserve within the novel their own structural integrity, as well as their own linguistic and stylistic peculiarities" (321).

it as coming not from the authentic subject of the diaries but from an adulterated source:

> It is written in a florid style and full of bombast, obviously not the work of the diarist I knew but one of his secretaries or priests. (573)

The "format" of a genre can render an identity – or betray it – and these possibilities have occupied the attention of new-rhetorical genre theorists, raising issues of genres' impositions of values, their coercion of the subject into standard social roles. Yet, when the Maharaj Kumar recognises the motivations of genre in his own writing, he also recognises genres' enactments of the multiplicity of *self* – even, as here, the alternation of selves:

> The agenda was to write two books. I wrote my autobiography on odd dates and the massive introduction to Shafi's book on *The Art and Science of Retreat* on even dates. (343)
>
> I wrote as usual with a long, firm and neat hand. But the language and the thought processes of the two texts were different without any conscious intention on my part. The prose of the "Retreats" text was formal and precise. I composed entire paragraphs, often several pages in my head [...]
> I did not have a plan for my memoirs but its language came as a shock to me. I tried to resist it, at times tore up page after page but finally gave in. I realized for the first time that my mind was a two-tongued instrument: an austere, distanced and deliberative high Mewari for the purposes of ratiocination and logic; and a cross between the language of the court and the colourful, pungent and coruscating dialect of the eunuchs, servants and maids in the palace. (345-56)

From a Bakhtinian perspective, it's important that mind is realised in *tongues*, language being the site of the person's "ideological becoming" (341). And, from a Bakhtinian perspective, the mind analysed here would be more than *two*-tongued: the military treatise is the expression of one plane in the social order; the language of the court another; the language of eunuchs another, of maids another, and so on. And the speaking subject is this confabulation of voices, some discrete, like the military voice; some promiscuous, like the repartee of the court and its folk.

Designing not only these interlocutions but also the Maharaj Kumar's reflections on them, Nagarkar tells us how a figure tells a story: as Bakhtin observes, "behind the narrator's story we read a second story: the author's story; he is the one who tell us how the narrator tells stories, and also tells us about the narrator himself" (314). The author stands in relation to the character's words, even as the speaking character himself takes into his own speech others' words and takes a position *vis-à-vis* these words. But not all chapters of *Cuckold* are told by the Maharaj Kumar, and the exemptions are patterned on at least one dimension: chapters for which the Maharaj Kumar is not the speaker are (with one exception) those which attend private encounters between the Maharaj Kumar and his wife. Late in the novel we hear what might be an explanation for this stylistic feature. Reading Mangal's last message to him, written in anticipation of assassination and received following the death of the Maharana, and then turning to a letter from Kausalya, the Maharaj Kumar reads her estimate of his own opportunity to be "the greatest Rajput ruler the country has ever seen. You have the vision and wiliness to beat all our enemies and become Maharana of the whole of India" (599). But this destiny is contingent – "Can you break with your wife?" – for the Princess's dominion is insidious:

> It took me a long time to realize this but I finally understood that she would destroy Mewar. The saddest part in all this was the influence she had over you. You seemed to *lose your mind* when you were with her. (598, emphasis added)

What does it mean for the Maharaj Kumar to *lose his mind*? How does this *loss* materialise in the stylistics of the Princess chapters?

Wallace Chafe's linguistic theories of consciousness can help us track the lost mind, and still remain within the domain visible from a Bakhtinian perspective. In a detailed technical analysis of a corpus of conversation and of literary and non-literary texts, Chafe in *Discourse, Consciousness, and Time* (1994) begins by demonstrating the fusion and fissure of the speaking subject: even as the "I" can recount its own experience, it splits from itself, into a Representing Consciousness and a Represented Consciousness, first along fundamentals of time and place, where a speaker (Representing Consciousness) tells *now* and *here* his or her experience *then* and *there*, that experience belonging to Represented Consciousness. This fissure – commonplace and plausible – between "proximal" and "distal" consciousness grows, in Chafe's analysis, to account for much more mysterious subjectivities at play between Representing Consciousness and Represented Consciousness. Especially mysterious is the position of the "unacknowledged self" – an agent of narration or of exposition traditionally identified as "third person." In Chafe's analysis, this conventional category, both catch-all and empty vessel, emerges as a site of great complexity and potential virtuosity. Where the "unacknowledged self" takes on the duties of the Representing Consciousness, we can meet – or, in a sense, just miss meeting – a narrator who plays no part in the events of the story. We might say that this speaker is not *embodied*, cannot be tracked down in the fictional world. But it can nevertheless disclose itself in tell-tale linguistic signs: time and place deictics, modals, evaluations, patterns of presupposition, and sometimes in simple-present maxims which can be assigned to no bodily figure but must go to this hovering intelligence. Yet so discreet can this narrating consciousness be that it can also dissolve into an absence, which in the purest form divests itself of all indications of position, these flowing usually to the third person protagonist, although they can also be distributed amongst several characters. We might ask if the possibility of the *lost mind* lies somewhere in these uncertain zones.

In the Princess chapters, readers are in the custody of an "unacknowledged self" as narrator: the Representing Consciousness is intangible, and all indications of subjectivity are assigned to the third-person figure. To begin to explore such conditions, let us go to third-person Chapter 16, where the Maharaj Kumar returns to the palace, and is about to go to bed when he overhears his wife's voice, and goes to her door. We are for this chapter provided with a third-person narrator, but that Representing Consciousness shares in every particular the limits of the Maharaj Kumar's knowledge: here, for example, there are no answers to the Maharaj Kumar's question beyond the evidence and reasoning he himself can bring to bear on the matter:

> Who could she be talking to? He had given strict orders the previous evening that the doors of her rooms were to be locked in perpetuity from the outside. Kumkum Kanwar could cook for her, bathe her and do whatever else her mistress wished but whatever happened, even if a fire broke out, she was not to be let out. (187)

What we can know of the situation is not only limited to what the Maharaj Kumar can know, in his position in front of the closed door of the room, but is also rendered according to his familiarity or unfamiliarity with elements of this segment of life at the court. He expects the doorkeeper, so, rather than "There was *a eunuch* outside her door," that figure appears as a *given*:

> *The eunuch* outside her door was fast asleep. He had a soft downy snore. When he exhaled, his mouth worked furiously to grab the air and eat it. (187, emphasis added)

At the same time, some features of this scene are radically unknowable – for example, the specificities of another's inferred dream:

> Was he the one talking? No, he was far too busy eating some *ambrosial stuff* of which he could not have enough. (187, emphasis added)

Other features (below) are points of speculation from this position of limited knowledge, modals (*seemed, must, sure*) indicating the processes of the Represented Consciousness evaluating immediate evidence and combining it with stored assumptions about the world. Deictic *this* anchors this consciousness spatially, close to the eunuch, and evaluative expressions indicate some standard by which appearances are judged:

> The Prince could hear his wife's voice better now. It *seemed* unlikely that she was conversing with *this* corpulent dead weight through a locked door. *Not bad looking* though. *Must* have cut a fine figure when he was young and despite the absence of extended genitalia. Was *sure* to have been popular with the queens. (187)

A Representing Consciousness with more elbow-room, with scope beyond the borders of the Represented Consciousness, might tell us *why* the Maharaj Kumar has to touch the eunuch:

> ... the thought of touching that genderless flesh was repulsive. The Maharaj Kumar had to grit

> his teeth when he bent down and slipped his hand in the eunuch's pocket. (187)

Instead, we are confined to what is established in the Maharaj Kumar's mind – the fulfilled expectation that keys are to be found in the eunuch's pocket:

> It took some time and trying for the Prince to figure out which of *the two dozen or so keys* fitted the lock on his wife's door. (187)

Thereafter the schedule of revelation is scaled exactly to what is known or new to the Maharaj Kumar himself – a pattern of definite and indefinite expressions signalling the pace of his awareness:

> He opened *the latch* softly. *Her bed* was made as his own had been on *the night of the wedding. Flowers* were strung from *the four posters* and lay crushed on *the mattress*. She was lying on her back, not a shred of cloth on her. Her clothes were thrown helter-skelter as if *someone* in *a rush of indelicate impatience* had disrobed her. He stepped over *the eunuch* and lightly closed *the door* behind him. When he turned round, he froze. She was staring at him. [...] He realized then that she was totally oblivious of him. (87-88, emphasis added)

Knowing only what the Maharaj Kumar can know, when he knows it, we have a previous claim corrected, even though this claim *she was staring at him* was originally expressed without qualifying modality as in *must have been a favourite*. The sequence of newness signals the subject's unfolding awareness, while deictic expressions – *the opposite wall, in front* – secure the (limited) position from which this spectacle can be understood:

> Against *the opposite wall* was *a low, red stool* barely three inches from the ground. *In front* of

> it was *a gold thali* filled to overflowing with *all manner of food*, most of it *sweets and pastries* made from milk and curds. No, he said to himself, it didn't look as if the meal was laid out for him. In one corner of the room she had drawn *an uncredibly elaborate painting* with rangoli powder of the Flautist and herself dancing the raas on the banks of the Jamuna. (187-88, emphasis added)

Is this a *lost mind*? It is attentive, speculative, inference-producing: what could we say has gone missing? At first a seemingly more eligible candidate for the *lost mind* might be the consciousness represented in Chapter 19, the record of the Maharaj Kumar sunstruck, dazed, truly out of his mind – yet, rendered in the same stylistic profile as the Represented Consciousness of the Princess chapters. Here the scope of familiar and unfamiliar, definite and indefinite, and the direction of speculation suggest a consciousness even more hindered, as the Maharaj Kumar reconnoitres from a very limited position indeed. His estimate of time is uncertain and iterative (*some days ago, a couple of days, a few days*), his discoveries trivial (*a mound of sand, a slow hissing sound*) – or alienating, as the flute he carries, something already known, becomes unidentifiable: *something hard*. Resources for his inferences are limited to the guilt he shoulders, the possibility that he might be a mass murderer, which haunts him throughout.

> He had abandoned Befikir *some days ago*. As if that wasn't bad enough, he couldn't now recall where he had misplaced one of his shoes. He sat down and scooped up sand with the remaining shoe and poured it out at the same speed he had seen it run down in an hourglass. There was *a foot-high mound* in front of him. He *must* have been playing Father Time for hours, *maybe* even *a couple of days*. Before that

> he had walked for *a few days*. At every step his foot sank irretrievably into the sand. He fought hard to pull it out but all that frantic activity only made the sand shift. There was *a slow hissing sound* and the foot was sucked in further. Was he getting a taste of what he had put the Gujarat soldiers through? Was this his final comeuppance? It couldn't be. There was no way he would have an easy and swift end, of that much *he was sure*.
> *Something* hard was poking sharply into his back. (236, emphasis added)

There are however in *Cuckold* more than just two profiles for the Representing Consciousness – more than the one acknowledged as the Maharaj Kumar himself and the unacknowledged one which is entirely dedicated to or hostage to the Maharaj Kumar's consciousness and only his. Around the wedding of the Prince hovers a reporting mind which is more mobile and resourceful. This Representing Consciousness makes an appearance after the wedding, when the party returns to Chittor from the bride's home. The occasion is told by a consciousness which can report some events which the Maharaj Kumar himself might have reported, had this been a first-person chapter.

> The wedding party returned home. Her favourite uncle, Rao Viramdev accompanied her to Chittor. She was allowed to bring a friend or servant along with her who would stay with her all her life. She brought her childhood friend and maid, Kumkum Kanwar. (71)

But this Representing Consciousness can also follow the bride and her maid, as the Maharaj Kumar may or may not have done:

> They had never been outside Merta and Kumkum was full of wonder and alarm at the sights, scenes

> and smells of Chittor. Merta was a small town compared to Chittor. Chittor was wealthy and worldly. It was filthy, spacious, corrupt, crowded and self-assured. Kumkum Kanwar could not keep a lid on her excitement. She tugged at her friend's sleeve, pointed breathlessly at the Victory Tower, she screamed with delight at the size of the custard apples, she was horrified at the boldness and number of the beggars, her eyes enlarged in disbelief at the variety of precious stones, pearls and jewellery exhibited so casually in the marketplace. Her mouth remained agape that whole day. (71)

Since Kumkum exhibits such plain external signs of her experience, possibly any watchful observer could have gathered evidence of her inner-state. The Princess on the other hand is less demonstrative – "Her young mistress was quiet" – so the narrator's disclosures suggest a greater privilege of access:

> But she was neither snobbish nor supercilious from a sense of inferiority. She was as eager, impressionable and excited as her maid. Since the time she reached her teens, she had always been shy and quiet. Her new status as bride to the Maharaj Kumar of Chittor had added an edge of reserve to her temperament because she did not understand the implications and nuances of entering such a large and alien household. She was at the epicentre when she would rather not even have been on the outermost periphery. (71-72)

The narrative disclosures follow the Princess's gaze, as it turns to the objects of her concern:

> Her husband did not speak to her the first six days of her stay. He looked pale and anaemic and hurt beyond mortal help. She tried to do

> things for him, get his slippers, fetch his saafa, button his kurta, dry his wet hair after a bath. He turned away. (72)

After following her to respite at her hometown, the Representing Consciousness restores the concerned gaze to the reticent husband. Seven weeks after her return,

> He looked more haunted than before she had left. There was a tightness to his mouth and his eyes were the water at the bottom of the hundred foot well in her home. (73)

But then within this paragraph the Representing Consciousness can turn from its investment in the Princess's attention – an investment even to the point of offering a figure of speech from the Princess's hometown: can turn on a dime to a following sentence which transfers nearly imperceptibly to the Prince's daily schedule, not immediately entering into it, but perhaps observing on the Princess's behalf, like a private detective surreptitiously trailing the husband while he is out of her sight, and providing some intimate findings:

> He no longer tried to sleep at night. He held himself erect, it was something his body could not unlearn after so many years of military training. But it was an empty shell that managed to be at work at six; conducted the affairs of the ministries under him, talked business, assisted his father in formulating strategy, attended official functions, presided at the small causes court on Thursdays, played cards on new year's night. But there was no person there, only the pain of not knowing and the fear of discovering the truth. (73)

With the last turn of this passage – to *pain*, *fear* – the Representing Consciousness enters into the Maharaj Kumar's experience.

The surreptitious Representing Consciousness of this chapter can follow Kausalya too – tracking her down in her own espionage as she observes the Princess's composing process –

> Kausalya wasn't quite sure whether it was something about the Princess' writing or the way she put it away that struck her as odd. She knew that her mind was working overtime these days imagining clues and omens in everything and everywhere. But you had to admit that it was a little unusual for a Princess, even a literate one, to be always writing. The Maharani, for instance, or even the favourite, Queen Karmavati, never wrote, or they got some scribe to do it. (75)

– and recording her inferences from other watchful experiences, knowing the measures Kausalya takes in absolute secrecy to gather evidence –

> It was a mystery where [the princess] hid all her writing material. Kausalya had gone through almost everything in her rooms. It had taken a long while. The only time you could search the place was when she was having a bath and when nobody was around. (76)

– and having access to affective responses and silent evaluations:

> It was a little disconcerting to find that she did not keep anything under lock and key, not even her jewellery. She was a trusting fool, she was. (76)

When she finds the Princess's compositions, indefinite expressions stage the moment of discovery:

> The pages were wrapped in muslin and, along

> with *an ink-pot and quills*, were stowed away in *a drawer* under the platform and the holy silk. (76, emphasis added)

We can only regard these sought-after pages from Kausalya's position, estimating the extent of her find – "There *must* have been at least four or five hundred pages there of which more than a half were full of written matter" – and inspecting them with the scrutiny of an illiterate person:

> The individual letters were beautifully formed like black studs carved with infinite care and often an entire sentence stood out like a necklace of black pearls. But if you took all the lines together, the total filigree work on the page *looked* a confused and convoluted mess. There were long stretches which *seemed* to have been written in a scrawl that was trying to catch up with her frenzied thoughts. (76, emphasis added)

The illiterate perspective of Kausalya is frustrated in its efforts at interpretation: "Kausalya could not relate the writing to its mistress. She was so neat, tidy and unruffled" (76). The surreptitious consciousness then follows the letters to the Maharaj Kumar's desk, and the literate mind – solitary yet accessible to this roving representer – attempts a reading:

> He went through the pages, ten, fifteen, a hundred times. There were places where he couldn't link the zig-zag of her writing. It rose from the middle of the page, went to the next one, came back to the margin of the previous page, gave up the sentence, started another, abandoned that, and tried to revive the earlier one. (78)

Painstakingly, the Maharaj Kumar decodes the pages and then names and evaluates the speech acts:

> It was a delirious raving, a mad outpouring of passion and plaint, the most abject grovelling and fits of temper and tantrums. (78)

But even this roving, adept and agile consciousness, surreptitious and penetrating, is not the whole story – or the beginning of the story. For, backing up, we find that the account of the wedding has still more facets to add to narrative possibility. Chapter 3 begins:

> He had been the most eligible bachelor in this part of the world. It took them a long time to find a bride for him. Two or three proposals along with horoscopes arrived every day. They had to appoint a full-time priest to go through the horoscopes and decide which matched his. There was no point in looking at the proposals first and getting excited about a few of them only to discover that Saturn was in the wrong house in one princess's case another princess had a malevolent Mars dogging her. (40)

Could the Maharaj Kumar have said this? "I had been the most eligible bachelor in this part of the world": would this have worked? Possibly, for this Representing Consciousness is one which presupposes assumptions which would explain the relevance of horoscopes: it is compatible with the Maharaj Kumar in this, and also like the Maharaj Kumar in being on site, as indicated by the proximal deictic *this* in "this part of the world." But this Representing Consciousness has further dimensions to it. The discussion of horoscopes is followed by a maxim in the simple-present tense-aspect characteristic of the expression of timeless truths: "Marriage is a two-way street." This is not beyond the scope of the Maharaj Kumar's position, nor, possibly, are the next statements, where the simple present of maxims then shades into a less general, more limited application, referring to socio-historically contained custom:

> The girl's people make overtures. But the boy's relatives don't sit on their behinds and wait for a pari or an apsara to drop out of the heavens. (40)

But then *you* appears – in this usage, a person deictic on the border between first person and second person. Hinged to the interests of "the boy's relatives," it suggests that the speaker is aligned there, but also suggests that this position is one which the addressee would know too:

> You make your moves too, prepare a list of the houses you would like to be allied with, then find out if there's a suitable unmarried girl there without a limp or a cleft palate or polio legs. (40)

But the very next sentence invokes another *you* – one specifically located in the history of the Maharaj Kumar's family – not the shared position of the prior *you*, but the definitive, exclusive one of a particular interlocutor:

> Do *you* remember the time the Maharaj Kumar's father, the Rana, got married? The king of Mandasaur had a fine, vivacious daughter.... (40)

The discussion which follows, describing the fate of an eligible girl who is overlooked, and developing an account of subsequent matchmaking and betrothal inquiries, suggests, if not a busy-body, at least a courtly gossip-historian.

Once the marriage is arranged, the Representing Consciousness appears to join the wedding party, a modal verb indicating his estimate: "It *seemed* as if the whole of Chittor was going to Merta for the wedding" (42). In a festive, party-going frame of mind, the Representing Consciousness then invokes that fraternal *you,* sharing the first-person position with the second person:

> Other people's marriages, your brother's, sister's or friend's marriages are fun. Not your own. Prior to the marriage, Ganapati, the Auspicious One, sat in the palace for seven days. Each day, they fed the groom such rich food, he would soon sport an enormous paunch and become the twin brother of the elephant-headed god himself. (42)

But even the friendly speaker, seemingly cordial to a compatriot listener, well established and satisfied, can hand off representation, and the Representing Consciousness slips into "unacknowledged" status.

> He [the Prince] was suddenly at the threshold. He had alighted from the elephant. The priest had performed the puja and tied a string around his father's silk purse to make sure that the Rana didn't spend even a copper coin while he was a guest of Merta. The drums and the trumpets were still blaring. If he turned around he would see his father, close family and half the clan behind him. (43)

The *suddenness* is a sensation for the Maharaj Kumar – or is it a general sensation? *The elephant, the priest, the drums* are all established in the bridegroom's consciousness, but in others' too, in all likelihood, although perhaps not from the same perspective. But then disclosures arrive which can only be derived from the Maharaj Kumar's experience and which include the abstract speculations characteristic of his mentality:

> But he felt cut off from them. He would have to make it on his own from now ... He felt abandoned and alone. Surely two steps in either

> direction couldn't make such an irreversible difference. It was absurd but true nevertheless. He thought of his bride whom he had never seen. (40-43)

Once it has signed off, the genial consciousness of the chapter's opening is gone – gone home. In fact, it is unthinkable that he abide, for the Represented Consciousness is now as intimate as possible in its scope, retiring to the newlyweds' chamber, from which even wedding-night pranksters have been expelled.

> He realized that her fear made him clinical ... She shuddered and moved away. He wanted to take her in his arms as he had promised himself when he was at the threshold. How could he convince her that he would protect her from all harm? He wished there was a lion or a tiger in the room .... he could kill it with his sword and make her understand that he was her shield. (44-45)

The catastrophic copulation follows, an occasion perhaps when the presence of even a minimally acknowledged Representing Consciousness would be scandalous, disgraceful – especially shocking, that is, when that position has, at the start of the chapter, had a slight but tangible social coordinate, a trace of *self*. Implicated in the gradual withdrawal of a consciousness with a public presence, the third person itself eerily suggests that certain things *can* be known by others.

II

Chafe's categories offer a more technical account of the Bakhtinian double voice, the stylistics of subjectivity, and the virtuoso domains of the Representing Consciousness. In the story-telling of *Cuckold*, the most pronounced feat of the Representing Consciousness is its disappearance or camouflage in the Princess chapters, its retirement into an "unacknowledged self." In these passages it is absorbed into the erotics of the royal marriage, and there is no doubt much to be discovered in this. Yet we could also take a different, possibly complementary view, a political one, for Kausalya sees military and national consequence in the Maharaj Kumar's *loss of mind*.

By itself the stylistic performance of the Representing Consciousness in the Princess chapters might be impossible to interpret – but it is not by itself: it is not the only narrative variable. There is in addition a Representing Consciousness which is also an "unacknowledged self" but one not devoted exclusively to the Maharaj Kumar. As we have seen early in the novel, it is able to move amongst the experiences of the Princess and Kausalya, and thereby trouble, just barely, the moral stillness or unrippled reflection of a single point of view. And on the threshold of acknowledgement near the beginning of the story, there is the genial voice of another Representing Consciousness, gregarious, public, posing a convivial *you* which may or may not be different from the confidential *you* of the Maharaj Kumar's own diaries. In an atmosphere of conspiracy and espionage, military and civil intelligence; under circumstances which obsessively measure loyalty, suspect betrayal, and calculate trust – under these circumstances it is no small matter that a rogue or free-lance consciousness roams these chambers. How perfect is the fusion of Representing Consciousness with Represented Consciousness in the Princess chapters? Where has the surplus gone? Are leaks possible? While the Maharaj Kumar is always trying to find out others' secrets, his own may be open. Could the *lost mind* of the Princess chapters be the predicament of a sentry asleep at his post, a failure to keep a lookout, the sign of a double-agent, the anxiety that we are going to be blind-sided – or that we already have been, but don't know it yet? *Information* is a precarious quantity, simultaneously securing and exposing.

The voice of modernity which cuts across the 16th century voice also privileges information – acquired from surveillance, and systematic data-gathering. This theme could recontextualise, or re-accent ancient practice, finding in it the seeds of modern consciousness and modern administration. But time may flow both ways, its current carrying the ancient values of factional loyalty and deadly subterfuge towards 20th century images of rational administration, bringing antique espionage face-to-face with modern surveillance – kingship in dialogic exchange with government. In Bakhtin's view, the truly dialogic situation is ever unfinished – its outcome ever unforeseeable, escaping control. And so even the very terms which – by espionage or by surveillance – privilege information and control also act on one another for outcomes which can never be controlled or concluded, and can only be awaited: having brought these separate discourses into contact with one another, the narrative cannot bring their exchange to a conclusion, for the words themselves are delegates of differences which can never be resolved – or cannot be resolved without some edict from the party with the upper hand. For Bakhtin, this is a novelistic condition – and a democratic one, defying edicts. It is also one which does not arrive automatically, and comes at some cost: the sacrifice of "that system of national myth that is organically fused with language" (369). The sacrifice is executed by the "relativization of literary-language consciousness at the deepest level, ... its re-tuning to a new prosaic key" (368); the developed "sense" that a national language is "surrounded by an ocean of heteroglossia" (368). This "sense" is not indigenous to all regimes, but is, rather, a political aspiration to "[re-tune]" conflict: the fact of a "community [being] torn by social struggle" (368) is not in itself enough to cultivate a dialogic imagination. Struggle or conflict alone, without a dialogised awareness of speech diversity and its uncontrollable but infinitely fertile productivity, cannot accomplish the "step forward" in knowing the word's "actual power to mean in real ideological life" (352). The step forward is propelled by a philosophy of language which acknowledges and registers the voices of others, forsaking control over the word in favour of attention to, incorporation of the alien word; forsaking perfect or unified understanding for the hazard – and promise – of difference. It is Nagarkar's great political and philosophical accomplishment that the peak of this novel's dialogism is at the level of rule itself: the discourses of traditional hegemony and those of modern administration in contact.

Viewed in the terms Bakhtin uses to analyse epic, a dialogic narrative like the Maharaj Kumar's memoirs opposes the values emanating from the dominating voice of the ancestor – the unitary "system of national myth." The Maharaj Kumar himself expresses his own reservations about epic. Outlining his motives in composing his memoirs, the Maharaj Kumar complains about the ahistoricity of ideas of the past which seal it off from time and devote it to triumph:

> The past was with my countrymen every moment of their lives. History for them was that fabled second chance. They could rework the past and get it right this time around. It was an act of faith and invention where defeats turned to glory; courage, bravery and heroism were chosen above vision or long-term gains and enmity was more precious than alliances. Best of all, you did not have to tot up the accounts and pay for the grandeur of your delusions or the vacuity of your mistakes. To them five

> hundred years ago was the same as yesterday, an episode outside the orbit of time. The past was never your responsibility. It was not the sum total of mankind's wisdom, errors and insights. It was not the torch that lit the darkness and choices of today. (344-45)

At the same time, though, the Maharaj Kumar has a reverent and knowledgeable regard for the august texts inherited from time immemorial, and, decently Machiavellian, he also recognises the value of tradition in maintaining order: "A kingship survives on institutions, and there's no greater institution than tradition" (165).

Like Bakhtin, the Maharaj Kumar also opposes poetry, but for less explicitly specified reasons. Reading the purloined pages of his wife's compositions, he finds

> ... quatrains and broken verses and entire poems. There were padas that she had started and scratched out. The lyrics were the only text that he didn't read. Poetry left him cold. His curiosity was intense but try as he might, he couldn't overcome his resistance to verse. (78-79)

While we might estimate Nagarkar's position *vis-à-vis* epic somewhere near the Maharaj Kumar's (and Bakhtin's), from the evidence of his arrangements for dialogic design, what can we make of his position *vis-à-vis* poetry? The Maharaj Kumar reconciles himself to some poetic expression as the narrative advances: even as he "[excoriates] the banality of besotted love songs to the Flautist" (415) he nevertheless responds to the music; and even as poetry was "the one-time bane" of his life, by the time he is beginning to read Babur's diaries, he "must confess that in the last couple of years, constant exposure has worn me down to the point that I am not only receptive to it but even look forward to it occasionally" (379). For his part, Nagarkar, in his "Historical Note," acknowledges the lyric legacy:

> A great number of [saints in India] wrote truly superb verse, lyrical, passionate, colloquial, abstruse, rigorous, humorous, romantic, austere, complex, playful. (608)

Although these qualities are not quite those which distinguish the writings of his own fictional Little Princess, and may not exactly describe the poetry of the historical princess either, Nagarkar appreciates the latter's capacity to invest a public national consciousness:

> The Indian imagination responded warmly to the romantic story of the Princess and her divine paramour, and her travails with her in-laws. She was a fairly prolific writer. Her love poetry was in the confessional mode and she has innumerable imitators even in this day and age. Her imagery, the turn of phrase and her work are part of the conscious and unconscious vocabulary of Indians. (609)

This surge of reiteration pours through the popular genres of the 20th century – cinema, plays, dances, poetry, painting, feminist commentary, as well as song:

> The Little Saint, as we all know, became a very big saint.... Her bhajans, love-poetry and other kinds of verse are sung all over the country. More singers have recorded her songs than those of any other poet or saint. The other great Bhakti saints may have been intellectually more robust than her but their fame is mostly regional. Her name is on almost every Indian's lips. (609)

In seeking *intention*, we might consider that the book's patterns of familiarity and unfamiliarity can have meanings in themselves, meanings in the seamless merging of the speaker's and the addressee's experiences of the world – and their sudden rupturing, along fissures which divide and subdivide *Cuckold's* audience: telling configurations of affinity and estrangement. In the monologic voice of (lyric) poetry there is, on the one hand, no danger of rupture, but instead, according to Nagarkar's estimate, a guarantee of the familiar, reiterated and multiplied; on the other hand, the poetic voice can promise no new coalitions, for it is only in the risk of estrangement that new affinities are possible. The dialogic design of *Cuckold* performs in these high-risk zones. It convenes readers globally but also disaggregates that audience; it invests in the privacy of the memoir but hints at a clandestine audience with unknown ambitions; it remobilises the past to negotiate uncertain terms with the present. That design is full of hazard: someone will not understand and, thereby knowing their separateness, may act on the sensation; a secret may make its way into the wrong hands, treacherously; the national sureties of an epic past may be exposed to provocations from beyond its borders. But these hazards are companions of possibility too. Right inside *Cuckold* itself there is an image of such conditions: the Maharaj Kumar's reading of Babur's diaries – collected by military intelligence, fragmented, overheard, antagonistic and at the same time, by virtue of their gaps and presumptions, an imaginary invitation to "get together one of these days" (435).

Works Cited

Bakhtin, M. M. *The Dialogic Imagination*. Trans. Caryl Emerson and Michael Holquist. Austin: U of Texas P, 1981.

Burchell, Graham, Colin Gordon, and Peter Miller, eds. *The Foucault Effect: studies in governmentality with two lectures and an interview with Michel Foucault*. Chicago: U of Chicago P, 1991.

Chafe, Wallace. *Discourse, Consciousnes, and Time: the flow and displacement of conscious experience in speaking and writing.* Chicago: U of Chicago P, 1994.

Clark, Herbert H. *Arenas of Language Use*. Chicago: U of Chicago P, 1992.

Dasenbrock, Reed Way. *Intelligibility and Meaningfulness in Multicultural Literature in English.* PMLA 102. (1987).

Giddens, Anthony. *The Consequences of Modernity*. Stanford: Stanford U P, 1990.

Giltrow, Janet, and David Stouck. "Survivors of the Night": The Language and Politics of Epic in Antonine Maillet's *Pélagie-la-charrette. University of Toronto Quarterly.* 71: 3. 735-53. 2002.

Nagarkar, Kiran. *Cuckold*. New Delhi: Harper Collins *Publishers* India, 1997.

Prince, Ellen. "Toward a Taxonomy of Given-New Information." Ed. Peter Cole. *Radical Pragmatics*. New York: Academic P, 1981.

Sperber, Dan, and Deirdre Wilson. *Relevance: communication and cognition.*1986. 2nd ed. Cambridge: Blackwell, 1995.

Interpretative Possibilities of Historical Fiction: A Perspective on Kiran Nagarkar's *Cuckold*

Anirudh Deshpande

I

> *You were Mewar's and my great hope ... You were meant for greater things. Highness. You have it in you to be the greatest Rajput ruler the country has seen. You have the vision and wiliness to beat all our enemies and become Maharana of the whole of India. Can you break with your wife? Only then will you be able to get the better of your brother and his mother and concentrate on Babur and our other enemies.*
>
> – Quoted from the last letter to Maharaj Kumar from Kausalya, his wet nurse and mistress, *Cuckold*, 598-600.

This paper examines the academic potential of historical fiction.[1] It is based on a selective reading of Kiran Nagarkar's historical novel *Cuckold*, which is set in medieval

[1] Based on a paper presented at a seminar on Kiran Nagarkar's Fiction organized by the English Department of the University of Mumbai on 7 march, 2001. A revised version was presented at the NMMI, Teen Murti on 4 September, 2001.

north India. Throughout the article some parts of *Cuckold* have been used as historical reference points to arrive at positions pertinent to Indian history in general and military history in particular. The paper is also an attempt to contextualise *Cuckold* and highlight its salience in the theoretical reconstruction of Indian military history attempted therein. On the whole, this intervention underlines the stimulus given to written history by well conceived, properly researched and elegantly written historical fiction. Having said this, I hasten to add that the argument that historical fiction inspires written history or the social sciences can be extended in equal measure to good fiction of any kind. Since fiction is located at the intersection of history and imagination its ability to raise questions and inspire research can hardly ever be underestimated. Given the contemporary circumstances in which history as a subject is contracting and general interest in it is declining one hopes this kind of inspiration generates a wider, and more critical, awareness of our past.

II

Early this year, and more than three years after it was published in 1997, *Cuckold* received the Sahitya Academy Award and Nagarkar was briefly in the news again. When the novel was published it got a few reviews. A good one was written by Khushwant Singh in *Outlook*. This made me buy the book and my interaction with the novel finally culminated in this paper. Had *Cuckold* won the Booker or Pulitzer Prize it would undoubtedly be better known if not actually more widely read. On 23 February, 2001 the city supplement of the *Hindustan Times* of Delhi did us the favour of carrying a small report on the novel and its modest author. This report, like some of the reviews I read, contained two errors. Firstly, it called *Cuckold* the story of the Maharaj Kumar, the elusive husband of the historical and legendary

Bhakti saint Meerabai. Secondly it misquoted Nagarkar by confusing the battles of Panipat and Khanua. Could the author of *Cuckold* have said that Rana Sanga and Babur fought at Panipat in 1526? The First Battle of Panipat, as all students of Indian history know, was fought between Babur and Ibrahim Lodi. According to the writer of this report, to claim that *Cuckold* is only the story of Maharaj Kumar is like suggesting that *War and Peace* is only a narration of events in the life of Count Bezukhov. It is true that the Maharaj Kumar is the cuckold in the novel and is metaphorically cuckolded by none other than Lord Krishna. But the canvas of the novel is much larger. It is an imaginary reconstruction of life, as it must have been, in medieval Mewar – the jewel of Rajputana, based on meticulous research by Nagarkar. It is a story as much of Maharana Sangram Simha and his times as it is of his family, kingdom. Novels like *Cuckold* cannot be reduced to simplified interpretations. It is a pity that such a work does not command larger attention in a country with a rich historical legacy. Indeed our media's attention to historical events reproduces the cavalier attitude of most Indians towards history. It is my humble contention that fiction has the potential of making historical subjects interesting. It can offer a path to serious academic history which, to begin with, intimidates the more curious amongst us. In this context, Nagarkar's novel offers a refreshing way of looking at the past, especially in an inter-disciplinary way.

Cuckold is much more than a narration of the events and experiences in the life of the Maharaj Kumar, the elder son and heir apparent of Rana Sanga the ruler of Mewar. It is an emotive account of the history of Mewar, mostly presented from the viewpoint of the Maharaj Kumar the hero of the novel. The political character of the Maharaj Kumar is essentially conceived as a counter to the milieu of feudal India with all its possibilities and problems. At places he reminds you of Muhammad-bin-Tughluq and at many places in the novel his attitude towards military and other matters are highlighted deliberately *in contrast* to feudal practice. By reconstructing the military experiments of the Maharaj Kumar, Nagarkar is able to critically examine the military mentality of feudal Mewar. This underscores the importance of examples to the study of military history and theory, as mentioned by Clauzewitz, the modern philosopher of war. This dictum has been put to good use in *Cuckold*. Since war is a human activity like social, economic and political activities its conduct is never free from the influence of social mentality. In fact military history is often little more than the examination of the dialectics of mentality and military activity. In this connection, *Cuckold* is an admirable commentary on the *mentality* of the warlike Rajputs. Much of this commentary is conveyed to the reader of the novel through the complex, contextualised, imagined and potentially progressive character of the Maharaj Kumar, about whom historians actually know very little. The very fact that so little is known of the Maharaj Kumar has given Nagarkar the freedom to create his protagonist.

This paper is not a general discourse on Nagarkar's acclaimed historical novel: rather it concentrates on the military aspects of feudal Mewar presented in *Cuckold*. Nagarkar has deftly illuminated the strengths and weaknesses of Rajputs, a first class "martial race" of north India. But he is not the first to have done so. His sources include chroniclers of the 16th century and historians like Tod, Lane-Poole and Ishwari Prasad. The scholarly works of Kasim Farishta as translated by John Briggs, Abul Fazal as translated by David Price and contemporary historians like Satish Chandra and Stephen Rosen give us a good idea of military practices existing in medieval India. But somehow historical fiction stirs the imagination unlike some types of academic history. While reading the exciting books by

G. A. Henty and W. E. Johns in school, it was difficult for us to grasp the overall intellectual potential of fiction. The theoretical and philosophical realms lying beyond the domain of imagined chivalry remained largely unexplored in the *genre* represented by authors like Henty and Johns. Compared with books like *Cuckold*, their very English perspective on European and World history does appear ideologically biased to the post- and counter-colonial scholar. But despite their limitations they have the ability to stoke the imagination of their adolescent readers. For a long time when I was in junior school, I remember, the exploits of Biggleswortth (the RAF pilot in Johns' novels) kept up my interest in the history of the two World Wars. However, the overall theoretical and philosophical concerns of *Cuckold*, not to mention its multifarious military implications, make it a mature, and superior, novel in many ways. Long after you have put it down after having read and re-read sections from it, the scenes conjured up by the author haunt your imagination. The questions keep coming back, pushing you deeper into comparative history.

As far as Indian military history is concerned, *Cuckold* reiterates the combination of individual courage with the freezing of the Indian way of warfare in medieval India. This freezing seems to have occurred in the ancient period although it appears most visibly in medieval India. According to Rosen's well-conceived volume, the ferocity of individual warriors was the chief characteristic of ancient and medieval Indian armies in comparison with the organisation and cohesion of armies brought into India by invaders from Alexander onwards. In the Ancient World, according to Rosen, two army models seemed to have emerged. The first was the professional army which became cohesive due to the long campaigns it undertook. These armies, like those of the Spartans and Macedonians and the Roman Legions, were divorced from their societies by means of military training, traditions, messing, campaigns etc. The second model was the largely temporary "militia-type" army produced by Indian society. These visually and statistically intimidating armies had a low degree of cohesion and, as a consequence, were usually defeated by smaller professional armies in pitched battles. A typical case of such a contest was the Battle of Jhelum between Alexander and Porus fought in 326 BC. Moreover, Rosen's framework suggests that the tactics adopted by an army depended upon the model it represented. The ancient Greeks and Romans had great faith in their spear-wielding infantry phalanx and used it as their main arm of attack and defence. The cavalry, contrary to popular opinion, was deployed in a fashion meant to outflank and confound the enemy: its job was to *assist* the infantry. In contrast to this, the Indians relied on war elephants and charioteers. Records indicate that on the battlefield[2] there was little tactical coordination between the elephants, chariots, cavalry and infantry. Contemporary observers noticed how the charioteers normally did not assist the labouring infantry and vice-versa. The elephants were generally deployed to protect masses of infantry from enemy attacks. But this stratagem backfired. When attacked, the elephants often turned upon their own massed infantry, triggering a wave of confusion, demoralisation and desertion.

Upon reading the account of the battle of Khanua towards the end of *Cuckold*, the reader is struck by the coexistence of bravery in men like Rana Sanga and his ally Hasan Khan Mewati with the military stasis prevalent in medieval India. Or else by the exemplary courage of Porus

---

[2] I prefer to call this the *chaturanga* or chessboard method of Hindu warfare. It rarely worked in the face of professional invading armies. The 'standing armies' of ancient Indian kingdoms were not professional in the strict sense of the term. They were rarely divorced from society and had no system of common messing, professional training or systematic deployment on long campaigns. They lacked the *esprit de corps* which characterised some of the veteran Roman Legions.

in the lost battle of Jhelum, or of Ibrahim Lodi in the First Battle of Panipat (1526), or even Sadashiv Rao in the Third Battle of Panipat (1761). It becomes difficult not to believe from this marked opposition of personal courage and military stasis that Indian military tradition, as cherished and borne by its ruling elites, was unproductive and even futile. The sustained combination of individual courage and group military failures in Indian history compels you to go beyond the battlefields in search of causes. Perhaps the answers can be found in what Nagarkar, in the voice of the Maharaj Kumar, calls the classic formation of the Indian armies of yore. This involved an excessive reliance on war-elephants – often with disastrous battlefield consequences. The elephant looks intimidating but is a difficult animal to control and use effectively, specially against artillery. If the *mahaawat* was speared or shot, the elephant was prone to panic, and trampled the men plodding and pushing along behind it. The *kshatriya* Hindu Raja, eminently exposed to the enemy in his splendid *howdaah*, was himself the cause of many Indian defeats. The moment he vanished from his caparisoned elephant, the army deserted. In sum, a semi-circle of war-elephants protecting a tightly packed army comprising cavalry and mostly untrained infantry was the classical battle formation of the Hindu ruling elite. The aim of the astrologer-assisted Hindu military elite was to use this mass as a battering ram. Defeat and retreat were almost invariably never thought of. A battle, in general, was considered decisive. The trumpeting elephants were used, I suspect, to produce a psychological effect on the enemy. The upper caste cavalry, unlike armies following the Greek method, briefly surveyed earlier, rushed into brief inconclusive charges. Is it possible that the infantry could not be used as a cohesive arm because of the caste system? Was the infantry shielded and kept apart because the *kshatriya* Raja could not trust the heterogenous masses?

Possibly the infantry could not stand shoulder to shoulder because the armies lacked unity, training, common messing and, above all, camaraderie born of shared military experience. The differences between a largely temporary, "militia-type" army and a professional army can be analysed in this context even with contemporary overtones.

But the amazing fact is the longevity of this deployment despite its proven inefficacy. In the period covered by *Cuckold* and during the Moghul rule in India, twice at Panipat and once at Khanua, the same deployment was resorted to with similar results. Surely, the refusal to learn from contemporary history is strange for battle-hardened kingdoms, led by a ruling elite immersed in martial traditions.[3] While discussing this inability to learn from historical events the timing of *Cuckold*'s publication should also be noticed. Here, taking the liberty of traveling freely in time, I am referring to the peculiar problems besetting India at the beginning of the 21st century. The widespread tendency of not learning lessons from history can be perceived all around us. The resurgence of religious intolerance and the growing popularity of vaastu, astrology, faith healing and charlatan "gurus" makes a sharp distinction between a people aware of their past and a people trying to escape into it. To a historian studying military phenomena in the context of "war and society" the military establishment

---

[3] Sources clearly suggest that the Rajput kingdoms of north and north-western India were perpetually at war with each other during the medieval period. Some of these kingdoms had, in fact, emerged from the Tripartite Struggle for Kannauj preceding the Ghazanavid and Ghurid invasions of the medieval period. By the early 16th century, when Mewar was almost continuously at war with Gujarat and Malwa, the Rajputs had already acquired a martial reputation largely due to the labours of men like Rana Kumbha and his descendant Rana Sanga. Much of this reputation remained intact during the Moghul period when Rajputs served in extraordinarily large numbers in the Moghul armies. Later, the British reinforced the self-image of the Rajputs by classifying them as a first rate "martial race" and recruited them heavily into the Indian Army. The martial self-image of the Rajputs is, therefore, not merely a product of British colonial needs and classification. The image is as much historical as discursive, and was sustained by the status of Rajputs as the ruling elite of Rajputana.

and popular attitudes towards it represent crucial elements of the social formation to which it belongs. As Rosen asserts: "If someone wants to theorise about Indian society and Indian military power, the understanding of Indian society that drives the theory must be set forth and justified." [1996: Preface] *Cuckold* opens a window to the integrated lessons of war and history.

I now concentrate on two events described in vivid detail in *Cuckold*. The first is the war against Gujarat which brings out the importance of military training and cooperation among social allies in a warlike situation. The second is the widely discussed and decisive battle of Khanua. In the first instance, in Mewar's war against Gujarat, the Maharaj Kumar is shown carrying out certain experiments in mobile warfare with the help of his Rajput and *Bhil* friends. The involvement of the *Bhils*, who are organised and led by Puraji Kika, their intrepid and cunning Raja, in a campaign against the well-equipped Gujarat forces is construed deliberately by Nagarkar to highlight the military possibilities inherent in inter-caste cooperation in medieval India. From the *Bhils,* Nagarkar's protagonist learns the art of a people's war, comprising tested components like surprise, masquerade, feinting, quick dispersal and rapid concentration of forces. This tells us that alternate methods of war were being practiced by non-Rajput warriors like the Bhils, in the forests and hills of medieval India. However, this potential for developing mobile warfare remained unexploited in feudal India for a variety of reasons. When the time comes, the Maharaj Kumar conducts war against Gujarat using all the means at his disposal. Finally a marsh, towards which the enemy cavalry is forced to hurtle, is utilised to trap and destroy the Gujaratis. But the hidebound Rajputs of Mewar do not learn a lesson from this campaign to develop a new strategy of warfare. Court intrigue, which also plays on Rana Sanga's vanity, puts paid to the Maharaj Kumar's experiments and denigrates his success against Gujarat. The Rajputs, Nagarkar's novel reasserts, knew how to fight and die for their notions of honour but they seemed to have drawn very few lessons on how to win at their favourite pastime. It is not surprising that the historian's search for the wisdom of a Tsun Tzu or Ibn Khaldun among their archives yields nothing.

The experiments in warfare against Gujarat, described in vivid detail in *Cuckold*, have their limitations considering the historical period in which Nagarkar locates them. Both artillery and matchlocks are conspicuously absent from the campaign. This absence of firepower is noticed once again when the grand Rajput army leaves for Agra. The hundred thousand strong Indian army, which marches out of Chittor to stop Babur, is shown to contain only a hundred matchlockmen and no artillery. Imagine how unsuccessful Mewar would have been in its campaign against Gujarat, in the fictional account given by Nagarkar, in the absence of the swamp! Personal bravery plays a role too. In a defining moment of the war with Gujarat, the Maharaj Kumar resorts to a masquerade to kill the Gujarati commander at great personal risk. He tries everything successfully against Gujarat – surprise, tactical manouevre, grouping and regrouping, and finally the annihilation of enemy leadership and forces.

Given its military experience, Mewar had the potential to institute regular training and planning, and to execute war exercises simulating the conditions of real war, in and around Chittor. The small anecdote of the Maharaj Kumar's visit to the Institute of Advanced Military Tactics and Strategy in Chittor should be seen in this context. (There is no historical evidence of this.) The Prince is "keen to enlarge the scope of the Institute to encompass the latest technologies" based on the "vague rumours of advances made by the Arabs, Turks and Portuguese in war materials...." The Maharaj Kumar notices that the "mechanics of retreat" are not taught at the Institute, and is made to prophetically say that "if the art of retreat is studied scientifically, you'll not only reduce loss of life dramatically, you may also live to fight another war." We know that Babur's life was a testimony to this adage. He had been defeated and hounded out of Farghana twice by the Uzbegs and always kept a rearguard ready during his battles. In comparison, the idea of retreat was anathema to the Rajputs. Their practices like wearing the *kesari bana* before the last sally and the fearful *jauhar* of their women testified to their do-or-die attitude.

Was the refusal of Rajputs to observe contemporary reality, grasp its implications and thereby develop a new synthesis of theory and practice, predicated upon the caste system? Rosen draws our attention to the relationship between Indian military weaknesses and caste. It is suggested that in the 9th and 10th centuries, rising Hindu conservatism and caste rigidity contributed to the easy fall of border territories to small groups of Turkish invaders. This often "led Hindu elites to regard the peoples of the border territories, who had become racially and culturally mixed, as 'repugnant' to Hindu sensibilities and not deserving of assistance ..." [1996: 117] This may not be an unproductive way of looking at Indian history. But plausible answers can also be sought in the peculiarities of regional feudalism, which spawned a frog-in-the-well mentality in Indian society during the medieval period. This mentality was nurtured by the highly insular Brahminical system as noted by scholar travellers like Al-Biruni in the 11th century.[4]

---

[4] Al-Biruni. *India*. New Delhi: NBT. 1993. 10-11. Biruni calls the Hindus "haughty, foolishly vain, self-conceited, and stolid." Furthermore the learned Hindus refused to acknowledge the advances made in scientific matters in Persia or Khorasan. The Hindus traveled little for fear of becoming impure and hence learnt little from societies placed outside the sub-continent.

Long before the battle of Khanua, the Ghaznavid and Ghurid invasions had driven home the point that the Indian dependence on numerical superiority on the battlefield created problems for their troops. The Second Battle of Tarain fought between Prithviraj Chauhan and Mohammad Ghori in 1192 has been accurately described by Satish Chandra as "more a war of movement than of position." The battle of Chandawar fought against the massive army of Jaichand two years later for supremacy over the Gangetic plain was similar. The Turks were renowned for using mounted archers in rapid outflanking movements. Earlier, speed of movement had also given the edge to the Turks led by Saladin against the heavily armed and slower European knights during the Crusades. We must examine these facts in the context of the training imparted to the Mewar soldiers by the Maharaj Kumar and his innovative friends. However, when we look at what was happening in Europe during the 16th century, the feudalism of the Rajputs assumes a new dimension.

Over the 16th century, a "military revolution" – a concept utilised by Geoffrey Parker – gathered momentum in some states of Europe. This development, which was concurrent with the Renaissance and Reformation, comprised two momentous changes in warfare. Firstly, the importance of a well-drilled infantry in the armies of certain European states grew in proportion to that of the cavalry. Moreover, in time, this infantry began to use muskets on an exponentially increasing scale, and by the 17th century, the infantry square, the well-organised system of marching and back-marching and volley fire had emerged. This had the potential of breaking the best of cavalry charges. Secondly, the importance artillery and its variety developed in tandem with the development of the infantry. While heavy artillery diminished the importance of medieval fortifications, the growth of mobile and light artillery progressively reduced the role of the cavalry in battles fought in the open. Since the infantry was also vulnerable to firepower, there was a move to introduce greater discipline in order to withstand losses. The growing reliance on firepower translated into constantly improving the design and accuracy of firearms, artillery pieces and types of ordnance used on land and sea. These developments comprised the basis of European military superiority over non-European regions from the 16th century onwards. For lack of time, I am not delving into the details of the productive deployment of artillery for use at sea, and consequent developments in naval strategy and tactics, which were occurring almost simultaneously. However, the "military revolution" had broader implications. It encompassed all military activities of the State like recruitment, supply and provisioning, military production, creation of uniforms and the regimental system, constant drilling and training and, above all, the development of institutions, academies, theories and a philosophy dedicated to the study of war. By the 17th century, war in Europe had become increasingly de-personalised and hand-to-hand combat was becoming rare. Personal courage was still important to prevent the infantry square from breaking under enemy fire, but the age of feudal chivalry was over.

The use of firepower was not unique to Europe. In the 15th century, the Persians and Turkoman peoples of Central Asia also started using artillery and personal firearms on a substantial scale. To the north of Afghanistan, the descendants of Changez and Timur were grafting firepower on to tactical mobility, a process which some Mongols had mastered. The addition of mobile and swivel artillery pieces to the system of using cavalry as a tactical reserve [here I am referring to the Mongol maneouvre called *tulughma*] was quietly ushering in a minor "military revolution" in the Ottoman territories and Central Asia. By the 15th century, the Ottoman Turks seemed to have overcome the problem of nomadic tribal divisiveness and rebelliousness by means of developing a centralised state apparatus. This state was dependent upon the Christian Slave Janissaries who formed a standing professional army of around 10,000, separated from Ottoman society and beholden to the Sultan for its position. With the help of this *professional* army the Ottoman Sultans successfully curbed the power of the rural and religious elites for a considerable period of time. In the 15th and 16th centuries, the Ottoman Empire was at its peak and its influence was felt from Central Asia to Eastern Europe. Its military methods were well known in Iran and areas now covered by Uzbekistan and Turkmenistan.

Babur had mastered the new forms of warfare before the First Battle of Panipat. The references to *firingi* and *zarbzan* shots in the *Baburnamah* confirm this. The tradition was deep-rooted in the Turkoman areas and continued in parts of Afghanistan, well into the 18th century. Studies prove that camel- and carriage-mounted artillery, designed for swift deployment and movement, constituted an important element of Ahmad Shah Abdali's army, which decimated the Marathas in the Third Battle of Panipat in 1761. Here a short description of Babur's military method will not be out of place. Sources continuously refer to his use of Ottoman methods [Chandra, 1999; Briggs, 1966; Price, 1984]. At Panipat, Babur placed his army to the right of the town, thus protecting his right flank. A large ditch was dug on the left and covered by branches of felled trees (*abatis*) pointing towards the enemy, to prevent the Afghan cavalry from charging upon the left flank. The front itself was arranged according to the so-called Rumi or Romi, i.e., Ottoman or Asia Minor fashion. Around 700 carts were strung together with raw hide ropes and between every two carts short breastworks were erected. The matchlockmen stood and discharged their volleys behind these temporary fortifications in a disciplined manner, along with the artillery.

The field cannons were placed in front of the barricades. Babur called this the Rumi method because it had been used to great effect by the Ottoman Turks in a famous battle with Shah Ismail of Iran at Chaldiran in 1514. The arrangement was defensive-offensive and amenable to mobility on the battlefield because the carts could be moved forward as and when required, without breaking the line. To this arrangement Babur added an innovation. In the line of carts, at critical moments during a battle, gaps wide enough for fifty to a hundred horses or men to charge were created at a bow shot apart. "The battle which followed," writes Satish Chandra, "proved to be a triumph of generalship over numbers" [Chandra, 1999: 30].

The main aim of Babur, after having chosen the battleground on the advice of his military engineers, and arranged his line, was to break the frontal cavalry attack of the Indo-Afghans. At Panipat, as Farishta writes, "Ibrahim Lodi drew up his forces in one solid mass, and, according to the practice of the Indians, ordered his cavalry to charge. This attack the Moghul army received so steadily, that the Indians began to slacken their pace long before they reached the enemy's line" [Briggs: 29]. The devastating nature of Babur's victory was due to his use of matchlockmen and mixed artillery commanded by thorough professionals. Even before the enemy's cavalry was engaged, its centre was bombarded by field cannons. Once the concentrated firepower of thousands of matchlocks and scores of artillery pieces threw the under-prepared enemy into confusion, the reserves were brought into play. While the enemy centre recoiled on itself and the air was rent with the cries of wounded beasts and dying men, the *tulughma* and Babur's advance guard multiplied the damage inflicted by the liberal use of gunpowder. The *tulughma* was a tried Mongol cavalry maneouvre. This involved wheeling a reserve body of mounted archers round your left and right flanks on the enemy's sides or rear in an attempt to confuse and demoralise it further. Thus the enemy was hemmed in from all sides and most escape routes were also closed. While the enemy flanks caved into its centre, the battle finished with the charging units of Babur's household guards, usually with great slaughter.

Similar tactics at Khanua yielded similar results. But the remarkable aspect of both battles was their direction and control. Without proper supervision and direction Babur's plan could have failed. In both battles, the centre was held by Babur who remained close to the artillery at the head of his personal guards. The artillery and matchlockmen, although under capable gunners, were personally supervised by him. The communication system of the Mongols stood in stark contrast to the confusion which prevailed in the Indian ranks. The Bakshi of the camp, with numerous attendants necessary to convey orders, attended the person of the king. In this way he could receive the final instructions of Babur, which were then "circulated to the different divisions through the *Tawatchies* and *Yesawuls* [adjutant generals and exempts] – the commanding generals being forbidden to quit their posts, on any pretext, or to commence action without express orders to that purpose" [Price: section on Panipat and Khanua]. The significance of communication can hardly be overestimated considering the fact that the front with its right – centre – left combination was often three layers deep. In addition the reserves, *tulughma* units and rear guard had to be managed. The entire front could easily be spread over a couple of kilometres with units fighting simultaneously at several places.

This description of the Turkish methods brings us to the second event which concludes *Cuckold*: the decisive battle of Khanua fought between a great Rajput-Mewati alliance led by the redoubtable Rana Sanga, and the

Moghuls led by Babur. Nagarkar is right in telling us that it was firepower which destroyed the Rajputs at Khanua. Both Panipat (20.4.1526) and Khanua (16.3.1527) established the superiority of artillery and musketry over war-elephants and cavalry. At Panipat, the inexperienced Ibrahim Lodi, according to Babur's estimate, brought almost a thousand war-elephants to crush the Moghuls but the Afghans failed to breach Babur's defenses. Earlier, as Nagarkar and other scholars assert, Rana Sanga had been in touch with Babur while he was the resident ruler of Kabul, a fact corroborated by Babur himself. If Sanga had diplomatic contacts with Babur and had actually invited him to India to get rid of Ibrahim Lodi, what prevented him from closely examining Moghul military methods? In the year between Panipat and Khanua, the Rajputs made no effort to study the battle in which the Delhi Sultanate perished.

Could this have happened because of the Rajput belief in astrology? A few days before the decisive battle of Khanua, the Rajputs had wrested the fort of Bayana from the Moghuls. This, and the size of their army, probably made them over-confident. It is important to remember that on the eve of this battle, Babur disregarded the demoralising predictions of Muhammad Sharif, an astrologer who had come all the way from Kabul with some reinforcements. The unexpected loss of Bayana coupled with Sharif's depressing predictions seemed to have precipitated a serious crisis in the Moghul ranks. How Babur became a *Ghazi* to overcome this is too well known to be repeated here. Sources mention that, after the battle, Sharif gained from Babur's generosity but was also reprimanded. Had Babur succumbed to astrological predictions, the fate of India might have been different.

The Moghul victories at Panipat and Khanua were spectacular achievements. However, to jump to conclusions on the basis of these victories would be incorrect. The Moghuls could hardly have been considered invincible, and moreover, Babur represented a social system which was similar to that of the feudal Rajputs. It is true, however, that Babur was a remarkable man in many ways. As a man of letters, professional soldier and general, he was far superior to the military leaders of the Rajputs and the Indo-Afghans. However individual brilliance should not be passed off as a substitute for systemic change. In history, the role of the individual must be recognised; but individuals are rarely in a position to transform societies through a few well-fought battles. Babur can be called innovative and successful to the extent that he understood the role of gunpowder in 16th century warfare. Rana Sanga was much older than Babur and militarily more experienced, but his mental attitudes and circumscribed area of operation limited his understanding of warfare.

What is a possible scenario if the Rajputs had abandoned their mental handicap about warfare? At Khanua the *tulughma* could have been neutralised by archers drawn in protective rows on the flanks of the main army. A reserve numbering a few thousand cavalry could have been kept outside the range of Babur's canons to be used in counter-*tulughma* operations on the lines suggested by Nagarkar. The dashing Hasan Khan Mewati or Medini Rai of Chanderi could have handled this. The battle could have been less haphazardly directed without exposing the supreme commander to enemy fire. In fact, a suggestion to this effect made by the Maharaj Kumar in *Cuckold* – that Rana Sanga be placed on a fifty-feet-high mobile tower outside the range of Babur's guns – is shot down by the treachrous Silhadi Rai at the last moment. Finally a contingency plan of orderly retreat could have been put in place to prevent the defeat from becoming a rout. In the event, these possibilities were eliminated by methods predicated upon an excessive reliance on elephants and cavalry.[5] Why the Rajputs did not attack Babur with the aid of a flying column while he was shifting his camp from Sikri to Khanua will remain a mystery forever. Ultimately, Khanua proves that it was Babur who exploited the enemy's weaknesses to greater advantage than Rana Sanga. That is the stuff military victories are made of.

The battles of Tarain, Panipat – I mean the first and third battles – and Khanua, raise the issue of a distinct "Muslim" strategy *vis a vis* a "Hindu" strategy. Some people suggest that the invading armies triumphed in India because of the internal divisions prevalent in the Hindu armies. There may be some truth in this. However, whether the core of Babur's army was cohesive because it was Muslim or tribal is a question which cannot be answered here.[6] If Islam was a unifying force, Ibrahim Lodi's army should have displayed better cohesion at Panipat. Social cohesion, however, is only one part of the story: technology, tactical methods and leadership all mattered. I do not wish to discuss the communalisation of Indian military history here. For our purpose it will be sufficient, and intellectually more productive, to highlight the differences between the Central Asian method of war and the traditions existing in the sub-continent. In contrast to the Indians who depended on numbers to overwhelm the smaller armies of the northern invaders, the poorer Central Asians and Afghans were swift

[5] The Rajput reliance on these animals should be understood in context. The elephant was kept for ceremonial purposes, to execute opponents and criminals, and to enhance imperial prestige. The horse gave the tribute and revenue collecting elite much needed mobility. The sword and lance wielding Rajput *sawar* was militarily superior to the cultivator in every possible way. The socio-economic conditions of medieval India did not produce the historical need for much military innovation. In such circumstances the military accent remained on numbers, and hand to hand combat in the last resort.

[6] The cohesion of Babur's army seemed to have broken down on the eve of the Battle of Khanua. Only his exceptional qualities, a political appeal to Islam, and disregard for astrology saved the day for the Moghuls.

adventurers *par excellence*. The Ghaznavids and Ghurids had to depend on light equipment, smaller contingents and speed, given the distance they had travelled from their power base. This seemed imperative because the invaders could never be certain of obtaining sustained local support in India. Hence operational mobility and the ability to concentrate forces at the right conjuncture of time and place made these raiders successful. Nobody can imagine that the Turks could have penetrated India with large unwieldy armies. In the first place, their revenues could never sustain large standing armies, and secondly, these armies would have created insurmountable logistical problems for their commanders. The Turks and Mongols had neither the time nor the resources to waste. In general, they sought brief decisive encounters and, hence, when the mammoth Lodi army showed no signs of activity in Panipat for a while, Babur needled it into action for his own benefit. The Central Asians were not prepared for attrition in potentially hostile territory. Babur's descendants, however, who became completely Indianised in the 17th and 18th centuries, failed to learn the relevant lessons from his strategies, thereby paying a heavy price to adventurers like Nadir Shah and his pupil, Ahmad Shah Durrani, and the Marathas.

III

In Europe, in the 16th and 17th centuries, near continuous warfare produced a "military revolution." The armies became larger; and the state structure raising and maintaining these armies became increasingly institutionalised and complex. Artillery, infantry and navies developed new forms and adapted themselves to technological progress. However, viewed in a trans – historical perspective, the development of military organisation, order, form, strategy and technology were not exclusive to Europe. There were other areas where the impact of war on society led to lasting changes in social formations. The importance of these changes appears even more striking in comparison with the military equilibrium achieved by the warring states of feudal India. In Indian history, from the exploits of Chandragupta Maurya and the south Indian Cholas to the tripartite struggle for Kanauj, there is no shortage of war. But let us examine what happened in ancient China.

In Chinese history, the period between 770 and 221 BC is known as the "Warring States Era." Out of this era grew the massive armies of up to one million, belonging to the larger states. Significant tactical changes also occurred simultaneously. Aristocratic charioteers armed with bows gradually gave way to massed conscript infantry, armed with spears and iron swords. By 221 BC, the Chinese "military revolution" had been accomplished and a system had been created in China which endured, with little change, for almost two millenia. The Great Wall of China and the enormous mausoleum of Prince Cheng, larger than the pyramids, guarded by an army of 6000 life-size terracotta figures, belong to this period. These figures narrate a tale of the amazing efficiency and centralisation achieved by China in the 3rd century BC. These statues are shown wearing standardised uniforms with colour–coded insignia denoting their units. In comparison, the regimental system in India was finally created by the British. While China stands out as an example of military innovation, countries like Vietnam are not far behind. The successful Vietnamese war first against the Japanese, then the French and finally the United States, during the 1940s, '50s, '60s and '70s was predicated upon the Vietcong's ability to learn the correct lessons from history and apply unorthodox military methods in the execution of a people's war. In their overall understanding of war, the Chinese and Vietnamese have generally been ahead of others, and many of their effective strategic traditions are, in fact, quite old.[7] Not to fight on the enemy's terms or by enemy standards is ingrained in Far Eastern strategic thought.

With this as a background, it becomes useful to ask how many units of Mewar we remember. Why is it that the warrior Rajputs, the favourite "martial race" of the British, never produced a proper treatise on warfare? However, they were not alone in Indian history in their peculiar attitude towards war, much of which was characterised by the *kesari bana* and *jauhar* – both wasteful exercises. Regarding artillery, except a Tippu here and a Ranjit Singh there, the rest of India seemed to share the Rajput view. Even the Marathas who had emerged as the foremost military power of 17th and 18th century India, relied far too much on cavalry and hand to hand combat with sword and shield. They remained singularly deficient in the production and use of artillery, and hence lacked the experience of fighting and winning large-scale battles. It was their ignorance of the "mechanics of retreat" and lack of careful deployment of artillery which led to their disorderly flight from Panipat in 1761. When confronting the Afghans, they departed from their guerilla tactics without understanding the modalities of modern war, and paid a heavy price for their ignorance. Once again they demonstrated their inability to deploy and use artillery at Assaye in 1803, and failed to win an otherwise hard-fought battle.

Had *Cuckold* been available at the court of Sangram

---

[7] During the anti-colonial wars of the 20th century, the Chinese and Vietnamese people led by their Communist Parties successfully adapted traditional methods of conducting protracted war to suit contemporary needs. Tradition was not blindly followed, but creatively reconstructed in a period when China and Vietnam were passing through a phase of total war. This creativity underpinned the success of the Chinese against the Japanese and the Chiang Kai Shek led Kuomintang during and after the Second World War. The Vietnamese were successful first against the French colonialists and later against the technological might of the United States.

Simha, it would have become great source material for strategic warfare. It is, however, a modern novel, a complex mix of history and fiction. This article has glanced at some of the military questions raised by it, but has deliberately provided only one reading of the novel. *Cuckold* cannot, however, be reduced to just the treatment of military matters. There is much more to it for historians who study the social, economic and political complexities of everyday life. In sum, novels like *Cuckold* are invaluable for changing popular perceptions of history. By locating the military problematic in the complex of systems, mentalities and technology, Nagarkar has reminded us of the comparative nature of history. War appears as a window to State formations in this paradigm and we come to realise that the causes of victory and defeat are not only to be found on the dusty battlefields of military history.

Works Cited

Chandra, Satish. *Medieval India: From Sultanat to the Mughals, 1206 – 1526*. New Delhi: Har-Anand, 1997.

———. *Medieval India From Sultanat to the Mughals, Volume II, 1526 – 1748*. New Delhi: Har-Anand, 1999.

Clausewitz, Carl von. *On War*. Princeton: Princeton UP, 1984.

Ferishta, Kasim Mahomed. *History of the Rise of the Mahomedan Power in India Till the Year A.D. 1612*. Trans. John Briggs. Vol. 2. Calcutta, 1966.

Parker, Geoffrey. *The Military Revolution: military innovation and the rise of the West, 1500 – 1800*. Cambridge: Cambridge UP, 1988.

Prasad, Ishwari. *The Mughal Empire*. Allahabad: Chugh Publications, 1974.

Price, Major David, ed. *Mahommedan History from the death of the Arabian Legislator to the accession of the Emperor Akbar and the establishment of the Moghul Empire in Hindustan – from Original Persian Authorities, Volume III, Part II.* 1821. New Delhi: Inter – India Publications, 1984.

Rosen, Stephen Peter. *Societies and Military Power: India and its Armies.* New Delhi: Oxford UP, 1996.

Stetler, Russell, ed. *The Military Art of People's War: Selected Writings of General Vo Nguyen Giap.* London: Monthly Review Press, 1971.

Sen, S. N. *The Military System of the Marathas.* 1928. Calcutta: K. P. Bagchi & Co., 1979.

Narrative Technique in Kiran Nagarkar's Fiction

Yasmeen Lukmani

Kiran Nagarkar's three novels, *Seven Sixes are Forty-Three* (translated from the Marathi *Saat Sakkam Trechalis* by Shubha Slee), *Ravan & Eddie,* and *Cuckold*, are as different in subject matter as in manner of presentation. However, there are similarities as well. In each of these, Nagarkar explores the psyche of his characters, to find out what makes them tick, and does this by making the reader see them in action, in relationships with others, and in the process of introspection. They are very much situated in the world around them – the Bombay of the '60s (*Seven Sixes*), lower middle-class Hindu and Christian Bombay of the slums (*Ravan & Eddie*), and finally in the last novel, *Cuckold*, 16th century Mewar, represented faithfully in terms of political and social structures, and yet in an idiom and sensibility which is highly contemporary. This tension between the two periods, the 16th century and the present day, instead of reducing authenticity adds, on the contrary, a dual perspective, enabling us to relive the already-lived life through modern eyes, enlarging our perception of the present through the understanding provided by the past. Narratorial perspective or the nature of the persona's voice, which is being projected, seems to be very important in Nagarkar's writing and as Berger puts it, "Perspective makes the single eye the center of the visible world" (16). The centre shifts and changes as the perspective changes.

Seven Sixes are Forty-Three and *Cuckold* have points in common which distinguish them sharply from the more robust *Ravan & Eddie*. One of the major differences is the nature of the characters – the two young boys, Ravan and Eddie, interested mainly in developing their physical prowess, they are action-oriented, non-intellectual and, are, by and large, non-introspective, though each discovers in himself a consuming passion for music. It is also the only one of the three novels, which is presented more or less entirely in third person narrative. *Seven Sixes* is written mainly in the first person, while in *Cuckold* there is a constant shift in focus from the protagonist's perspective to that of the narrator/author, and both protagonists are highly sensitive in their intellectual and emotional apprehension of reality. I would like to argue that in Nagarkar's work, the use of first person narrative allows scope for self-questioning, self-analysis and disquisitions on life as such, and on a myriad specific issues. In *Ravan & Eddie*, that is, in third person narrative, there is also a great deal of discussion and analysis, but on more impersonal issues, issues which are related tangentially to the story, for example the disquisition on Hindi films (which the writer himself classifies as "utterly unnecessary"), or the meditation on neighbours. These are hospitably received in the novel largely because of the exuberance with which they are presented, and which is so much in keeping with the mood of the book. They are very different from the outpourings of the Maharaj Kumar's mind, or those of the protagonist in *Seven Sixes* which are personal, and expressive of their personalities, their doubts and desires. However, they do have the usual dose of analysis, irony and sharp wit.

In both *Seven Sixes* and *Cuckold*, one suspects that the mental make-up and sensibility of the protagonists comes remarkably close to that of the author, and the "I" mode allows the author to express the inner world of these characters from very close quarters. It is almost as if there is an identity of vision, a coalescing of personalities, of mindsets. In *Ravan & Eddie* particularly, and even in the parts of *Cuckold* where the third person is used, there is automatically greater distancing and objectivity.

It seems as if the degree of distance from the narrative and the objectivity/truth value of the narrative is connected with the presence or otherwise of a narrator different from the omniscient novelist. The act of juggling between the two perspectives, however, adds a new wrinkle to the complexity of experience presented in the novels. In *Ravan & Eddie* as well, right in the middle of third person narrative, there are first person sections, without any warning, without any mention of the person whose cogitations are being expressed. For example, Eddie overhears his grandmother egging on his mother to re-marry. We are not told that Eddie is anywhere on the scene, eavesdropping or otherwise, but suddenly we get,

> And I thought you were on our side. How could you do this to me, Granna? It was shameful the way Granna was carrying on, trying to get his mother to marry Machado, Furtado, Figuereido or someone as bad. What did they need a man for, they had got along fine without one for the last eleven years or so and would do so for the next hundred. (154)

The introduction of the first person mode, makes the gravity of the situation for the little boy more immediate, and hence more dramatic. But there is a quick reversion to the third person, using the word "Granna" as a means of bridging the first person-third person divide. This is one of the many instances of free indirect discourse in the novels. This aspect will be discussed later.

There are a large number of deliberate authorial intrusions or disquisitions on topics set off by the story being told. We are dragged out of the story and made to consider ethical or socio-cultural issues or the history of a culture, issues which stem from the storyline. These are mini-essays with headings, and in Chapters 6 and 12, there are even two such perorations each. These are directly addressed to the reader by means of the author deliberately stepping out of the story, and since such a large number of these digressions appear, one could perhaps have been pardoned for wondering whether they were a backdrop to the story, or the story the backdrop to the digressions! The drama of the events and the rambunctious humour which is so prominent a part of the book, however, make us keep our focus on the story. The digressions are a means by which the subjectivity of the author emerges without the use of the first person.

Moreover, in addition to these labeled digressions, there are many instances of cogitations by the characters, reflecting on their situation and way of life, eg. the opening page of Chapter 13 has the author commenting on (not digressing from) the parallel lives followed by the two boys, each going his separate way in the same direction. This moves on to reflecting on what makes communities which otherwise have so much in common, diverge so drastically, and then what made the parallel lines followed by the great lovers of the past cross. Again, in Chapter 14, Parvatibai cogitates on the ways of the gods and fate, and their effect on her life. These again widen the scope of the novel and our awareness of the complexities of the issues it is dealing with. While the digressions are a means of pontificating about life, the cogitations open up the internal life of the character. It is true that the characters in *Ravan & Eddie* are earthy and incapable of the subtlety of the self-questioning indulged in by the protagonists in *Seven Sixes* and *Cuckold*, but lower middle-class and semi-educated though they may be, they are also deeply concerned with the basic issues of life, and this is brought out through their thoughts.

There are other ways in which we move out of the main storyline and enrich it, such as the two dreams that Ravan has. In Chapter 7 we watch Ravan in the throes of seeing himself as Krishna desporting himself with the Sarang girls as gopis. In the other dream, we have Ravan as a one-year-old, taking off with his kite, cavorting with it, careering through air, and flying through the air in a supreme moment of joy into the arms of the sky (318-22). Both these dreams allow us fresh insights into Ravan's character, the way in which he can totally abandon himself to the freedom of the elements, to the movements of his body, and his total absorption in music. Eddie, on the other hand, with the same propensities, expresses himself in a different way. He is able to take on a completely different persona when required, for instance when he is forced to manufacture stories for the edification of Father Agnello, thus satisfying the adults who would have been happy with nothing less than a confession, never mind if he hadn't done any of the forbidden acts he narrates.

Ravan's dream of free-floating with the kite, and later, the two momentous encounters of the two boys are also worth noting. In the first of these (327-28), the bodies of Ravan and Eddie are locked together in a battle for regaining their sanity in face of the terror of encountering the suspended figure of Shobhan who had hanged herself. It was an interlocking in which there was simultaneously sinuous grace, a terrible beauty, a struggle for power, and a movement towards harmony. It was also the embrace of deadly enemies. In the second such encounter at the end of the book (end of the Epilogue) we have a perfect fusion of opposites, a fusion of planes and angles in motion, of the interaction of the two practitioners of two different martial arts, two life-long enemies intersecting in total surrender to the forces of space and motion, leading to complete harmony. The marked similarity between the two encounters of the boys makes a narrative link and it makes possible thematic cohesion, even linking Ravan's dream of floating with the kite. These moments of complete abandon, whether due to absorption in *Dil Deke Dekho* or *Rock Around the Clock*, or these three instances mentioned above of surrender to the forces of motion and freedom are akin in depth and magnitude to the erotic and spiritual heights reached by the Maharaj Kumar and the Princess (not in consort, but each individually) in *Cuckold*, or the soul-searing particularity of death through war in the same novel. Or the erotic abandon, and the deeply sensual quality of pain, the latter particularly which is so remarkable in *Seven Sixes* ("Because pain and suffering have no memory. You may have seen and experienced everything but for pain and suffering there is only the first time, act one, scene one." 208). In all of Nagarkar's work, we see the quality of living life to the fullest realisation of possibility, according to the individual predelictions of the characters. There are other ways in which the novels are linked. Commonality of image or aspects of experience do not make for narrative technique and so will not be explored here. In a sense, though there is far greater subtlety in *Cuckold*, the task of exploring the complete abandonment to the deepest rhythms of life shown by the two young lower middle-class lads, is a tremendous achievement and more difficult to capture, particularly as the protagonists do not draw as much sympathy as those in the other two novels. Thus, there appear to be thematic links across the three novels.

In *Seven Sixes*, while first person narration is used by

and large, with the protagonist at the centre of all activity or as the perceiving and interpreting eye, occasionally there is third person narration, as in the opening scene of the book when Pratibha is beaten up and ends up burning herself to death. It is not an occasion on which Kushank, the narrator could have been present. A great deal of objectivity is achieved however, by the frequent use of dialogue in first person narration. Sometimes it is even unclear whether a statement is made by the protagonist or the author, as in the first two sentences of the passage given below:

> However free a man is, he manages to tie himself to something or to someone. Psychology and philosophy may offer a hundred explanations for this tendency, but you can't escape Human Bondage. Whether you like the bonds or not, whether they're from the past or the present, the point is, you're bound. There are a thousand ways of freeing yourself if you really want to, but you remain tied.
>
> You choose a person to communicate with. In solitude, in a crowd. Whether he can hear you or not. Whether he has forgotten you, or you no longer exist for him, you keep talking to him. But rarely can you find two people who talk to each other.
>
> When I first saw you, your eyes seemed extraordinary. Even through your glasses, I had never seen eyes that were so wide, and which hid so much. If I had walked straight through them for a mile or two, I still wouldn't have found you. (91)

The first two lines above are a general statement. Then from "Whether you like the bonds or not ... who talk to each other" the protagonist/author gets into an interactive mode, and attempts to involve the reader. The interactivity of the generalised "you" then changes to the character "You" who is never named but seems to be the chief person the protagonist loves. It is extremely rare to find such centrality being given to the second person pronoun. It emphasises the atmosphere of conversational openness that is characteristic of the book. She becomes even more special because she is not named. It is almost as if the book is addressed to her, as she is being referred to as "you." It also introduces, along with the digressions, a strong sense of alienation in the Brechtian sense. We are involved in the story and yet from time to time stand back from it.

Cuckold, the latest and most mature of his novels, is basically told in the first person, as part of the memoirs of the Maharaj Kumar. The author's third person narrative comes in at intervals, punctuating and differentiating that which is presented in the first person. Though the three novels are as different as they can be in subject matter and in general effect, there are great similarities as well. The nature of the authorial voice, the use of the first person, and the nature of the movement from first to third person, as well as the unabashed use of digression, all bear testimony to the pen of Kiran Nagarkar.[1]

Cuckold begins with first person narration. At the start of the first chapter, the Maharaj Kumar is seen conducting a session of the small causes court, where an aged dhobi claims that his wife is unfaithful. Thus, at the outset, his position as the Crown Prince is established, while one of the major themes of the book, the nature of marital fidelity, is also introduced. The Maharaj Kumar's thoughts and feelings on the occasion are brought out, here, as in the other sections

[1] There are several aspects of content which also recur, though it is not possible to deal with these here. To mention a few: The question, 'What difference does it make?' relating to whether life is meaningful, is raised both in *Seven Sixes* and *Cuckold*; the concept of the inseparable link between opposites or sworn enemies (Ravan and Eddie, the Maharaj Kumar and Shri Krishna); and the image of the double helix that intertwined the very essence of their lives occurring both in *Ravan & Eddie* and *Cuckold*.

of Chapter 1 and in the rest of the book. He analyses his own motives, those of others, and interprets the actions of others: "Did I really expect her to smile demurely and tell the court who she was sleeping with? ... Her breasts, the colour of fine sand at Pushkar, were exposed for a brief second. I could feel Mangal's eyes at the back of my neck" (1). He goes off into disquisitions at different times about a variety of matters, whatever seems to stem from the scene being dealt with. There is an interesting account of Jain food which, the narrator remarks, though severely circumscribed, "seems to suggest that what it lacks is but superfluous" (4). In addition, a little later, he pontificates on Jain finances and systems of earning merit. We move from a semi-objective description of a scene by the protagonist to statements of his own pet views. As the whole is (perhaps arguably) part of a memoir (though we don't know this as yet) the musings do not seem extraneous to the whole. In any case, they fit in with the tone and the mood, and seem perfectly natural. In *Cuckold* we have the cogitations of the protagonist, reflecting his perspective, what he sees and hears, while in *Ravan & Eddie*, we have disquisitions by the author which are only thematically or tonally linked.

Indications of the book's being part of a journal are provided from the beginning. The opening line, "The small causes court sits on Thursdays," through the use of the present tense suggests the protagonist's musings on habitual activity, not just the description of a scene. It then follows in the past tense, past continuous and past perfect. A little later he says, "I like to be at work by six thirty in the morning" (6), again suggesting the tone of a friendly discussion with a peer, or a potential reader. It is only as late as Chapter 27 that the writing of the autobiography is mentioned (343-46). That is, at the beginning of the novel, we are plunged into the narrative directly, with only a few indications in the style (such as the use of the present tense, mentioned earlier) to suggest that the story was at a remove from primary reality, filtered as the reality was through the viewpoint and written word of the protagonist. The tension between the protagonist's personality and the nature of the varied experiences with which he is dealing is articulated by the self-conscious and analytic Maharaj Kumar:

> I was amazed to discover such a strong, personal tone in my narrative. I am not a man to let my guard down, whatever the occasion or provocation. Or so I thought. Instead here I was, if not baring my soul, certainly throwing my usual habit and mask of caution to the winds, telling it all, taking swipes at myself and at my relatives including Father, meditating, digressing despite an ingrained habit of disciplined progression. I was alarmed by this openness and my willingness to express an opinion on any and every matter. Should I abandon the project? Was it getting out of hand? I had to admit that it was. But to censor it would be tantamount to a kind of doctoring. (346)

This statement attacks directly the problem of accounting for how the introverted Maharaj Kumar came out into the open and made available for public consumption such unsuspected aspects of his nature.

Thus we have the narrative filtred through the personality of the Prince, a personality with many facets, having a sensibility which resonates to the many complexities in life, and who probes into issues, pursuing them to their natural conclusion, as well as having a child-like appreciation of the beauties of nature and the world. And as we have seen, it is not just the flow of events, but introspections and disquisitions on life that come alongside the narrative and are as much a part of the memoirs. The memoirs end at the close of the last chapter, when the Prince says,

> I have almost finished my last entry. In a minute now I'll seal these bits of my memoirs and hand them over to the messenger and ask him to head for Chittor. It is merely a matter of time before His Majesty's assassins come for me. (600)

After this comes the Epilogue, in which four possible ways are put forward in which the Maharaj Kumar's life could have ended. This necessarily could not be done by the Maharaj Kumar, but by the omniscient novelist, who perhaps is not-so-omniscient after all, since he doesn't have the one authoritative ending to offer us. Another possibility is that it is part of the re-telling of the tale by Sajani Bai.

Sajani Bai, the great singer who performs at court, is finally also one of the great recorders of history. At a feast to celebrate the conquest of Malwa, the following conversation takes place between her and the Rana:

> "We rework our own memories and reinvent ourselves to suit our tastes and predilections every day. Who is to notice a hiatus in history a few centuries down the road?"
>
> "Why is it so important,' Father spoke almost inaudibly, 'to remember, Sajani Bai?"
>
> "Because otherwise our lives would be lies and we may never tell our children to speak the truth again."
>
> "Will you be the remembrancer of Chittor, Sajani Bai?"
>
> "I would be honoured, Your Majesty." (474)

Again at the end, in the Epilogue, when the most dramatic of the death scenes of the Maharaj Kumar is being outlined, we have the suggestion that there are other and perhaps truer forms of history, such as the songs of traditional singers,

> He brought his double-edged sword down, swift

> and hard just as he had imagined he would. Was his hand stayed in mid-air? Did it at least make a slight nick in the beatifically smiling face or torso of the marble Flautist? Sajani Bai is silent on the subject. (602)

However, the Maharaj Kumar is almost wiped out of history, He is presciently aware of this:

> I am the missing page that is not missed, the hiatus that may be skipped. (Epigraph heading the Epilogue, 601)

Again,

> I am sure there will be a school of historians in the future who will put forward the theory that the black sun in my vision was not due to chance or bad luck. (578)

The narrator/novelist needs to put in an appearance, not only at the end but also right through, at various points in the novel. When he enters the picture, he does so quite unobtrusively, in fact the tone of the narrative hardly differs, whether it is the Maharaj Kumar speaking or the narrator/novelist. Thus, apart from the slight distancing brought about by the use of the third person, there is not much difference in the nature of the experience presented. There are only 14 chapters out of the total of 50 (including the Epilogue) which are presented through the third person, indicating that this is the less preferred mode for Nagarkar to present his work in *Cuckold*. The chapters in the third person are: 3, 6, 8, 10, 12, 14, 16, 19, 25, 28, 31, 39, 45, and the Epilogue. They are spread out over the whole novel, but not in any markedly even fashion. The use of the third person is required to take care of a variety of situations involving the narrator, the Maharaj Kumar, of which he:

(i) could not have had firsthand knowledge (eg. Ch. 3 – the Princess' life before coming to Chittor)

(ii) could not have known about or which occur when he was not present (e.g. Ch. 6 – the Princess coming to her married home; Kausalya's conversations with her)

(iii) would be unwilling to talk, being very personal matters, (e.g. the wedding night when he forcibly sleeps with his wife, 45-46).

The third person also gives a measure of objectivity to something which could conceivably exist only on the psychological plane (eg. 149-52, the Prince's first encounter with Bhootani Mata) and also subsequent encounters, (Ch. 19, 248. Ch. 31, 417).

The importance of the third person narrator's point of view comes out in statements like the following,

> He sat her down. *He controlled the pitch and timbre of his voice.* "Do not sing. Is that understood? I will not have you sing under my roof."
>
> "Why?" *she asked innocently* or at least she did a fine imitation of innocence.
>
> "Because princesses don't sing for the public, at least not in this house. Tawaifs do." (147, emphasis added)

The underlined parts require the presence of an outsider, in this case, the narrator looking back on the situation in his memoirs, in order to be able to perceive the situation, objectively. This involves judging the control of his voice by the protagonist, and next, realising both that the Princess "asked innocently" (an objective view), and simultaneously, "or at least she did a fine imitation of innocence," thus putting across a more biased view, which would be closer to the first person viewpoint, a reflection of the Maharaj Kumar's thoughts. There is a mixture of the outsider and the protagonist's viewpoints.

The next passage also shows the authorial stance of standing back, however slightly, in order to see the two of them from the outside, though the Maharaj Kumar's tone of voice appears.

> *"She was a deep one. He had to hand it to her, it was, frankly, close to a master-stroke in the escalating war of nerves between him and her."* You want a name, say it again, you want a name, you really and truly want the name, how many months had he pursued her with that one single question, here it is, she had thrown a name at him casually, like a bone to a dog, go ahead, chew on it for the next seven hundred years, for all I care. (102, emphasis added)

The complexity of pronominal use indicates a complexity in the perspective on the characters. Simultaneously, the Princess is "she" and also "I." With the use of "I," we penetrate into her mind, as interpreted by the Maharaj Kumar, and finally as this is presented by the author. Similarly, the Maharaj Kumar is simultaneously "he" and "you." The use of "you" for the Maharaj Kumar and "I" for the Princess, leads to objectifying him and personalising her.

Again, the underlined words below indicate the need for authorial statement, coming over and above the narrator's account. This statement would not have been possible coming from the protagonist, or the narrator looking back on the situation. However, the rest of the passage brings in the Maharaj Kumar's perspective, as well as his looking at himself as "you."

> He threw his head back and laughed. *A loud, unambiguous, unforced laugh.* "The bride of

> god, how's that for a conundrum? Try and figure that one out, my friend. You had to admit that she was a wizard at sowing confusion and slipping away. Put yourself in her shoes, you are having one hell of a roaring, ear-splitting, torrid affair, they get you married to some young bloke, the future king of the most prestigious kingdom in the community. Do you keep your secret to yourself, no sir, you are a plain-speaking, honest person. On the night of your wedding you tell your husband the truth, and nothing but." (102-03, emphasis added)

The frequent use of the second person pronoun "you," as in the above, moves away from the distancing brought in by the use of the third person into what becomes an interactive position. This could be interpreted as interaction with the reader. Or as the Maharaj Kumar's voice seems to be inlaid into the third person account, it could be his own soliloquising, the "I" getting submerged in the "you." Thus the voices in the passage merge in complex ways and defy strict pronominal designation. The use of the "you" takes the narrator (of the memoirs) away from the events he is presenting. The use of "you" seems to act as a bridge between first person (the protagonist speaking) and third person narration (the protagonist as narrator looking back).

The second person address occurs from time to time. It has links with the perorations which are a direct form of address to the reader, and also with first person narration, that is, as the first person voice speaking to itself. It also provides links across his books with the character You in *Seven Sixes*. In the two passages given below, the "you" involves the reader in a discussion, and personalises the situation for him/her:

> Boom. Boom. Boom. Boom. You can make that sound with your mouth. Not at all scary, is it?

> Hear one of those cannons shattering your eardrums and you lose all confidence and sense of purpose. It's worth pointing out that the cannons didn't do extensive damage to our people; after all the Padshah had only seven of them and it takes a while before the gunpowder compartment cools and you can clean the barrel, reload it and fire. (582)

> Will somebody enlighten me about the way the human mind works? From the day I got married to her, Greeneyes has told me to keep off her. Now I'm married the second time, never mind that it was against my wishes, and all she spends her time doing is wooing me. (548)

The speaking voice is used, introducing a conversational tone. This is one of the ways used to show the Maharaj Kumar as one who never stands above us, being always on the same level or even lower, and always willing to point out his own shortcomings.

We even have a change in first person narration, from the use of the first person to the third person in the same paragraph. This is the reflection of a complex series of mental moves between degrees of objectivity in the analysis of character.

> That sounded lame. It would be a risible and inadmissible plea even in my own small causes court. If the Maharaj Kumar of the realm was going to be in the dark about his wife's movements, he had better become a hermit and go into the mountains. Because if he couldn't take care of his wife, how was he going to look after his subjects and his kingdom? Did I not know it was Janamashtami, the Flautist's birthday? (166-67)

There is a shift from the first person perspective to the

third person and back again to the first person. While referring to himself as "he," he is looking at himself through the eyes of others, and when he speaks through the pronoun "I," he is looking through his own eyes.

In addition to the Maharaj Kumar's voice (first person narrative), the narrator's voice (third person narrative), with occasional direct appeals to the reader through both these voices, there is also the use of free indirect speech, in which the narrator's voice coincides with that of a character, or sometimes of several characters. Let us look at some examples:

> "A simple question, who will be king when your father is no more?"
>
> *There, the sacrilegious, forbidden words had been spoken and the earth hadn't cracked open, their uncle had not been smitten by lightning and the heads of the three princes were still on their shoulders.... The audacity of the thought was breathtaking.* No, it was a little more than that. It was an awesome idea, one that froze the blood in your veins, gave you cramps in the pit of your stomach and made your tongue so heavy, it was impossible to utter a word. (59, emphasis added)

The three brothers, that is Rana Sanga in his youth and his two older brothers, are seen reacting in their thoughts to the question raised by their uncle. The underlined section appears both as the narrator's comment and as the actual thoughts of the three brothers. The next quotation is slightly different.

> No, it certainly wouldn't do to earn the Devi's displeasure. (62)

This is an instance of the narrator's voice coinciding with that of the character(s), that is, of the narrator's father and brothers, as well as of the protagonist himself (looking back on the situation in his father's youth). A number of viewpoints are thus brought in.

The use of free indirect speech brings the third person chapters closer to those in the first person. The supposed objectivity of the narrator coincides with the perspective of the character(s) and makes for a smoother flow from the third person to the first person chapters. In the following instance, we see the interpenetration of the protagonist's voice into that of the narrator. In fact, though it is the narrator who is nominally speaking, since this is third person narration, what follows is not the narrator's but the character's view. So, it is more than free indirect speech, it is entirely the protagonist's narration through the voice of the narrator.

> She was lying. Trust her to come up with someone as absurd and incredible as Shri Krishna for her paramour. A simple straightforward man was not good enough for her. Only a god, one of the most powerful, important and beloved of gods would do. You couldn't fault her for under-reaching, lack of imagination, or low self-image. It was so far-fetched, so utterly beyond the probable and the possible, some credulous fool might just give it credence. Shri Krishna. Ha. Make it a ha, ha. (91)

Sometimes, on the other hand, free indirect speech projects both the protagonist's and narrator's thought into the narrator's voice.

> It was time to go to the bride's house and get married. (43)

In both the passage above and the last quoted line it is almost as if at some points in a third person chapter, we have the Maharaj Kumar's thoughts presented directly, the difference between the two quotations being that in the second it is both the narrator and protagonist speaking, and in the first, though it is the narrator who is speaking, the views expressed reflect the immediacy of feeling of the character.

A subtle mosaic of viewpoints on the characters emerges through the shifts in perspective between first and third person narration, with even the technique of directly addressing the reader, or what I have called "second person narration" being brought in from time to time. The difference is mainly in terms of being able to see the protagonist visually, from the outside, instead of being part of his consciousness, or directly calling for participation by the reader. The whole tenor of the novel is built on subtle shifts in position between the narrator's perspective and that of the protagonist, and it is possible that the narrator is not just the Maharaj Kumar speaking through his memoirs. Since nothing in this regard is clearly stated, it is perfectly possible that the memoirs were edited by someone else (perhaps the author?) or altered in the telling by, say, Sajani Bai.

There are other shifts in perspective as well, such as the constant movements between centuries, the 16th century and the present day, which affects the way in which action is regarded and characters are interpreted: particularly, issues relating to warfare and the whole system of retreat, and the manner in which sexual relations are regarded. Humour also plays an important role in distancing the event from the character: the Maharaj Kumar's wry reflections, self-deprecations, with occasionally a more robust type of humour, enable different degrees of distance from the reader.

There is, however, a tonal link between the different parts of the novel which seamlessly merges the protagonist's voice with that of the narrator, and the other voices and perspectives in the novel. With all its variations, the tone remains remarkably constant right through, and acts as an effective link. It is by turns analytical, wry, self-deprecating, playful, witty. The tone is the resonance of the Prince's personality which comes out through all his thoughts, feelings and actions, at times ironical, tender, contemplative, overwrought, and a host of other factors. It is as varied as his personality and is a major cohesive element. This tonal connection is even made, in a sense, with the Acknowledgements section of the book, before the novel begins, in which wit, humour and gratitude all coalesce in such a way that the real life persona of the author, Kiran Nagarkar, seems to merge with the rest of the book. This brings to the fore the suspected similarities in the personalities of the author and the protagonist.

Another narrative technique employed is the use of epigraphs at the beginning of the third person chapters. Let us analyse this. The epigraphs seem to undercut the seriousness of the issues being dealt with in the story. The irony counter-balances the fervour, eg. "Ah yes, the truth. What a to-do we make of this word when we all know we would be so much better off without it." (Epigraph to Ch. 6, at a time when the Maharaj Kumar is desperately trying to discover the name of his wife's lover).

The epigraphs occur only in the third person chapters. In these chapters themselves, while it is the narrator (the writer of the memoirs) who presents the events that occur, most of the time Nagarkar ends up reflecting the feelings and views of the protagonist. In the epigraphs, however, much of the time, it appears to be the narrator, or even the author speaking in his own voice and speaking tongue-in-cheek. The irony is in synch with the generally ironic approach of the Maharaj Kumar, but nevertheless, most of the time it seems to be the author speaking. We are thus, made to move to another level of abstraction: general comments are being made, touching on the story, but also standing on their own, and could apply to many other events outside the novel as well. Thus, while the author, and of course the narrator can identify with the Maharaj Kumar to a very large extent in the story, he can simultaneously undercut the passion and suffering depicted through the use of the ironical epigraphs.

In the epigraphs to some of the chapters, however, that is, in four of the fourteen epigraphs, it appears to be the Maharaj Kumar himself speaking, because they are written in the "I" mode. In one of these, the protagonist goes in for a severely ironical look at himself, which is both funny and full of pain, but not cynical: "We were that rarest of couples. Even after years of marriage we were madly in love. I with her and she with somebody else" (Ch. 14). The cynicism displayed in these epigraphs is really a defense mechanism on the part of the protagonist, trying to protect himself from the enormity of the revelations that are being made about him. So these occur in the first person. Here, it is as if the protagonist was looking over the shoulder of the author as he was tearing open the tortured and intensely private aspects of his life. On the other hand, it could be an instance of the author's total identification with the protagonist/narrator. Thus, we are constantly standing on shifting ground, perspectives change and intermingle. There is irony upon irony, including the final irony of not being able to identify the voice in the epigraphs.

Pithy as they are, the epigraphs might appear flippant, but this is deceptive. In one instance, a comment is being made about both the Prince and Princess, without privileging the Prince. Both of them appear to be fighting for themselves alone. "Identical twins are close. But true enemies are closer" (Ch. 31). The final embrace is of opposites, of enemies; and in the final analysis we can only be *against*, not *with* people. In the chapter containing this epigraph, the Maharaj Kumar plays *raas* with his wife and they are like lovers, but we know that the union is based on a falsehood, and that the Maharaj Kumar is deceiving himself. Thematically speaking, the sentiments expressed in the epigraph take us back to the two occasions on which Ravan and Eddie are involved in a deadly embrace.

In another instance, where the second person is used, the epigraph deals with unequal power relations, "You can exorcise the devil. But how do you rid yourself of a god?" (Ch. 16) In that chapter, the Maharaj Kumar sees his wife in the act of making love to Krishna, and he feels that he should quit while there is an iota of dignity in him. But the quality of her ecstasy, her joyousness, overpowers him and he realises that all that he wanted was just her. Finally, in the epigraph to the Epilogue (where the death of the protagonist is described in various different versions) it is the protagonist, not the author, who speaks in his own voice and comments wryly on the course of history, "I am the missing page that is not missed, the hiatus that may be skipped." – what price his memoirs and his role in history? Since no records exist, we do not know if he did indeed have a role in history. Moreover, to have him commenting on his own death and being able to predict his non-role in history is alienation of a very high order.

Let us now turn to the songs sung by the Princess. These constitute another narrative technique. The songs are not what tradition claims she wrote: they are specially written for the Little Saint of the novel and portray a radically different Meera from the stereotype we have known over the centuries. They play their own role in the narrative structure. Like the aphorisms, they provide occasion for the expression of passion, lyricism, irony, and become a means not only of expressing the soul of the Princess, but of adding another perspective to the story that is being unfolded. Both the epigraphs and songs bring in new approaches to godhead, and the line between divinity and humanity becomes illusory. The giver and the taker seem to get conjoined, and poison and ambrosia are not so easily to be separated. Even a god requires a devotee to paint him vermillion in order to come into his own. And even a god is bound by duties and responsibilities. After all, "What is a saviour if he will not save?"

Most of the songs that clutch at one's heart occur in the third person chapters. These are the chapters which are embroiled in emotion. They are also the chapters which carry the epigraphs. There are four such songs occurring in Chapters 8, 12, 25. Other songs occurring in the first person chapters give an insight into the meaning of the narrative, for example, those in Chapters 15 and 24, which deal with issues relating to god and man (woman). The final verses sung by the Maharaj Kumar spontaneously at Bruhannada's funeral pyre, are from the *Gita* (546-47). Unlike the songs sung by the Princess which juxtapose opposites through both passion and irony, the song that the Maharaj Kumar sings is sober and restrained, though it maintains the supreme paradox accepted by tradition, that is, of life and death being one and the same. Throughout the novel we are more conversant with the Maharaj Kumar's viewpoint than his wife's, but in his song he doesn't open up his soul the way she does. He remains his usual rational self, but without the habitual irony that is part of his perspective on life. The Princess's songs supplement and reinforce the picture that we get of her through the eyes of the Prince, and at the same time, give her an added dimension. Also, in addition to revealing the character of the Princess a little more, her songs, like the epigraphs put forward by the author, are a means of commenting on life as it is being portrayed in the novel.

Another tactic used in the novel is the use of letters (written variously by Kausalya, Leelawati, Mangal or the Rana), excerpts from Babur's diary, and occasionally notes made by the Maharaj Kumar in relation to his plans for future action. The purpose of the letters and the diary, while carrying the narrative forward, and providing variety in presentation, is also to give voice to the characters whom we would otherwise see only through the eyes of the Maharaj Kumar or the narrator/author. This is a means by which they can be given a three-dimensional reality. Babur is the one person the Maharaj Kumar respects and wishes to have as a friend, sees him as an alter ego, but knows that they are destined to be enemies. In a sense, the epigraph in Chapter 31, "Identical twins are close. But true enemies are closer" can apply in a totally non-ironical manner to the relationship in the protagonist's mind with Babur. Nagarkar solves the problem of the Maharaj Kumar getting into Babur's mind by a rather modern and dubious method: getting intelligence or snooping around through a spy and thereby getting hold of pages from Babur's diary.

There is also frequent use of digression in *Cuckold*, as also seen earlier in *Ravan and Eddie,* whether in the first person or the third person chapters. In a sense, digressions are similar to the mode of second person narration, in that the narrator has to step out of the narrative and directly address the reader.

> "I have avoided speaking about the rights of succession as much as the other forbidden subject which tears my guts and paralyses my mind. But Prince Bahadur has touched a particularly raw spot and the least I can do is to gain a degree of relief by talking about it." (54)

The words "I have avoided speaking about ..."; "gain a degree of relief by talking about it" suggest that a reader is being addressed, however indirectly. The time of writing about this was much later, at Kumbhalgarh, not at the time when he had just given Bahadur asylum, yet a sense of immediacy is conveyed, as if the events presented occurred just here and at the present moment.

Again, his cogitations on the nature of honour (given

below), though germane to one of the important themes of the book, are given as existential questions addressed to the reader, questions which apply to far more than the events being dealt with here. His mother's viewpoint is also presented (through the stories told to him in childhood) which is very different from his own, and is meant to indicate something of the generally held position on the subject.

> What was a Rajput's word worth? Not much. It cost Rathor Jaitmalot and his sons their lives. They did brave battle. They stood their ground while Prithviraj and Jaimal slashed and struck them from their horses and Sangram Simha made his escape.
>
> Should Rathor Bida not have given his word? Should he have broken it? Where does one draw the line? When my own mother, the Maharani and at least nominally, the first among queens, told me this story and she told it often and when she forgot to, I forced her as a child to tell it again till I had fallen asleep, there were no villains, only heroes. Prithviraj, Jaimal, Surajmal, Bida and his sons, Sangram Simha, all of them.... Perhaps I am the only one who gets all hot and bothered with the thought of such wanton blood-letting. (65)

The Maharaj Kumar frequently announces that he is about to make a digression. He draws the narrative line plainly, but also demands the right to comment on the situation in front of him and on life as such.

> "Which brings me to a brief digression. Being in the right has got nothing to do with courage or exceptional bravery." (57)

> "A long circuitous digression that nevertheless reflects on Kausalya." (136)

The protagonist's comments (not too distant from the narrator's/authorial comment) have been raised to a level of profundity and insightfulness not usually to be encountered. It is the conscious mind analysing, dissecting, finding parallels, drawing generalisations, forming images, reaching out to a symbolic meaning. Events usually spark off deeper connotations, brought to us directly by the cognising mind. Authorial comment is nothing new. Fielding certainly addresses his reader frequently in the course of *Tom Jones* and takes a hail-fellow-well-met attitude. George Eliot, in a less obtrusive manner, steps back and analyses her characters and the events. But there is a distance between them. They are out there, and she stands above and outside, judging, criticising, presenting. Nagarkar follows in the same tradition, and makes no attempt to achieve verisimilitude by removing the author and narrator from the scene.

We are, in fact, at a far remove from verisimilitude. Instead, Nagarkar grapples with issues of godhead and fundamental principles of warfare which strike at the roots of the concept of honour. He also brings to the surface the deep fears of mankind and the horrors that fate can hold in store for us, through, for example, the figure of Bhootani Mata. Though she is given concrete form, she does not inhabit the same level of reality as the rest of the characters. The lack of concern with mere verisimilitude is very obvious in the way in which he does not attempt to provide an entirely authentic picture of 16th century Mewar. In some respects, it is an extremely accurate rendering. The historical research is very carefully done, and yet there is a great deal of latitude in the characterisation of the Prince and Princess. Nagarkar allows himself full scope in developing their characters, since very little is known about Bhoj Raj, the Maharaj Kumar, and moves far away from the Meera of tradition who has been sanctified beyond all credibility as a person. As with the songs we are aware of someone doing this, researching and/or inventing.

While the narrator analyses in retrospect the protagonist's thoughts and behaviour, the protagonist himself also lays bare his mind, his pressing concerns, and his assessment of people and situations. There is no attempt even at a verisimilitude of consciousness, by reflecting through a stream of consciousness every thought that passes through his mind and that of others. The author/narrator dwells on what he considers important and necessary in the mind and life of the protagonist.

Other narratorial techniques are also employed by Nagarkar to offset the limitations of first person narration. Stories are told by others to bring in incidents of which the Maharaj Kumar could have no first hand knowledge.

> There were many legends about the Devi. One of them Kausalya told me when I was a child. (60)

The use of Bhootani Mata can almost be considered similar to the telling of stories. She is certainly not a person on the same plane of reality as the rest. It is worth noting that almost all her appearances take place in third person chapters, suggesting a perspective which mingles belief in both the material and non-material, or purely psychological, reality.

Another technique is the use of time. Just as Charani Devi (Ch. 5) swallows up all time in bits and pieces and then brings them out very gradually, so also does Nagarkar unravel the story he is telling. But it doesn't come out in a straight line of progression. The primary aspect of time in the novel is a mixture of the elements of the 16th century and the present day, but there are also frequent movements back and forth in time within 16th century Mewar which suggest the omnipresence of all the events which have occurred, particularly in their bearing on those which are currently being described. We have the Princess being labelled a *tawaif* (whore) long before the description of her marriage and her rejection of her bridegroom. We see the Maharaj Kumar from his own perspective as involved in a variety of activities, both personal and in relation to running the State, before we see him from the outside as "the most eligible bachelor in this part of the world." Thus, the novel begins somewhere closer to the time of writing, and periodically goes backward – to the protagonist's wedding; to the fight for succession between Rana Sanga and his brothers, to Sumitra's death (Bahadur's illness takes him back to Sumitra's illness, 96-101). Again, after realising that it is Lord Krishna who is his wife's lover, he goes back in time to his own childhood and his close personal relationship with Krishna (Ch. 10). When dealing with Adinathji's illness he goes back to Kausalya's background and the way the Maharaj Kumar and Mangal grew up together (Ch. 13). The passages going back in time all seem to occur in the first person chapters, not as part of his third person narration of the memoirs/ Sajani Bai's retelling of the tale/the author.

This backward and forward movement in time enables a play between the immediacy of experience and the filling in of past events. The flow of the novel is such that in spite of this movement, there is an inexorable thrust forward, which seems to take care of changes in time, perspective and sensibility. There are even major breaks within chapters, like scenes in a play, or quick cuts and sudden switches in a film. Since the novel deals with such a wide canvas, it has to turn its attention to a variety of different matters, and a clear separation has to be maintained between each of these. The gaps in cohesion within chapters, as well as between chapters, make for clear-cut narratorial breaks in time and event, nevertheless, the architecture of the novel has been very carefully constructed; the breaks between chapters seem to be carefully organised into a pattern. One of these patterns is the link between third person chapters. The same topic is picked up from one such chapter to the next, with the other chapters in between dealing with, in the main, quite different matters. These chapters also contain an opening aphorism, and occasionally a song by the Princess, which is of great significance to the meaning of the novel. The diegesis, or referential action is not necessarily identical with the narrative material. What is included, what remains unsaid, what is highlighted, gives rise to the particular character of the narrative.

The chapters presented in the third person deal with passion, and the intensity of emotion in the Maharaj Kumar's dealings with his wife, variously referred to as Greeneyes or the Little Saint, depending on his perspective at the time, and of the Krishna element in his life and hers. Thus, it is both erotic and spiritual absorption that infuses these chapters. It is also significant that almost all mention of Bhootani Mata (the psychological or pseudo-spiritual element) occurs here. The chapters presented in the first person, on the other hand, deal with matters of state, the Maharaj Kumar's vision of how he could transform Mewar, with warfare and new conceptions of the conduct of war, and his various other liaisons and friendships. The weaving together of these two different kinds of subject matter in the two different types of narrative perspective help to set up a new kind of novelistic architechtonics. It helps to provide another kind of structure and another kind of principle of organisation. It is also a means by which we can continue to see the Maharaj Kumar in first person narrative as a rational human being, whose outlook on life can be trusted; while treatment of eroticism, issues of godhead, and the pseudo-spiritual, all issues which deviate from the purely rational, being too private to be exposed to public view by the protagonist are dealt with by the narrator.

The difference in treatment of the Maharaj Kumar's relationship with his wife in a first person chapter in comparison with third person presentation is great. When recounted in the "I" mode, it is hardly ever dealt with in the highly charged manner of the third person chapters. The use of the first person also seems to bring in a variety of topics in different scenes, unlike what happens in the third person chapters which are relatively much briefer and more often than not, concentrate only on the relationship between the Prince, Princess and the Blue God. It appears that shifts in perspective, however subtle they may be, are required in order to handle the burden of the ideological schemata being introduced.

However, the Krishna theme can be introduced by the character when speaking in his own voice, if excruciatingly private matters are not being dealt with, in order to establish the Maharaj Kumar's notion of honour, and determine his concept of retreat in warfare, thus establishing Krishna's centrality in the life of the Maharaj Kumar as well as that of his wife.

> Unlike Krishna, his own people, despite their great valour, needed to convince themselves almost on a daily basis that they had not lost their spirit. Whence this insecurity, he wasn't able to say. Why did the Rajput code of honour and chivalry always devolve upon the sacrifice of their own lives? Why were they always afraid of being seen as pusillanimous? It left no room for manoeuvering and for any other options including machinations, a concept which the world owed largely to Krishna.
>
> Krishna had no problems putting his tail between his legs and retreating. One would have thought he would be in one hell of a rush to terminate his uncle, the tyrant Kansa who had killed every one of Krishna's seven siblings.

> Instead, Krishna stayed away from him as long as he could (109).

It is also noteworthy that many aspects of cinematic technique are introduced in the novel, but in such a restrained and understated manner that they do not draw attention to themselves. There is a constant shift in focus, from seeing a panoramic view – of the city, of crowds assembled to hear the Princess sing, the lay-out of the army, to the closer focus on the more personal lives of the main characters and in going where an actual camera cannot, into their heart and soul. The narrator might suddenly zoom in on certain characters at first seen in the distance. From the top of the Victory Tower, the Maharaj Kumar says, "Look at that woman rubbing charcoal powder mixed with a bit of opium into her gums" (49). Perspective, as we have seen, also changes from that of the Maharaj Kumar, to that of the narrator, as we shift from the first person to the third person chapters and various combinations of these positions. The device of the freeze is also used frequently to bring time to a standstill while the Maharaj Kumar, and sometimes the narrator, go into physical descriptions of space, colour and sound. There are also other ways of stalling the action, of turning an event around in order to consider different aspects of it, through the use of epigrahs, song, stories of the past. These are what give richness and multidimensionality to the relationship between the Little Saint, Lord Krishna and the Maharaj Kumar.

The 20th century concern with disjunction and relativity owes much to the technique of the edited film, which moves from one image or locale to another without obvious cohesive links, using the principle of montage. The third person chapters in *Cuckold* provide an example of a novelistic adaptation of this. The action of one of the third person chapters is interrupted by the first person account, and then the action is picked up in the next third person chapter from where it was left off. This is readily seen in the movement from Chapters 3 to 6 to 8 to 10 which deal with the Maharaj Kumar's relationship with the Princess, while the in-between chapters are about quite different matters. The long first person chapters are broken into many parts through quick cuts and sudden switches. The relative distance of the narrator/author from the action, the degree of their participation in the action, and the extent of the specificity of detail transform the objects being described. The distance and angle of each individual "take" in cinema varies, so also in *Cuckold*, the changes in treatment of aspects of the referential action, whether through perspective, digression, epigraph, etc. are a means of providing different angles on the action.

In a sense, the past is already encapsulated and made available through the memoirs of the Prince, or perhaps, the re-telling of the story by Sajani Bai. Events are, therefore, not unfolding one after the other, demanding that we sit on edge to know what happens next. There is action and progression, but simultaneously, there are prolonged moments of stasis, where the inner movement of life is explored and the meaning of honour, responsibility, duty, joy, passion, action and reaction thrashed out. The ultimate moment of stasis is the death of the Maharaj Kumar. The fourth ending provides a graphic image, not action as such. In any case, the effect of alienation that is produced by the four endings suggested by the writer, is to move us out of the action proper to contemplate this history of the "hiatus in history," that is to say, the Maharaj Kumar. As Cohen puts it, "Once time in the novel is conceived of as physical, malleable, and above all, artificial, as is the case with cinema, the flow of time loses its relentless forward motion and the very notion of chronology begins to seem foreign.... [This leads to an] attempt to capture the present moment, to extend it, to memorialize it, to reinforce it against the inroads of past and future." In order to express the relativity of space and time, many writers, like Virginia Woolf, Naipaul, and Rushdie in *Midnight's Children*, make use of parenthesis as a central device. Nagarkar, however, achieves this effect through the use of multiple perspectives, and a number of alienating devices mentioned above, which make the reader stand back and reflect on the action, instead of being swept away by it.

It is worth noting that the narratorial techniques used are contained within the world that the novel establishes, and the creation of this world can be considered the overarching narrative technique. The world presented here has the Maharaj Kumar as its central point. Everything else that occurs is linked in some way with him. The main events are the running of the state, warfare, and human relations, particularly sexual relations. Lord Krishna plays an important role in this. His centrality is attested by the fact that the title of the novel suggests the primacy of the aspect of cuckoldry supposedly perpetrated by Shri Krishna. Thus, Krishna, the Maharaj Kumar's personal god, with whom he had a special affinity, and from whom he learnt to rethink issues relating to personal responsibility and the conduct of warfare, is revealed to be his rival and his wife's lover. The Maharaj Kumar feels totally betrayed – at one stroke he is deprived of both his god and his wife. Some time later, he begins to emulate the Blue God, and to appear before the Princess in indigo paint. She accepts him, imagining that he is Krishna himself. From being a supplicant of Krishna, now he dons his mantle. He realises at some point that his wife in fact does not see through the disguise, but genuinely thinks he is Krishna, which discourages him and makes him stop his nocturnal visits. However, matters take a very different turn at the very end. Escaping from his assassins, he goes to wreck vengeance on Krishna in the Baswa temple. "Even the gods," he muttered, "must get their just deserts" (601). He raises his sword to strike at the statue of Krishna, but just then the Blue One speaks to him about the complete pointlessness of enmity, considering that "you and I are one. My flute and song are on your lips. We love the same woman. Why, you fool, no power on earth can separate or divide us" (602). In the meantime, his enemies were closing in on him, but at the very last minute, just before he could have been caught and killed, the god embraces him. He disappears within Krishna, enfolded in his arms, with only a little bit of his turban hanging out of the marble.

The world of *Cuckold* incorporates the role of Krishna, the protagonist's wife's lover, who is also the protagonist's own mentor, in two ways: firstly, as regards his value system, the concept of honour, duty, responsibility; and secondly, in warfare, the concept of retreating to live to fight and win another day. Again, though cuckolded by him, the Maharaj Kumar is finally contained within him. His realisation at the end that the only woman who mattered to him was his wife makes all links come together. Both embrace and have been embraced by Krishna, and by the end, the Maharaj Kumar responds to the primal quality in his wife and knows for sure that she is the one woman for him. Side by side one has to take account of the scene where the Princess breaks two coconuts in front of Krishna's statue, and calls on Krishna to worship her. The principle of *So'hum* (That I am, or God is all and therefore I am God) has been carried to its logical conclusion. Thus, God and man are seen to be identical. This is why, with these overarching positions, in spite of its huge canvas, the book maintains a sense of tautness and purposeful direction. This conceptual, philosophical aspect is the larger principle which links together all aspects of the book.

The role of history, of collective memory in presenting a true and unbiased picture of reality is a major concern of the novel. It is extremely ironical that the role of the Maharaj Kumar is so minimal in the real life records of these events. Historians do not remember the Maharaj Kumar at all, and he seems to have foreknowledge of this in the novel. Is the novel dealing with history, or is it fiction? Why, when there is no "historical" record of the Maharaj Kumar, is this being presented as the "truth"? Certainly, there is the interweaving of factual truth as in the excerpts from Babur's diary, the known facts of the Mewar kingdom and the wars that were fought, with fictional devices leading to an impression of the truth, such as the memoirs of the Maharaj Kumar, and letters from various persons.

Thus, it is the combined efforts of the historian, personal memoirs (within the novel these are the Maharaj Kumar's), fragments of a diary/letters (Babur's) that are available, and the rendering of Court musicians that all build up to a history of the period. Nagarkar took up the task of trying to recreate the figure of the Maharaj Kumar, who has been side-lined by history, using whatever material was available, and creating his own when none existed. He does this by means of a number of devices, some of which have been analysed in this essay.

Works Cited

Berger, John. *Ways of Seeing*, UK: BBC & Penguin Books, 1972.

Cohen, Keith. *Film & Fiction, Part II: Exchange*. Yale: Yale UP, 1979.

Nagarkar, Kiran. *Seven Sixes are Forty-Three*. Brisbane: U of Queensland P, 1980. Reprinted by Vikas Pub. House Pvt. Ltd., 1981. Translated from the original Marathi, *Saat Sakkam Trechalis,* Bombay: Mauj Pub., 1974.

———. *Ravan and Eddie*. New Delhi: Viking, Penguin India, 1995.

———. *Cuckold*. New Delhi: HarperCollins *Publishers*. India, 1997.

Romance, Realism and the Postmodern in *Cuckold*

Hira Steven

Kiran Nagarkar's *Cuckold* is a multifaceted, multilayered work which, like its central motif Shri Krishna, is difficult to pin down, slot and categorise. Is it a romance or a realistic novel? Or, is it a modernist/postmodernist work? Again, looked at in another way, is it a historical novel or a philosophical novel or a psychological novel or a love story? As a matter of fact it is, or at least has elements of all these.

For its novelistic form and method Nagarkar draws on the old and the new as it suits him. Critics like Irving Buchen often maintain that experimentation springs from the pressure of the novelist's vision which finds the old forms inadequate for its expression. I suspect that in all but the work of groundbreaking writers, it springs as much from the pressure, conscious or unconscious, of current literary trends. However, in Nagarkar's case, I am inclined to discount the pressure of contemporary novelistic trends, since in many ways *Cuckold* goes so blatantly against these. Here is a historical novel essentially in the realistic mode, containing at the same time, a great deal that belongs to the currently discounted romance tradition, with several passages which could by hostile critics be termed purple patches. Nagarkar, then, seems to draw, as it suits him, on elements of romance, realism and, to a lesser extent, on postmodernism, as well as on a variety of types of novel.

The world of *Cuckold* is the world of 16th century Mewar, a world which appears to be straight out of romance. Belonging to the past, distanced from the reality of the reader's life, it is a world governed by rigid codes of chivalry, honour and loyalty, which are accepted on authority and never questioned. It is inhabited by several larger than life characters. For example, we have Adinathji, the Jain Finance Minister and moneylender to the State, Prime Minister Puranmalji, Rana Sanga (except in the last chapters), and slightly lower down the social ladder, Mangal Simha the Maharaj Kumar's companion and the Rajput equivalent of a gentleman in waiting who later becomes Head of Intelligence. We also have Mangal's mother Kausalya, the Maharaj Kumar's *dai* (wet-nurse), nursemaid, adviser and concubine. These come across as larger than life characters, always in control of themselves and others, acting out of clear cut motives, never manifesting anxiety or doubt. When, for example, the Maharaj Kumar approaches Adinathji for money for the Gujarat campaign, Adinathji, ultra smooth and courteous has Maharaj Kumar completely in his hands. Mangal has eyes everywhere, can anticipate what is required of him, possesses a loyalty that cannot be shaken and to whom "people listen even when he is not speaking."[1] Ultimately these characters and the world they inhabit are static, not subject to change and development.

---

[1] Kiran Nagarkar, *Cuckold* (Harper Collins India, 1997). Afterword. 604. One might point out here that history is not used by Nagarkar with that "intense self-consciousness" which Linda Hutcheon sees as the mark of post-modern historiographic metafiction. (Hutcheon, Linda. "Historiographic Metafiction." *Metafiction*. Ed. Mark Currie. Longman, 1995). In other words, Nagarkar does not question the conventions and assumptions either of historiography or of historical fiction, though he *uses* history with a degree of freedom that some may see as postmodern.

This is also the world of the historical novel, and whatever Nagarkar may have said about history having inveigled itself into the work against his intentions, *Cuckold* is a historic novel on an epic scale. It deals with momentous times in the history of Mewar and its neighbouring states when the course of Indian history might have taken a different turn. As a historical novel it focuses on kings and princes, alliances and battles, providing also a fascinating account of intrigues and power struggles within Mewar and the neighbouring states. At the same time, however, it puts under searching examination ideas of kingship, valour, loyalty and codes of chivalry and honour, beside invoking vividly a sense of the lived reality of the times – the reality of ordinary people living ordinary lives. These last two aspects of the novel take it out of the world of romance into the realm of realism.

This combination of realism and romance is achieved by presenting a romance world through the eyes and the mind of the Maharaj Kumar, the protagonist and first person narrator in most of the chapters of the novel. He belongs to the essentially romance world of 16th century Mewar, and yet he does not. He is a Rajput, heir to the throne, his right being questioned only by those who would aspire to it by any means possible. At the same time, he possesses an essentially modern sensibility albeit conditioned by his Rajput upbringing. The result is a fascinating blend, as we have seen, of romance and realism.

Unlike Adinathji, Puranmalji, Mangal and others, the Maharaj Kumar belongs clearly to the tradition of the realistic novel. He is presented in all his complexity, shown acting out of mixed motives, often unsure of himself, combining admirable and reprehensible qualities. However far removed from the reader in time and social position he is subject to recognisable emotions, problems and dilemmas. Most importantly, he is not static, but grows and develops with experience. As such, *Cuckold* is also a psychological novel presenting a fascinating study of a character with many truly admirable qualities who is nevertheless a loser both as a Prince and a lover. He is intelligent, energetic, self aware, constantly examining his own motives and the values by which he and his countrymen live, open to new ways of looking at things. He is also a man of action truly concerned to improve his State. Yet, he never manages to carry his countrymen with him and never succeeds to the throne which is rightfully his, eventually becoming, to use Nagarkar's phrase, " a hiatus in history."[2] There are several reasons for his failures. For one thing he is too far ahead of his times. Relatedly, he perceives and acts on the larger view and so loses the support and confidence of his people. "Why can't I be a good Rajput and see things simply, in black and white?" he asks himself (191). The Maharaj Kumar's problem is the problem all visionaries face – (I don't mean visionaries with a mystical vision. The Maharaj Kumar is a practical visionary.) – the problem of having to deal with people who will not look beyond what they have been taught to accept as right and best, and being able to carry them with him. The problem is aggravated in the Maharaj Kumar's case by his habit of constant self-examination often leading to self-doubt. He underestimates himself and overestimates the adverse response of others to his actions. For example,

---

[2] Kiran Nagarkar, *Cuckold*. 473. The passage from which this phrase is taken is one of the few instances in the novel where Nagarkar looks at himself looking at history, revealing the kind of self-consciousness about the use of history referred to in the above note. Sajanibai has just sung a song which gave the Maharaj Kumar pleasure, but at the same time he says it aroused painful memories. Sajanibai replies, "If we consign a song to amnesia because of the burden of our memories, then it is possible that an entire people will push a dastardly act or even the life of one of their own into the black hole of oblivion merely to seek forgiveness and absolution." "Do you really think one can wipe out people and events that easily?" "We rework our own memories and reinvent ourselves to suit our tastes and predilections every day. Who is to notice a hiatus in history a few centuries down the road?"

during the campaign against Idar when the Maharaj Kumar is leading the Mewar troops for the first time, he handles an extremely tricky situation involving his rebellious cousin Tej in what to us seems a masterly fashion, catching Tej off guard and knocking him down. But in his own estimation he had "certainly made a lasting impression on [his soldiers and royal peers]. They were dumbstruck by how low I could stoop" (216). Later in the same chapter, when the Maharaj Kumar is on the point of imposing a crushing defeat on the Gujarat troops, using all the wiles at his disposal he says, "I am no man's equal in treachery and deceit.... Expect the worst from me. I will always improve on your expectations" (229). The advice given to him by an old crone when he is faced by a crowd of dangerously hostile citizens who blame the cholera epidemic on what they perceive as the treacherous means used by the Maharaj Kumar to defeat their enemy, is most apt: "Don't take shelter behind your shyness. In your position, it is no virtue. Get yourself a trumpet and blow it" (310). All this bears out the truth of the observation that others (barring a few exceptions) take you at your own estimation of yourself.

This portrait of the Maharaj Kumar emerges through the first person chapters. Given the ability of the character to examine himself with honesty and to accept his defects, he seems by and large to be a reliable narrator. However, the third person chapters very subtly, and realistically, expose the limitations in his perception of himself. In the first person narrative he comes across largely as clear headed, active, possessing sound values, essentially a gentleman. The third person chapters reveal another side of him – pathetically enmeshed in his love-hate relationship with his wife, often cruel, clumsy, out of control. These switches between the first and the third person narrative which can be seen as an experimental device, eventually and paradoxically make for greater realism, dealing with painful and deeply embarrassing episodes in the protagonist's life – his relationship with his wife whom he discovers after his marriage to be betrothed to another. As Nagarkar asks in a recent interview, "Would this proud man, however candid about other areas of his life, be able to talk publicly about his wife's escapades?"

A word here about what is termed realism in the novel. Most discussions of realism[3] focus on the content of the work, rather than the form. They see "realism" as involving, among other things, truth to life in the presentation of character, scene and social setting; closeness to the experience of the reader; the use of contemporary middle-class values and perceptions. Most discussions also touch on language, but mainly to comment on the use of prose rather than poetry. What these discussions tend to ignore is the extent of convention that exists in the handling of form in the realist novel; in other words, to narratology. In the third person novel we have the convention of the omniscient narrator who can travel over vast areas of space and time, and can enter at will not only into the minds, but the subconscious of his characters. First person narrative is even more problematic. It is never made clear why and for whom the protagonist is writing. The first person narrator re-creates whole scenes and extended dialogue in great detail. Did he or she actually remember all that? Again, in most successful first person novels, there is a holding back of knowledge regarding the outcome that the narrator already possesses, for the sake of suspense, as the scene or events are unfolding. And relatedly, there is the problem of shifting perspectives: most scenes and events are presented from the limited

[3] Kettle, Arnold. *An Introduction to the English Novel.* Hutchinson and Co. 1951. Vol. I. chapter 2. "Realism and Romance"); Watt, Ian. *The Rise of the Novel: Studies in Defoe, Richardson and Feilding.* Penguin Books, 1972. First published 1957); Levine, George. *The Realistic Imagination; English Fiction from Frankenstein to Lady Chatterley.* Chicago: University of Chicago Press, 1981.

perspective of the narrator at the time of the action being described, while from time to time the older narrator comments with the knowledge gained by the time of writing. Many first person novels fall back on farfetched methods to present events at which the narrator was not present, like detailed letters and reporting by another character (again with detailed dialogue and scene setting). While *Cuckold* is not entirely free of these essentially nonrealistic conventions, yet its handling of the first person narrative form is closer to realism in its actual sense, in spite of the strong elements of romance. As the Maharaj Kumar informs the reader in chapter 27, he has started writing his autobiography during a period of exile and forced idleness at Kumbhalgarh. In the last chapter the protagonist says, "I have almost finished my last entry. In a few minutes now I'll seal these bits of my memoirs and hand them over to the messenger" (600). In the same chapter, the Maharaj Kumar gives us his reasons for writing his autobiography. They are, first, "to take a cold, dispassionate look at my life, find out where I had gone wrong" so that he could succeed in doing what he had so far tried hard but failed to do – carry his countrymen with him into a new way of looking at life. His second reason was to counteract the Rajput conception of history: "History was for them that fabled second chance" (344). That is, failures in life could be corrected through the telling. The Maharaj Kumar's aim then is to counter the prevailing romanticised history, (which reinforced the prevailing romanticised view of life), with the history of his times as it really happened – with all its mistakes and failures.

The language of this autobiography, the protagonist maintains in the same chapter, came to him as a shock – "a two tongued instrument: an austere, distanced and deliberative high Mewari for certain purposes of ratiocination and logic; and a cross between the language of the court, and the colourful, pungent and coruscating dialect of the eunuchs, servants and maids of the palace" (346). Also as a surprise to the normally reserved and cautious protagonist came the laying bare of himself, the "telling it all" (346) that he finds himself doing. All this reflects clearly the awareness on the writer's part of the artifices of the first person narrative form and his attempts to counter them.

As we see, then, the realistic novel is not entirely realistic in its handling of form. With regard to its novelistic content too the term "realism" needs to be examined. In the course of its development, the shifts in the novel from realism, to modernism and the stream-of-consciousness, to postmodernism are all basically shifts in pursuit of prevailing notions of reality. As these change, the novel changes to reflect these. The realistic novel reflects what is perceived as a stable, shareable reality, based on the grand narratives of religion and society. Modernism with its fragmented narratives was an attempt to reflect the prevailing sense of breakdown of social and political structures, of cultural traditions, of religious beliefs and consequently, of values and attitudes in the early part of the 20th century. Paradoxically, postmodernism attempts to reflect in its form, or rather in its playing with or discarding of form, its new notion of reality – that what we call reality doesn't exist, that life is undecidable and full of "ontological uncertainty."

To what extent is *Cuckold* postmodern? Taking into consideration its view of reality, it is not postmodern. One would class it as realistic in that the text does not draw attention to itself but is "transparent"; its primary concern being to communicate a reality that is taken for granted as universal and shareable. True, the protagonist, and through him the novelist, questions accepted values and codes of behaviour. More importantly, the protagonist at several points voices his sense of doubt about the elusiveness of truth. This questioning of reality and truth, one might say, is surely postmodern. However, the postmodern questioning of truth leads to an ultimate throwing up of one's hands at the impossibility of finding an answer, and a consequent falling back on insouciance and play. *Cuckold* on the other hand, through its protagonist, questions accepted ideas in an attempt to arrive at the truth. His questioning is a quest for truth rather than a denial of the possibility of truth.

An interesting question that strikes one here, and which I am not competent to explore is, does the Hindu ethos obviate the postmodern crisis? Perhaps the 20th century crisis regarding the perception of the human world, leading to the absurdist, existentialist, modernist and postmodernist movements is a phenomenon confined to the Christian West. Christianity provided, on the whole, clear answers to the eternal questions of life. When Christian belief began to weaken there was a crisis. In India such a crisis is perhaps impossible since Hinduism is already in one way profoundly postmodern in positing the relativity of truth – or at least of the human perception of it.[4]

Nevertheless, there are elements in *Cuckold* that are experimental and even postmodern. The device of switching between first and third person narrative, while certainly not new (Dickens had used the device as early as 1852-53 in *Bleak House*), is nevertheless a departure from the general run of novels which are termed realistic. But this device as we have seen is in the cause of greater realism. The switch from the real to the unreal in the presentation of Bhootani Mata does fall into the realm of the postmodern in its undecidability. She begins in the "real" world, when the Maharaj Kumar, driven to desperation in his attempt to discover his wife's

[4] Since this article was written I came across the following interesting observation by Manjula Padmanabhan in a review of *Cuckold* which seems pertinent: "The Prince's moral universe is the traditional Hindu one, where the quest is for a personal definition of Truth rather than unquestioning faith in any one doctrine." *Outlook*, March 5, 1997.

lover, decides to consult the old woman who lives in a cave forty miles from Chittor and who is reputed to perform arcane rites. But the actual cave leads him into a labyrinth in which he is almost immediately lost. He can see nothing. He is knocked down, lifted up, stripped and licked all over. He has visions of surrealistic horror that overgo Bosch. Finally, he sees Bhootani Mata first as a toothless old hag, then suddenly transformed into a young woman with a lush body and breasts which are full and firm. Is it magic? Is it delirium? Or have we moved entirely out of the realm of the novelistic real (in which magic and delirium have a place) into the realm of postmodern uncertainty and unconcern? Bhootani Mata appears only in the third person chapters, thus suggesting that she belongs to the unacknowledged areas of the Maharaj Kumar's psyche. There are repeated accounts of her lacerating him. In chapter 14 her hair "swished through the flesh of his face" and his skin was being shredded (151-52). In chapter 25, "Bhootani Mata was slashing his body, long clean gashes from which the blood welled up eagerly" (327). Bhootani Mata also puts curses on him: "May everything you touch turn to ashes. May all those who are dear to you rue the day they came within your ambit" (417). And she makes dire predictions: "People who are totally unaware of the pact you made with me will pay the price of your sins and the vagaries of your mind" (495). Does Bhootani Mata then belong in the labyrinthine recesses of the Maharaj Kumar's subconscious? Is she a manifestation of his constant self-doubt which leads him to lacerate himself and to somehow hold himself responsible for whatever disasters befall those around him? In that case, Bhootani Mata is one of the devices contributing to *Cuckold* as a psychological novel. And yet, one is never certain. As the Maharaj Kumar says, in one of the rare references to Bhootani Mata in a first person chapter, "Who is she stroke fate stroke the void" (475).

As a psychological novel then, *Cuckold* draws on

elements from realism (mainly) and postmodernism. Romance, as noted earlier, also plays a part in the psychological exploration of the Maharaj Kumar who as narrator, however questioning and modern his sensibility, nevertheless projects a romance world due to a conditioned sensibility. However, at its core *Cuckold* is a philosophic novel. Its main theme is the single, simple versus the multiple and complex. It is evident in the protagonist's questioning of the Rajput code of honour and chivalry already discussed. For the Rajputs fighting according to the accepted codes of honour and bravery is more important than winning battles. "What fool will not win by deceit, dishonour and guerilla tactics?" asks a member of the black flag welcome orchestrated by Vikramaditya on the Maharaj Kumar's return to Chittor after his triumph over the Gujarat forces, through the use of unorthodox tactics, "We are Rajputs here, not cowards."

This theme is also evident in the extremely interesting extended debate on the concept of loyalty between the Maharaj Kumar and the eunuch Bruhannada, who remains unquestioningly loyal to his masters Queen Karmavati and her son and heir aspirant to the throne, Vikramaditya, in spite of the attempt on his life by the latter. The gist of the debate as well as the Maharaj Kumar's philosophy comes across clearly in the following passage:

> "Do we stick to people, however mistaken or evil they may be, merely because we were born on their side or should we owe our loyalty, not to people or institutions but to values? Bhishma may have served humanity better if he had had the courage not to follow tradition blindly but to weigh in on the side of right, especially because he was perceived as a man of great moral fibre."
>
> "You've got it wrong, Highness. Go back to

> your *Gita*. Whichever side of the river you are born, the *Gita*-god tells us, whichever caste or profession you belong to, be true to it."
>
> "So he does, Bruhannada, so he does. But gods too may be wrong occasionally and one must have the courage to go against them, perhaps even contravene their fiat." (533)

This theme of the single, simple and unchanging versus the multiform, complex and changing is most importantly manifested in the central motif of the novel, "the *Gita*-god Shri Krishna, Krishna, Bal Krishna, Flautist, Giridhar, Gopal, Govinda, Atmaram, Shyam, The Peacock-feathered One, Vasudev, Kanhaiyya, Kanha, Murlidhar, Kaliya Mardan, Nagar, Madhusadan, and (the possessor of) a thousand other names and aliases" (103). The other gods who were the Maharaj Kumar's heroes in his childhood were static as he realised as he grew up. Whatever happened to them, in the end they remained the same. "The one exception was Shri Krishna." The following passage needs to be quoted at length since it is central to the novel and the Maharaj Kumar's philosophy.

> There was not one Shri Krishna but at the very least, three or four. He was protean and changed his role according to the circumstances in which he found himself. You could not put your finger on his character and say, yes this is him. He defied definition. You could never predict how he was going to act or react. Did he have principles? Yes, he did. And yet, if the occasion called for it, he kept them in abeyance, changed them or forgot them. Was he ruthless and unscrupulously opportunistic? Sometimes. But the Flautist wouldn't have framed the questions quite that way or would have subtly side-tracked them while answering them. Over-simplification was easier to handle but it was also dangerous.

> Nobody had a monopoly on truth. And your perception of the truth changed depending on your past experience, your family, clan or professional loyalties, your cultural background and what you wanted out of life. Was Shri Krishna dynamic because he saw the larger picture or did the canvas grow wider and far more complex because he responded differently to each set of circumstances and problems? (106-07)

As the passage just quoted indicates, the theme of change is also reflected in the relationship of the protagonist with Krishna. In his early years Krishna was his hero to the point of imitation and identification. As he grew to adulthood, the Maharaj Kumar saw Krishna in the role of mentor, from whom he learnt many lessons both as Prince and more especially as leader of his troops. (Chapter 10 is especially important here.) Krishna taught him not to "indulge in heroics ... [but] to wait and watch, ... negotiate, avoid confrontation as far as possible." If statesmanship did not work, to become "wily and devious." He taught him not to be afraid of "putting his tail between his legs and retreating." "Perhaps what the Maharaj Kumar owed most to Krishna was a habit of mind: don't take anything on authority.... Re-examine. Question. Doubt" (108-09). As the Maharaj Kumar grew older, though he never rejected the lessons learnt from Krishna, the early identification cooled into separation and then, after his marriage into bitter enmity, until sustained hatred led him to ultimate union.

In spite of the theme of change, in many forms, running through *Cuckold*, the novel then hints at the ultimate oneness of all things. One finds this in the meditation on "So'hum: I am that" in chapter 27. But it is most marvelously brought out by the "ending." Some have seen four alternative endings to *Cuckold* (discovering another postmodern element), but the novel in reality has only one, which occurs at the end of the last chapter, which is the end of the autobiography. The assassins are almost upon him as the Maharaj Kumar completes and hands over to the messenger these bits of his memoirs. That is the last *fact* we have about him. The novel thus has an open ending, characteristic of many modern novels. The *Epilogue* that follows does not have four endings but tells of four stories floating around of the Maharaj Kumar's disappearance – that he was killed by the assassins, that he escaped to Mandu and married Leelavati,. that he became a mendicant and joined the followers of the Little Saint, and a fourth. As the narrator in John Fowle's *The French Lieutenant's Woman* says, "Whichever ending is the second (in our case, whichever ending is the last) will seem, so strong is the tyranny of the last chapter, the final, 'real' version."[5] Readers of *Cuckold* will embrace the last version not only because it is the last but because of its wonderful poetic rightness. The final confrontation of the Maharaj Kumar with his rival, ending in final union in the Flautist's embrace.

Works Cited

Buchen, Irving H. "The Aesthetics of the Supra-novel." *The Theory of the Novel: New Essays*. Ed. John Halperin. New York: Oxford UP, 1974.

Fowels, John. *The French Lieutenant's Woman*. 1969. New York: Vintage Paperback reprint, 1996.

Selden, Raman. *A Reader's Guide to Contemporary Literary Theory*. 2nd ed. Brighton: Harvester Press, 1989.

Theme and Variations: Reflections on Nagarkar's *Cuckold*: An Exploration Of Human Loss and Redemption

Jacquelin Singh

Kiran Nagarkar gave the title *Cuckold* to his second major work of fiction in English. He didn't call it *The Maharaj Kumar of Mewar*, or *The Little Saint*, or *The Last Days of a Rajput Kingdom*. He called it *Cuckold*. So it must be assumed that this is where he wants our attention to be fixed as we read this novel set against the background of the kingdom of Mewar in the early 16th century.

In its simplest, most basic meaning, cuckold is of course the label given to a man whose wife is unfaithful to him. Usually we think of an old man with a young wife: a figure of fun and perhaps even pity. His bride has been taken away from him body and soul; someone else has appropriated her for himself. The factor of marriage is always there. A single man may be in a similarly unenviable position, but he is not likely to be called a cuckold: no marriage vow has been broken, no adultery committed. On the other hand, the idea of the woman (married or not) being despoiled is a constant in any relationship forbidden by the rules of the particular society she lives in. She has been defiled, ruined. The seducer is frequently characterised as a debauch, a rake, dashing, even. But evil. A wrecker. There is always an air of secretiveness, and even glamour about the whole business of cuckoldry with its tainted whiff of illicit intercourse surrounding the deceivers. It is interesting to note that the word *cokewold* (according to *Webster's Ninth Collegiate Dictionary*, 1990) entered the English language in the Middle English period during the 13th century, as if the phenomenon had had no name before then, or at least not in the written language.

If wider implications of cuckoldry are considered, then this appropriation can be expanded to include more than the act of cheating a husband. It can also include the taking exclusive possession of someone (other than a spouse) or something belonging to another, to take or make use of without authority or right. And so the object of this "looting" can be a person or a thing. Further, the idea of cuckoldry can be stretched to include the preventing of someone's attaining something that is rightfully his or hers (a kingdom, for example). Even further out: cuckoldry can work upon its object, making the "seduced" one indifferent or even hostile where attachment formerly existed: the ultimate estrangement. Alienation itself, a component of cuckoldry, implies the giving up of the values of one's society and family.

In all times and in all places, human beings have experienced loss and betrayal in one or more of these ways. It is this fact of life that draws Nagarkar's attention throughout the work as he focuses on the protagonist, the Maharaj Kumar of Mewar. The cuckold of the title. Betrayals and losses take place against the historical action that thrums away in the background like the constant sound of a *tanpura* on which the notes of a *raga* are arranged as pearls on a string.

When the early 16th century Rajput prince, the Maharaj Kumar of Mewar, returns to his father's kingdom flush with triumph at having routed the forces of the Sultan of Gujarat, he and his army find no cheering crowds to greet them. Instead, there are jeers and black flags. He has led his men to victory, but not on Rajput terms, or according to the Rajput code of honour. This episode appearing in the first half of *Cuckold* finds the prince in undisguised conflict not only with the enemies outside his father's kingdom, but with those inside the palace itself. It is a confrontation that he has been heading towards from the beginning and that leads inexorably and with a fine logic to the denouement.

The novel takes place at a time when the course of India's political destiny is about to undergo a change so vast that contemporaries caught on the brink of it cannot begin to foresee the outcome. The work is, however, a good deal more than a recounting of events leading to the coming of the Moghul dynasty signaled by Babur's victory over Delhi. In fact, Babur plays a very minor role in the book, "offstage" as it were. Although we never actually "see" the raider from Kabul, we are treated to glimpses of him during his march toward Delhi through bits of his diary smuggled out by means of an intricate intelligence web. They contain lovesick verse as well as coldly thought out battle plans and add a third dimension to the familiar, two-dimensional profile of the Babur of miniature paintings. There are the battles Mewar wages in turn against the Sultanates of Gujarat and Malwa, inadequate dress rehearsals for the final confrontation with Babur's army for possession of Delhi. At the same time the struggle over succession within the Chittor palace itself proceeds.

Far more than the usual action-packed historical novel, *Cuckold* is a work of substance that exists on many levels. It is the story of a love so overcharged that it has its being in a feverish, overwrought world hardly recognisable as our own. It is an exploration of the nature of kingship and statecraft. It offers a fresh vision of sainthood. It questions sexual identities. It contains depictions, deftly drawn, of the confusion and mayhem of the battlefield. It is a panegyric to the power of music. "There is only one art on earth which echoes the perfection of God," the Maharaj Kumar declares in a scene where he is practicing the flute. "It is music. And in music, the most perfect and complete godhood lies within each note. You cannot add to it nor can you subtract from it. It has no reason and no rationale. It is sufficient unto itself" (250).

In the course of events remarkably compelling personalities come to the fore. They love, hate, manoeuver, conspire, and engage in intrigues and deceptions. They tantalise, lust after, and shamelessly manipulate one another. Amidst a scene of some of the most despicable betrayals, the profoundest loyalty and rare courage are displayed.

Each character, no matter how minor, is distinct, unpredictable, capable of surprising us, and fully rendered. The book has its share of villains, but they are never completely evil. Vikramaditya, the third son of Rana Sanga, the King of Mewar, and stepbrother of the Maharaj Kumar, is stupid and cruel, but at the same time the Maharaj Kumar, after listing his many faults, says of him: "What a handsome head my brother had ... Even the most disheveled and disreputable clothes only enhance his casual and offhand charm" (32).

Vikramaditya's mother Karmavati is the Maharana Sanga's favourite wife and as close to being a thorough villain as can be found, yet the prince says of her:

> "Her eyes fell upon me. She smiled, gloating from ear to ear. I realized for the first time why someone like Father must find her hard to resist. She had a harsh kind of beauty but the source of her attraction was a lascivious obstinacy. Women were supposed to give in or give up. She never did. She would outlast us all. I bowed down deeply to her." (286)

His words prove to be prophetic. Another complex character is Bahadur Shah, the second son of the Sultan of Gujarat. He is impetuous, impulsive and sadistic; at the same time he is a gourmand who enjoys life to the full and whose company is much sought after. Then there is the chief, all-powerful eunuch of the palace at Chittor – who fathers a child! And the Maharana Rana Sanga himself, battle-scarred and gruff, and struggling with his own stubborn attitude toward his eldest son and rightful heir.

An engaging character is Kausalya, the Maharaj Kumar's *dai* or wet nurse and the widowed mother of his best friend Mangal Simha. She plays many roles in the Prince's life that make her indispensable to him. Then there is the relationship that eludes description – the Prince's with Leelawati, the winsome, nine-year-old granddaughter of Mewar's finance minister – who bears no resemblance whatsoever to Nabokov's Lolita.

Further, there is the Bhootani Mata. Is she a figment of the Maharaj Kumar's tormented imagination? Or flesh and blood seductress, hag, torturer, succubus, disturber of his dreams and haunter of his worst thoughts? She curses him saying, "May everything you touch turn to ashes. May all those who are dear to you rue the day they came within your ambit" (417).

Dominating the community life of Mewar from within the zenana and without is the wife of the Maharaj Kumar variously called "Greeneyes," the "Little Saint," the "Princess." Their unconsummated marriage gnaws at the core of the Maharaj Kumar's tortured ego and is the reason for much of his suffering.

Throughout, Nagarkar plays on the theme of cuckoldry with many a variation. In the person of the introspective hero he gathers the various notes of the *raga* together to achieve an artistic exploration of this very human concern in all its nuances. It is well worth the reader's while to pay attention to how he does it.

In a court scene well into the novel, a musical presentation by the singer Sajani Bai is awaited. The Maharaj Kumar reflects on the power of music. "The *alaap* is the part of our classical music that I like best," he says. "Anchored in the scheme enunciated at the very start, you are free to explore the full range of the human condition." Nagarkar could very well have been describing his own method of working when he tells how the singer "lays out her palette, the range of colours she'll be using. With measured strokes, both subtle and broad, she sketches in her themes and concerns though there is nothing sketchy about this" (177).

Thus, *Cuckold* opens from page 1 with a most ordinary incidence of cuckoldry, classical in its simplicity, like the first notes of the *alap*: a young teenage wife is suspected by her old husband, a dhobi, of infidelity. He has brought her for punishment before the "small causes court" presided over by the Maharaj Kumar. She in turn accuses the old man of impotency. It's all rather amusing, and the Maharaj Kumar orders the dhobi to a brothel to prove his counter claim to potency. Meanwhile judgment on the washerwoman is deferred until the results of her husband's night out are declared. The Maharaj Kumar warns the dhobi: "Even if you prove your virility with Rasikabai [the brothel's famed expert] you'll still need to produce proof of your wife's unfaithfulness" (2).

> Meanwhile, Sunheria, the young woman, offers herself to the Maharaj Kumar, turning the cuckold of the title into a co-partner of deception himself. To add further piquancy, the Maharaj Kumar's wife Greeneyes, dresses the washerwoman like a bride in borrowed clothes when the young girl shows up at the palace for the first of many assignations with the prince. After a week, the dhobi and his wife again

> appear in court before the Maharaj Kumar. "...it was to this white-haired, toothless and turbaned ruin of a husband that my heart responded," the Prince says...." Who should know a faithless wife better than I?" (18)

Sunheria turns out to be no ordinary playmate-of-an-evening. The simple incident of cuckoldry with which the book begins takes a new twist. The washerwoman brings a measure of peace not only to the Maharaj Kumar's unfulfilled physical hunger, but also to his tortured inner life. She offers up an entirely new way of looking at the world that he envies but cannot adopt: "She did not expect anything, she did not wait for anybody, she was never disappointed ... Because she did not think of the next minute and the next meal and the next day, there was never any rush. Whatever she had to do, she could do today, tomorrow, maybe never" (122). Before long, the girl becomes important to him: "Sometimes she came, sometimes she didn't. I was terrified when she did [lest the dhobi name him as co-respondent] and distraught when she didn't" (122). He goes on to wonder in an engaging vignette of a woman going through utterly feminine gestures: "Is sex watching Sunheria put on her anklets? Is it seeing her shake her hair loose, gather it together and twist it into a bun? Is it taking vermillion powder on her right index finger and zeroing in effortlessly to the dead centre of her forehead and spreading a perfect *tika* on it? Is it her hands cupping together to hold water from the bucket, closing her eyes and splashing the water on her face?" (123)

Eventually, the old husband becomes increasingly suspicious and jealous and beats the girl-wife without mercy or let-up. While the prince is away from Chittor on an extended campaign, Sunheria turns the tables on her tormentor and smashes his head with the clothes beater. In jail, awaiting the outcome of the trial, she hangs herself, certain that she will receive the death sentence. On the night of his return the Maharaj Kumar learns of Sunheria's suicide. He goes to bathe in "his" river, the Gambhiree. "Mother," he screams silently, "unburden me" (176). But there is no compensation for the loss of Sunheria. The waters of the river neither cleanse nor offer him the oblivion he seeks.

Early pages of the book are lightened by the bright presence of the nine-year-old Leelawati. She is all innocent fun combined with intelligence and beauty, a lively young girl-woman testing her feminine skills at getting her way while at the same time sharpening her own intellect against the formidable wit of the Maharaj Kumar. He enjoys her sense of curiosity and her delight in discovery. Her skill with figures rivals even that of her grandfather, the Finance Minister of Mewar. They play an elaborate game of gift giving, each preparing surprises for the other. More often than not, Leelawati's gifts are artifacts she has herself fashioned for the Prince. His gifts to her are costly gems and even a horse to ride. The Maharaj Kumar describes a chance meeting with her thus: "Leelawati was sitting on a swing in the palace. Without meaning to, I ran towards her. She flung herself from the swing straight into my arms and hugged me. She wouldn't let go of me and I wasn't about to let go of her. To be trusted so, without any reservations, I too must have been up to some good in my past lives" (115). Of course the time comes when he has to let go of her; the fact that she reminds him of his favourite sister Sumitra who has died tragically at a young age makes this second loss all the more painful. At first he suspects that Greeneyes may have planned some mischief when he discovers she has invited Leelawati to the palace. "What was she up to? She had already driven a wedge between the Flautist and me. Did she now plan to deprive me of this child too?" he wonders. (116)

But the actual occasion of loss is no such trivial incident. To the humiliation of being upstaged by his half brother

Vikramaditya, who has won over Rana Sanga, is the Maharaj Kumar's having to witness the ruin of Leelawati at the hands of this same brother. Vikram has been witness to an innocent exchange of banter and tomfoolery between Leelawati and the Prince and takes advantage of the assembled dignitaries' presence at a durbar to "explain" the reason for his elder brother's limp. "[the Maharaj Kumar] was gamboling with the fair Leelawati," he says "... on the lush lawns of Atithi Palace where he slipped and fell a little foolishly and happily over her. A small price to pay for such delicious company, wouldn't you agree, my friends?" (287) However untrue or however jokingly the slight is delivered, it proves beyond any doubt that the girl is guilty of lewd behavior and condemns her in the eyes of the citizens of Mewar. Her considerable beauty and the dowry her grandfather can pay are of no consequence. A suitable marriage does not lie in Leelawati's future. Demands from the Maharaj Kumar and Rana Sanga himself for Vikramaditya to apologise prove futile. Shortly after this, Leelawati disappears from court. No one knows where she has been taken until it is discovered after many days that her grandfather has had her locked up like a prisoner in his house. Vikram had effectively dropped the curtain on the Maharaj Kumar's relationship with Leelawati once and for all.

And the variations proceed. Kausalya who was the Maharaj Kumar's wet nurse, is from the beginning a constant in his life. The Maharaj Kumar tells us this about her: "Kausalya had presence, a charisma that stayed in your mind. If the men in my own family had kept off her, it was not only because she was withdrawn and was the Maharaj Kumar's dai, it had something to do with fear. If you knew what was good for you, you did not cross Kausalya. She had the most direct eyes I had seen. They saw through you and your intentions and told you to stay off" (143). She becomes in turn: his initiator into sex, his faithful lover, comforter, loyal counsellor, wise adviser and the intelligence through which he on more than one occasion is enabled to see the reality around him even more clearly than is his wont. In a relationship that is almost incestuous, he finds the anchor that steadies him throughout the many crises that arise. This still young and beautiful woman has made the prince her life's work. She is more ambitious for him than for herself and threatens even the Princess with retribution should the Princess do the Maharaj Kumar harm: "... what strange witchery do you practice upon him that he shuns all those who love him, even me who would give my life for him?" she asks Greeneyes. (74) "... Whatever your devious designs," she tells her, "and however subtle, I'll get you. Then God help you" (75).

The Maharaj Kumar's obsession with his wife causes a temporary estrangement between him and Kausalya, although she seems content as long as she can simply be in his presence occasionally. "Never mind if I did not talk to her," the Maharaj says, "... see her even when she was in front of my eyes; it mattered little or not at all that the new woman [Greeneyes] had turned my head and there was nothing but cold hatred and a disowning of the past in my eyes, just so long as she could get to see me every once in a while" (141).

When an honored guest of Mewar, Prince Shehzada Bahadur of Gujarat, is injured during a hunting trip with his hosts, Kausalya nurses him back to health. An infection turns into gangrene, and it is she who takes it upon herself to see to it personally that he is taken care of and that his life is saved. The result turns out to be devastating. After his recovery, Bahadur, who has during his stay in Mewar gained the reputation of a sadistic lover amongst the women of the harem, makes a startling request: "May I have her?" he asks the Maharaj Kumar, referring to Kausalya. The startled Prince is too nonplussed to answer as he says to himself:

"And you think you've seen everything and what you haven't you've had the sense to imagine: every possible scenario for anything and everything in the world" (133). To his guest he gives the offhand reply that the matter is between Bahadur and Kausalya. Later, when he has time to think about it, he fears that his feigned indifference may lead to yet another loss of a beloved. He wonders how another man's desire can rekindle a passion that was thought dead. "... Bahadur's interest in her was like a bushfire," he declares. "The more I tried to put it out, the more it spread" (141).

However, Kausalya proves to be even more resourceful than usual. Without refusing the honored guest of Mewar (a slight that could have unhinged the delicate relations between him and his hosts) she manages to make herself inaccessible by deliberately rubbing a highly toxic herb all over her body. The resultant rash is hardly a sexual turn-on, and her loyalty to the Maharaj Kumar remains intact and as steadfast as ever. Until she too mysteriously disappears from Chittor.

A fresh variation on the *raga* is begun as the Maharaj Kumar is persuaded, for reasons of state, to take a second wife: Sugandha, the daughter of Medini Rai, the Rajput prime minister of Malwa and later an ally of Mewar. Sugandha is depicted as charmingly innocent and wanting to please. But she is in for disappointment. As the Maharaj Kumar describes it, "I am convinced now that wedding nights don't suit me" (460). And, indeed they do not, as he finds himself unable to perform. "My world had lost its moorings if I could not depend on sheer, straightforward lust," he says, as even this has been taken away from him.

It doesn't take long for the restless Sugandha to search around elsewhere, and she doesn't have to look far: Vikramaditya is only too willing to oblige her and at the same time to indulge yet again his appetite for humiliating his brother. He and Sugandha make a public spectacle of their affair, going out of their way to flaunt the relationship. The Maharaj Kumar explains, "My own response to discovering that I was a cuckold a second time round was mixed and did not entirely do me credit"(498). He goes on to say that he is in a way glad that Sugandha is having a good time, but he also feels protective of this second wife of his: he fears what may happen to her, given Vikram's character and Rani Karmavati's using the girl as a pawn in the persistent game she plays to advance the fortunes of her son while damaging as best she can the reputation of the Maharaj Kumar. A rumour that Rani Karmavati has even played procuress circulates amongst the palace regulars.

When Sugandha stumbles onto the knowledge that Vikram is not only a tormenter, but also a threat to her husband's life, she tries to warn the Maharaj Kumar, and they enjoy a reconciliation of sorts. When she later announces she is pregnant, the question concerning the paternity of the child inevitably arises. But before she gives birth to it, the foetus inside her dies and takes her away also. "And I, what did I do?" the Maharaj Kumar asks. "I bet I bled internally, my backbone and brains cracked with the sheer weight of my megalomaniac guilt. I had little doubt that it was I who was responsible for Sugandha's condition" (558).

As for the Prince's marriage to Greeneyes, it is "the stuff of bad nautanki plays," he says, "Man, Woman. And lover. Except that the last one was an almighty god" (89).

The picture we are given of Greeneyes is like the constantly changing image seen in a trick mirror. One is invited to reconcile the portrayal of a powerful spiritual figure with that of a young woman who delights in gambling at cards and cheating at chess. She is a charmer who flies into tempers that are suspiciously calculated, short-lived, and somehow forgivable. Who enjoys setting off her considerable beauty with carefully selected clothes and jewels, showing a rare sense of colour and harmony. Who sings and dances like a nautch girl. Who can be single-minded and passionate and manipulative to an astounding degree. Who has qualities of leadership even a statesman could admire. Who leaves others wondering if she is making fools of them, being vastly cleverer than she pretends, and even perhaps enjoying their puzzlement and discomfort.

On their wedding night itself the Princess from Merta claims to be betrothed to another, and that "other," it is finally revealed after many months, is Lord Krishna. This startling announcement, at first disbelieved by the Prince, leads to dismay and apprehension. "What little he had seen of her told him that she was devious beyond anyone he had known. She was full of surprises, each greater than the previous one and they were all unpleasant and disturbing. He felt a shimmer of fear under his skin. Who was she? What was she up to?" (103)

In a sense Greeneyes has never been the Maharaj Kumar's, yet her choice of a lover manages to put a twist to the dagger inasmuch as Krishna has always been the Prince's "best friend," as he describes the god of many names, "my confidant and preceptor. This Blue God with the flute and the peacock feather stuck in the band around his head" (102). The Prince wonders if Greeneyes knows what the Blue God means to him and if she is deliberately taunting him. He has never told her of the special corner Krishna has in his heart. The Maharaj Kumar reflects on every aspect of the Flautist from the Bal Krishna whom he has left behind as he grows to manhood, to the mature Krishna of the Bhagavad Gita. The god has seemed to grow with him. He reminds himself that what he owes most to Krishna is a habit of mind: "don't take anything on authority ... Re-examine. Question. Doubt. And if need be.... swim against the tide" (109). When planning strategy and during crises, the Maharaj Kumar invariably refers to Krishna's acts and puzzles over their meanings. To realise he has been made a cuckold by the one he has all along turned to is more than the Prince can bear. On her part, Greeneyes has not only deprived her husband of herself, but of his god as well. He who was his mentor, comforter, and guide becomes in an instant an object of hatred, a symbol of loss.

"Is there anything more painful and lonesome than betrayal?" the Maharaj Kumar asks himself. Greeneyes has meanwhile made a public drama of her love for Lord Krishna, singing and dancing in gaudy clothes in delirious devotion to the Flautist, and earning the condemnation of the royal family and the entire court at Chittor while firing the religious spirit of the common folk who throng to watch her performances. The scene is at the Brindabani Mandir. The Prince goes on to tell himself that,

> "Worse than loss are the tricks that memory plays. I looked at the Flautist. It was like meeting a dear friend after a period of years. My first impulse ... was to touch him as I had done when I was four or five years old, but the priest came forward to greet me and the spell was broken. We were finally face to face. Two mortal enemies. Correction. One mortal and the other divine and immortal. I was overtaken by such a strong wave of loathing I wanted to strangle him till the last breath had gone out of him and then snap his neck" (171).

Greeneyes goes from nautch girl to saint – the Little Saint – as she further works her spiritual powers on the ordinary citizens of Mewar. By a series of good works she earns their devotion, and they credit her with their overcoming the cholera epidemic that at one point besets them. Further, she gains political importance by the trust the Maharana Rana Sanga comes to place in her. She even seems for a time to get the better of the worst of the court intriguers: Rani Karmavati and her number one henchman, the chief eunuch. Throughout, she performs all – but the most important – of a wife's duties with care and solicitude.

Finally, in a desperate attempt to reach his wife, the Maharaj Kumar disguises himself as Lord Krishna, smearing his body with indigo dye and arranging a peacock feather in his headband. He goes so far as to master the art of flute playing, dances the dandiya and even turns into a woman, just like the god. This new game appears to work. Time after time the Little Saint seems to be unaware of the charade. "Krishna Kanhaihyya, Krishna Kanhaiyya," she calls him. He feels his wife must surely know it is all make believe. He finally decides that he will never enter her bed again; yet he does for one last time. It is then that he comes to the painful realisation that, "she didn't love him, he didn't figure in her night life. The person she held in her arms, talked to, played with and found new ways to love was not he but her lover and god. She was not aware of him, so he wasn't even a lie." In the rare self-knowledge at his command, he realises that, "She had never seen through his game, it was he who had decided to deceive himself ..." (566).

The day the Maharaj Kumar leaves for battle against Babur, he spies his wife in meditation in front of the god. She garlands herself with marigolds, adorns her forehead with turmeric powder and then adds a vermillion sindoor. She breaks a coconut into two and places the pieces in front of herself, commanding the god to worship her, saying: "There's as much of the divine in me as in you" (568). The Maharaj Kumar is at first horrified, but comes to understand that her faith is merely making a final leap to the logical conclusion of "So' hum" – "I am that." "She could change roles with the Flautist," he says, "She was the substance and the power and the force that was God" (568).

The Maharaj Kumar himself comes across as a decent man amongst rogues. He is insightful and able to understand well enough the various forces that come between him and what he prizes most. But he proves powerless to help himself as he experiences one loss after another – of the people who mean most to him; of things he holds most dear, of even his god. Finally, the throne of Mewar itself eludes him, thanks to the machinations of Rani Karmavati on behalf of her son Vikramaditya and the inability of the besotted Rana Sanga to see through the tricks his favorite plays. Thus she manages to deprive the Maharaj Kumar of that which he wants above all else in the world. In the process she exploits the mistrust every Rajput king inevitably felt toward his successors and parlays it into an insuperable barrier between Rana Sanga and the Maharaj Kumar. For his part, the Prince finds it tragic that he and his father can never be close. "Awkwardness is what binds father and son together," he says, "I love him dearly and don't know how to express it and so make all kinds of wisecracks about him to myself" (203).

Besides making sure the Maharaj Kumar will not succeed his father, Rani Karmavati manages it so that it is impossible for him to realise other "worldly ambitions" as he calls them, like enlarging the kingdom of Mewar and within Mewar itself, bettering the lives of its people by getting an efficient water and sewage system in place. And finally a conspiracy headed by her ends in the murder of Rana Sanga and Mangal Simha, the Maharaj Kumar's best friend. With an admirable economy of means, Nagarkar describes this loyal companion and head of intelligence at Mewar in a one-sentence cameo: "When Mangal is silent, everybody listens." (464)

So, why is Nagarkar telling us all this? Why should we read this book, anyway? Why is he taking up our time? We are busy people. What are we supposed to make of all these losses that he has his protagonist suffer? All this play on the idea of cuckoldry and its many manifestations? The piquant humiliations? The predictable defeats?

One could say that to observe the "game" being played

over and above the pure plot line is a pleasing – even aesthetically satisfying – way to spend time. Something akin to listening to good music when the rhythmic element plays hide and seek with the melodic line. One can think offhand of only one other contemporary writer who can pull off such a tour de force with words alone: A. S. Byatt in *Possession*. But what does it "do" for the work as a whole? Taken alone, the losses that the Maharaj Kumar endures remind us of what we all experience to some degree. To the extent that we can identify with a prince of bygone days, the book becomes not "just a good read" about a particular time and place: it enters into the universal.

More important even than the theme of cuckoldry and its variations is the way the protagonist responds to the vicissitudes that plague him. Experiences that would destroy the strongest amongst us leave him intact. Although he can acknowledge his shortcomings, it does not diminish his self-esteem: he knows who he is and what he is worth. This is possible because he is able to look at himself and the people and happenings around him with rare objectivity. It frees him from self-pity and at the same time allows him a measure of self-mockery, as in this passage from a scene in which he is kept waiting inordinately long for an interview with his father. In an interior monologue he says, "Good tactic, that. Let the arrogant son-of-an-untimely screw stew in his own juice. These youngsters think they own the earth including their elders. Best to take them down a peg or two before they get completely out of hand. By now I'm really getting into stride, doing a piteous number that would make stones weep: you never loved me, Father. Where my soul was, there's a void and scar tissue" (202).

In a more serious mood he says, "My transformation from Maharaj Kumar to a nobody was now almost complete and that deck of cards called the fates would have to be shuffled to a freak statistic for me to be in the running again. But it had nothing to do with self-esteem. The mediocre will often find solace in identifying a scapegoat, even if it means pointing the finger at themselves. I have been down but the almost extinct Maharaj Kumar had no intention of giving up" (344).

And in another context, the Maharaj Kumar reflecting on the unfaithfulness of his second wife Sugandha and her affair with Vikramaditya says,

> "I was seeking martyrdom, nothing else. I wanted my forbearance and quiet dignity to be perceived as heroic and turn the whole of Mewar against my brother and wife. Humiliation was not a new sensation for me. Few people in Chittor have had my experience and expertise in it. And yet, despite the fact that I had crystallized my objectives so clearly, it took hours of coaxing myself in the morning before I could muster the courage to show my face to the members of my extended family, or worse, make a public appearance."(499)

Nagarkar adds emphasis to the quality of objectivity in his hero by his choice of point of view. It is always a big issue when one sits down to write fiction. Who is going to tell the story or through whose sensibilities will it be told? It is a pleasure to see how this very technical decision contributes to the characterisation of the Maharaj Kumar. The author has chosen two points of view here: the first person narrator (the Prince) and the third person observer who has access to one or more characters' thoughts. Nagarkar does this seamlessly, while we are not looking. The effect is to allow us into the Maharaj Kumar's innermost feelings while giving weight to his ability to see things straight. Using the third person point of view solves the additional problem of how to handle scenes where the protagonist cannot be expected to be present.

There is yet another technical decision Nagarkar has made that turns out to be "right" and that is worth mentioning. He states it in a note at the very beginning, before starting his story: "One of the premises underlying this novel is that an easy colloquial currency of language will make the concerns, dilemmas and predicaments of the Maharaj Kumar, Rana Sanga and the others as real as anything we ourselves are caught in...." The effect is to force us to compare our own times to the past, and to regretfully admit that things haven't changed all that much. The greed for power has not diminished, and the civilising of human relationships still has a long way to go. Again, universal concerns.

Finally, a protagonist whose inner light enables him to redeem his dignity – even as all is lost – is well worth reflecting on. A man who in spite of all the agony the "Little Saint" has put him through can declare in the last entry of his memoirs: "There is only one woman for me.... It is my wife. I will follow her to Brindavan, to Mathura, to the gates of hell, even to heaven, if the gods will have me," deserves our attention (600). He makes it possible for us to recognise the potential in ourselves to overcome the destructive power of loss through the redemptive might of self-knowledge.

Note: all quotations from the text are from the Second Impression of *Cuckold* (HarperCollins *Publishers* India Pvt. Ltd. New Delhi, 1997).

History and Humour: Strange Bedfellows

C. T. Indra

We are living in an era of demythologisation and desacralisation. Nothing is certain. We are tired of grand narratives which look suspiciously like special pleading to our sceptical dispositions. Sociologists and cultural historians have studied the Bhakti movement and the vast array of literature it has produced from perspectives very different from the ones that marked traditional hagiographies and histories. Counter-culture movements have thrown up formidable challenges to orthodoxies of various kinds. The result is that much of the writing produced in the last two to three decades has been intensely preoccupied with ideological issues of centre and margin, the oppressed and the oppressor. In this earnest preoccupation one sad casualty is humour. This is why a book like Kiran Nagarkar's *Cuckold* is a welcome exception. Its unusual title relating to the Saint Meera's relationship with her husband, the Rana of Mewar's son, and her devotion to Lord Krishna, is provocative and iconoclastic.

The aim of this paper is to focus on the wide range of humour and wit used by the novelist directly and through the device of the memoirs of the protagonist to chronicle the Maharaj Kumar's life, as a Rajput Prince, statesman and warrior, and as a husband. The protagonist does this with singular honesty, self-analysis and self-deprecation. The novel, mainly written in the form of the Maharaj Kumar's autobiography provides, at the same time, a chronicle of Mewar in the 16th century when Babur invaded and took control of Hindustan. Thus the book straddles an intensely sensitive private sphere as well as a public one, and each will be dealt with separately, after a general analysis of the humour in the novel.

HUMOUR: ITS RANGE AND FUNCTION

An amazing variety of humour is in evidence in the novel. The gamut of tones ranges from whimsy to broad comedy, from irony to the macabre, from wit to farce and the bawdy. Moreover, the humour interpenetrates the more serious issues being dealt with, and often conveys the protagonist's clarity of insight into the real issues involved, with a self-deprecating awareness of public opinion and of how he is forced to handle matters. The opening chapter in which the Maharaj Kumar presides over a session of the Small Causes Court is an instance of the fusion of the ridiculous and the intensely serious. A young woman married to an aged dhobi is being tried for infidelity: "An old, bent dhobi, I would have sworn it was the same washerman who besmirched Sita's name and obliged Lord Rama to banish her into the wilderness some two thousand years ago, was now casting aspersions on his wife's virtue" (1). The subject of injured conjugal rights, here thrown in casually and peripherally, is at the same time the chief motif in the personal life of the Maharaj Kumar. Hence, it is a masterly opening chapter presented with a sense of the ridiculous, and makes the reader instantly aware that this is no ordinary chronicle. Some time later, at night, the

Maharaj Kumar's trusted lieutenant, Mangal, announces a woman to the Maharaj Kumar:

> "Which woman? Can't she wait till Thursday for me to look into her case?"
>
> "It's the woman whose husband was complaining that she has been faithless." He was talking in conspiratorial tones.
>
> "I did not ask for her."
>
> "I know. But I thought Your Highness might perhaps enjoy a new face."
>
> "Did she want to come?" That was the trouble with trusted old retainers. They think they know your mind better than you.
>
> "Gladly."
>
> "And what about her husband? What if he cites me as the co-respondent in the case?" (12 -13)

Nagarkar's wit, through the words of the Maharaj Kumar, spares no one, not even himself. In the same first chapter he speaks of his scheming brother Vikramaditya deliberately creating a scandal out of his wife's dancing and singing in public view, and reflects his own bitterness at his wife's behaviour: "Yes, I was aware of that. Since then he had not only had the pleasure of peering under my wife's *delirious* petticoat, he had composed doggerel of such scatalogical merriment that the whole town was gyrating to it" (21). This is savage humour aimed at Vikramaditya, his wife, and himself, all at the same time.

Some scenes and descriptions border on the burlesque. Take for instance, an important meeting the Maharaj Kumar had with Lakshman Simhaji, the Home Minister, Pooranmalji, the Prime Minister and Adinathji the Finance Minister, on the tricky situation of having to arrest his brother, Vikramaditya. The seriousness of the situation, both for the Maharaj Kumar, and for Mewar, is deflated and at the same time paradoxically intensified by the accurate verbal description of the surfeited Home Minister easing himself after a meal: "I forced myself to eat. I envied my uncle Lakshman Simhaji, not because he ate heartily and picked up either his left or right buttock to allow for a smooth passage when he broke wind, but because he alone out of the four of us was not exercised by the implications of what we were doing" (31). Again, a combination of wit and seriousness is evident in the scene of the Maharaj Kumar visiting Adinathji for dinner. Aspects of Jain cuisine are dealt with in pithy detail and he admires the completeness and variety of such a circumscribed diet (4), while the Jain proclivity for moneymaking is summed up with great wit and perceptiveness:

> The Jain mind is an abacus. It sees everything in terms of numbers. Like interest, you earn merit.
>
> You give alms, you earn merit. You feed the poor or the Digambaras, you collect some more merit. Pacifism is a capital investment of a high order. It's a kind of super-compound interest scheme with an eye on both heaven and earth. Extend the metaphor and it has a foot in the here and now, and the ever-after. Let's look at the latter first. The more merit you earn, the more you are likely to abridge the number of reincarnations you have to go through to reach the kind of enlightened state which gets you to moksha. In the meanwhile, just see how profitable the fruits of non-violence are in this life. You stay pure while someone else, someone like me and my Rajput clan, does the sinning and the killing. While you religiously refrain from bloodying your hands, you lend vast sums of money to finance the mightiest armies at miniscule decimal point percentages which add up to monstrous sums as interest. Whatever the outcome in the killing fields, we

> warriors protect you. We often die; you live unscathed to finance another war. And here's the best part: thanks to in-laws, nephews, cousins and the whole unbelievable complex of the extended family, your interests are safeguarded in every way, and you emerge substantially richer whoever wins, be it friend or foe. (5-6)

This is a double-edged compliment to the money-lending community and the sharpness of the wit serves to qualify the Jains' contribution to Mewar and bring out the Rajput Prince's awareness of how the Jains seem to have it both ways.

The Prince was weighed down by responsibility for Chittor in his father's absence on one of his campaigns. His position, however, is all the time systematically undermined by his second mother, Queen Karmavati, and her son, Vikramaditya. The insecurity of his position often forces the Maharaj Kumar into wit and irony. At the same time he accurately captures the crude sarcasm in the jibes of his brother, for example when Vikramaditya is brought in manacled, which makes the Maharaj Kumar's "heart miss a beat" (31), in his predicament at having to try his own brother, particularly in the context of the political uncertainties prevailing at the court:

> What court are you talking about? This sad circus with three superannuated clowns and a spineless prince whose wife is a common nautanki girl? Look after your own affairs, heir-aspirant, instead of pretending to look after the business of the state. I have a suggestion for you. That wife of yours, the whole city knows, dances for free. Why not become her pimp? That way, you'll have something more worthwhile to do with your time and you'll even earn some money. (32)

There are other parts of the novel where the tone descends to the grimly macabre, even horrifying. Nothing better illustrates this than the battle scene in which he slays Zahir-ul-Mulk, the Gujarat Commander-in-Chief. The antipathy of the Maharaj Kumar to taking human life could not have been more effectively underscored. Consider the minute and accurate description of the killing on pages 261 to 262 and what follows: a revolting, grotesque but clinical description of a particular man's death:

> You could see the profile of the cut now, there was far more neck on the right than the left. How is it that two-hundred year old trees don't spurt all over and make a fuss of themselves when they are axed? Red rivulets were racing down his armour. The veins in the stump of his neck distended to accommodate the free flow of blood. Where the column of the neck was higher, the blood shot up four or five inches, took a downward turn and subsided. Every time the body twitched, a transparent red bubble formed at the jugular. When it broke, a fine spray fell all around. Already some of the descending streaks had begun to congeal. I had killed countless people but it was the General's beheaded neck that would keep me company whenever I had a fever or was delirious. (262)

Although there is no overt satire in Nagarkar's treatment of the themes of injured gender interests, the novel occasionally has heavy doses of the grotesque and the bawdy, especially in those sections where the Maharaj Kumar engages the subliminal sexuality in his personality. In his somewhat cynical representation of the unvarnished impulses and drives in human nature, particularly relating to desire and power, we have what we may call "dark humour" or "black comedy." Sometimes, the effect of this kind of comedy is macabre or bizarre, sometimes, grim and horrifying. In Chapter 23, when Kausalya brings in the pubescent twin call girls, Raat and Din, to take the Maharaj Kumar's mind off the non-availability of his wife, he is completely nonplussed and quite unable to respond to these girls who are doing their utmost to give him a good time. The pathos and horror of their situation strike him forcibly. The gap between what one would expect of a romantic love scene and the sordidness and bizarre nature of the situation gives rise to dark humour:

> These two, however, were rare birds. They looked young and eager and uncertain and yet every now and then I had the feeling that they had seen more of life than the great sages for whom the past and future were interchangeable. Their names were Raat and Din. They were identical twins. Their parents, pimp or whoever named them must have had a juvenile turn of irony or twisted sense of humour. After a while I began to suspect that they were playing some kind of game with me. If I called Raat and held her hand, she smiled shyly and said "She's Raat, I'm Din." (300)

A little later, Kausalya opens the door very slightly because she must make the girls leave urgently:

> "Will you please excuse the young ladies?"
>
> I did not ask what, why, wherefore. Kausalya is not in the habit of intruding on a private party.
>
> "How much time do they have?"
>
> "A minute and a half at the most."
>
> They did not wait for me to ask, request or order them to leave. The customer's pleasure was the only thing that mattered. Raat, maybe it was Din, tossed her breasts

> into her blouse and locked them up for the night while the sister tied the strings of her ghagra. They tried to put the musical instruments back in the corner of the room. (304)

Kausalya has to usher the girls out because His Majesty disguised, looking "like an elephant trying to move about incognito" (304) is at the door to discuss an important State matter. Livelinesss, exuberance and the bawdy seem to go together in this extract.

The news of Sunheria's suicide while he was away at war, makes the Maharaj Kumar express himself in an agonised soliloquy, where intense grief merges with dark humour:

> Come back, laundress, I swore at her, come back. You better explain yourself. I have got eighteen months of clothes to wash. Get to work, woman. I want them cleaned of all the blood on my hands, don't forget the collar and the cuffs and my conscience. I don't want to see a single speck of guilt, did you hear me, I won't have anyone suspect that I wiped off ten thousand men one early morning and followed up with several thousand more as the months progressed, go on, bash my clothes, my brains and body till I am a virgin, just the way you were supposed to be despite our sexual discourses over the years and starch me crisp like thin flat steel plate. (277-78)

One notices how effortlessly the Maharaj Kumar has created a textuality which embeds his grief at not being able to save her into the normal aspects of her workaday life, in the profoundly honest injunction, "don't forget the collar and the cuffs and my conscience."

THE PRIVATE SPHERE

The term "cuckold" has the distinct suggestion of Elizabethan and Jacobean comedy, in which the deceived husband grows horns and thereby betrays the infidelity of his wife, thus becoming the butt of ridicule. Cuckoldry is a notion typically part of European/English sexual mores of the past. The Indian novelist has transposed this motif to an Indian context, conflating it with our sexual mores. It is a daring move on the part of Nagarkar to make the most endearing among the Hindu gods, Lord Krishna, the Giridhara Gopala, the villain of the piece and equally daring to bring Meerabai down to the human level. Making Krishna the villain leads to a debunking of the celestial status of the Blue God or Neelameghanshyama. The term "cuckold" is first mentioned prominently in the description of the Janmashtami festivities (167). Subsequently, it is occasionally very judiciously used (see page 212 where in a brilliant turn of self-irony, the Maharaj Kumar tells us how "the budding poets in the army are busy composing limericks about the cuckold and coward") to purchase sympathy for himself without falling into self-pity. Even when he gets married a second time, to Medini Rai's daughter Sugandha, he is destined to become a cuckold, this time because of human duplicity in the form of his brother Vikramaditya who will stop at nothing for a fling, or to humiliate the Maharaj Kumar.

The complicity between comedy and cuckoldry needs to be pursued a little deeper. Comedy often deals with men and women in the lower strata of society and gives them the freedom to indulge their whims and fancies. Often, hierarchy is flouted when comic characters engage in banter and outwit their social superiors. Kiran Nagarkar subverts this traditional generic feature by making no less a person than the Crown Prince the object of public ridicule, or presenting him at times as a sulking, impotent husband airing his discontent in writing. The Prince's expression ranges from the savagely ironic to the deeply moving. Meera's mystical love when presented in diachronic terms (as opposed to its reification in the synchronic accounts of centuries of paeans sung in her praise) foregrounds the plight of the husband who cannot see his rival in tangible terms and hence feels even more insecure and incensed. The unravelling of his rival's identity makes him react with sardonic irony. When the Princess calls out to Krishna to vindicate her honour,

> They call me tart, harlot, whore
> Slut, strumpet, fornicator.
> Tell them I beg you
> I beseech you, tell them
> Save my honour, beloved, save my honour (168)

her husband remarks with superb irony, "There is some misunderstanding here, my dear wife, I believe it is my honour and the honour of Mewar which needs safeguarding" (168). The agony of the Princess's soul expressed in the song, and the self-irony on the part of her husband combine to create both a comic and moving effect.

We must proceed now to the more intense deployment of the same method for purposes of desacralising and demythologising the Meera legend. This begins as early as pages 13-14. Paradoxically, it at once subverts the piety of the Princess and yet confirms her status as a miraculous "Little Saint." The main purpose is to take a fresh, unfettered look at the hagiographic history of Meera. By a brilliant stroke of the author, the legend of Meera becoming a saint unravels itself in front of the very eyes of her aggrieved husband. The Princess does achieve sainthood in the novel, hence, hagiography is preserved to a certain extent, by revisiting it in contemporary terms. She was initially slandered as "slut" and "harlot," and referred to as the

"Royal Whore" by Queen Karmavati and others. She is considered a blot on the name of the royal family of Mewar by all and sundry, till gradually she acquires a following and is regarded as a saint, especially after her near death in the cholera epidemic. As the Maharaj Kumar wryly notes, the public celebration of her recovery ensures her acceptance as a saint. He describes her being weighed in gold in ironical terms, culminating in the brilliant acidic sentence, "... imperceptibly my wife began to rise. It was a thrilling sight, the ascension of the Little Saint" (330).

At the same time we see that she had other more human features, as well. We are made to see her as a bold Rajput woman who can ride and even hunt without missing her mark. The iconic Meera with the *ektara* strummed by her lyrical fingers, the pallu modestly covering her head and the eyes half indrawn, is supplanted by an agile Meera riding a horse and bringing down a male barahsingha with one unerring arrow. She is also shown as an able manager of the zenana, sporting the bunch of silver keyrings so typical of the traditional daughter-in-law in the upper-caste and aristocratic societies of India. She is even capable of jealousy towards the second wife of the Maharaj Kumar. Her solicitous care and nursing of her father-in-law, the great Rana Sanga, and her adroit cheating at chess or cards, which the Rana himself treats with indulgence, completes the vignette of the domestic portrayal of the Princess which is a far cry from the mystical damsel of Meera lore.

She has also acquired some amount of political power, and has been able to make the Rana consider her views. At Kumbhalgarh, her husband is at his ironical best when he says,

> In a few years' time Father should hand over the command of our troops to my wife. She'll sing and dance and the people of Gujarat,

> Malwa, Vijayanagar and Delhi will catch the fever, disown their kings and follow her wherever she goes. (341)

Behind this ironical acceptance of her power is also the idea of her enormous contribution to the Bhakti movement, and that Bhakti was the force that made India a nation in medieval times.

There is definitely an impish attempt at remytholgising this famous pair. The Maharaj Kumar rails at his wife to reveal the name of her lover, and finally discovers in Chapter 10 that it is Shri Krishna. The Princess's songs, occurring on pages 91, 92, 93, 94 are not the songs tradition has ascribed to Meerabai. They have been created to fit the image of this new type of Meera.

> If he won't come soon
> Let him come late
> I will wait

There is also bawdy irreverence in depicting the Maharaj Kumar's relationship with a woman whose other-worldliness is built on her complete absorption in the Blue God, and her spiritual passion is usually expressed in sexual terms. "Finally, her name itself became synonymous with the faithless wife as mine became interchangeable with cuckold" (316). The sublime episode in Meera's life of telling the great Rupa Goswami that there is only one male in the world and that is Krishna, is used to great effect in the novel, because with grim irony, the Maharaj Kumar has to admit that he himself is not male enough. The reiteration of the word "cuckold" requires no elaboration. If Bhakti poetry is rewritten in a contemporary idiom, stories relating to Krishna lore are retold with irrepressible wit and brilliant sarcasm: "The women did not have to wait in a queue to share their beloved. He was sufficient unto all of them without having to divide his time amongst them. There were always as many Flautists as there were gopis in the picture." The punch line comes at the end: "He was sure he had walked into a pichwai painting except that the Princess had taken care to eliminate the competition altogether" (415). The reader of the novel recalls the *raas leela* but in an entirely different spirit.

The Meera of tradition, the most sacred of female saints has been defamiliarised. We see her primarily in her role as wife who refuses to perform her wifely duty to her husband, and flaunts her love for Krishna. As the story is presented as mainly a first person account by the Maharaj Kumar, her husband, the novel centers on him and not her. We see her from his eyes and have to sympathise with him in the raw deal he is getting in his married life.

There are two traditions to the making of the Meera legend. One is the time-honoured orthodox Bhakti tradition which saw the travails and tribulations of Meera as testimony to her matchless devotion to Lord Krishna. The other is the more recent feminist tradition which has refused to romanticise the sufferings of women like Meera and Andal, the 7th century saint from Tamil Nadu. A feminist reading of Meera's story would foreground the fact that she made a breakthrough in patriarchal society, forging her own way, and refusing to be bound by tradition and custom, a fact which was glossed over by the traditionalists by making her into a saint (a person to whom convention does not apply). In fact, the Historical Note at the end of the novel says, "In the 1980s, it was discovered that like Saint Joan of Arc, she was one of the earliest feminists" (609). The Bhakti movement, in which Meerabai was such an important figure was the path of the individual seeking his/her own absolution, freedom from the priesthood, freedom from oppression, but it did not finally manage to eliminate caste and oppression, so we are told by unorthodox readings of the Bhakti movement, by contemporary sociologists and historians.

Our author seems to have cast his novel in a post-feminist framework and even seems to reverse the victor-victim paradigm when he presents the "thwarted" husband as really being the deprived one, and the victim of the Princess's refusal to live up to her marriage vows. The interior monologues of the Prince, for example,

> She was a deep one. He had to hand it to her, it was, frankly close to a master-stroke in the escalating war of nerves between him and her. You want a name, say it again, you want a name, you really and truly want the name, how many months had he pursued her with that one single question, here it is, she had thrown a name at him casually, like a bone to a dog, go ahead, chew on it for the next seven hundred or a thousand years, for all I care. (102)

and the explicit accounts of his own desperate sexual escapades in his attempt to make his wife respond, make us sympathise with the male rather than the female in this marriage relationship. The implied ideological premise of the novel seems to negotiate a space for man in this gender drama and its dialectics.

The Epilogue, the third person last chapter, relates the stories floating around about the Maharaj Kumar's disappearance. After the defeat of the confederate force of the Rajputs, under the Mewar Rana by the Moghul Babur at Khanau, and the Rana's subsequent poisoning by malcontents spurred on by Vikramaditya, the Maharaj Kumar, pursued by the treacherous compatriots, runs to the temple of the Blue God at Baswa which has a marble image of the Flautist. After the usual banter, this time with an undertone of urgency, we find the much maligned Maharaj Kumar merging into the equally maligned Blue God:

> The six were already closing in on him, sword ready for the kill. It was then that the Flautist embraced the Maharaj Kumar. Terror and astonishment struck the six men. One minute the Maharaj Kumar was here, the next he had become invisible. (602-03)

Who can fail to recall the mystical end to Meera when she reaches the Dwaraka temple and appeals to Krishna as Dwarakanatha to open the doors and take her? Does the author here suggest that his hero is in the same position and finally achieves beatitude? Here could be an attempt to build a male legend to supplement and fill out the female legend. Certainly, both the Prince and the Princess seem to achieve beatitude in their very different ways.

THE PUBLIC SPHERE

The method of subversion/desacralisation/ demytholgising, through the use of humour, enables Nagarkar to question without destroying. This method is evident also in the accounts touching the public sphere of the Maharaj Kumar's life. The chief target of the attack is the Rajput idealisation of heroism and honour, and the mindless mythicisation of war as an expression of valour and honour. Look at the tart comment, "We fought well, all fifty thousand of our warriors. But on the enemy's terms. By noon we had lost seven hundred and fifty men" (213).

As a chronicle of the "decline and fall" of the Rajputs, *Cuckold* compels the modern-day Indian to think of our history more critically, instead of eulogising our somewhat feudal notions of prestige and honour. The Maharaj Kumar employs his customary self-irony in depicting the courtiers' and the public's perception of his apparent lack of political wisdom.

> This was the first battle the troops were fighting under the Maharaj Kumar's command. What kind of signal was the Rana's eldest son sending to our armies, and more importantly to the enemy? Who would ever take the Mewar armies seriously again? The Rana had spent a lifetime building a reputation which was the envy and awe of the most powerful kingdoms in the country. And now, with one thoughtless gesture, the heir apparent had brought down this carefully wrought edifice of determination and deterrence. (214-15)

This is a superb instance of mimicking the voice of the public. He builds up a panegyric to exalt the line of Kings of Mewar going back to Rana Kumbha, but laces it with irony especially at the expense of the poets and the bards who created a wholly adulatory image of the rulers. The function of humour and irony here is to undercut this received chronicle by a more meditative and self-examining approach, thereby decentering the kernel ideology of the Rajputs. It is doubly enlightening because it is penned by a Crown Prince who is himself decentred:

> We are a country of bards and minstrels and story-tellers and troubadours. They never tire of telling stories of the heroic exploits of my ancestors. Of Bappa Rawal. Rana Hameer, Choonda and Rana Kumbha. I think we breathe in less air than we inhale these stories. Our anecdotes are all history. The bedtime stories of our children are about these larger-than-life monarchs and warriors from the past. Our arteries and veins are clogged with them. Sometimes I think we have no present, only the past. (54)

There is also unmistakable disapproval of the mindlessness of traditional notions of heroism.

> They turn the fratricidal and bloody struggles that always preface the assumption of the throne after a king dies, into a hundred or thousand pretty couplets about heroism and valour. They cannot see death's head above the crown of each king. And absolutely nobody calculates the cost of all this insane and internecine bloodshed to Mewar. We are our enemies' best friends. (54-55)

The portrait of Rana Sanga all through the chronicle is an index to the complexity of the Maharaj Kumar's emotional and intellectual make-up, and his relationship with his father. There is no doubt respect for the Rana's well-worn Rajput markers of self-esteem. However, the son cannot help gently and lovingly undermining the stature of his great father because his ideology of war is seen by the Maharaj Kumar as unimaginative and counter-productive. The fact that the Rana himself was a product of such inherited and unthought out political principles is brought out by the ambiguous eulogy he occasionally bestows on his father.

There are brilliant pen pictures of various political types whom we see and hear in important as well as unimportant moments in this crucial phase of Mewar's history. Here, the author allows what Bakhtin would call "dialogism" and "multi-voiced discourse" whereby we discern that not everything is hunky-dory with the Rajput way of life. The motivation for repeated wars, battles, skirmishes – all appear to the Maharaj Kumar as unwise and counter-productive, but his wise counsel is disregarded and he is looked at by his contemporaries as a nincompoop. That is the undoing of Mewar. The Crown Prince's views are exceptional in feudal times because instead of war, he gently promotes peace and the containment of war. Instead of heroic defeat, he proposes the strategy of retreat (209). Instead of being hailed as a victor when he returns from war, having won, with the fewest losses ever to be incurred by a conquering army, he is reviled by his countrymen for dastardly behaviour, for tricking the Gujarat army into getting sucked into the bog in the crucial battle against Gujarat. This was considered absolutely un-Rajput-like and unorthodox. The Crown Prince was a modern egalitarian ruler who was a misfit in the feudal set up. There is much space given in the novel to his plan for building an underground sewerage system and making civic amenities available to the subjects. This is seen by his contemporaries as much too down-to-earth a concern for a Rajput prince. Behind this obsession with public projects is a caring ruler in the making, who cannot succeed in achieving his goals. He has to fight not only for political power but the power to govern wisely. He has also to reassure everyone in the court that he has no evil designs upon the Rana, his father. There are of course contrary perceptions which are fuelled by the second mother Queen Karmavati and her volatile and vain son, Vikramaditya. The Maharaj Kumar goes out of his way every time to state that his spirit was one of conformity to tradition and loyalty to his liege. This is politically true but this conformity is itself an art of subversion because he hopes to educate the entire power echelon of Mewar in order to install a sagacious policy of governance.

The chronicling of Mewar history reaches a crucial point with Babur landing across the Sindhu river. The contemporary relevance of this historical fact cannot be ignored by the reader for it makes us rethink our sense of national identity and our religious strifes. The Maharaj Kumar is witness to the diachronic making of the Babur legend because he is his direct contemporary. Reading through snatches of Babur's diary, the Prince becomes an admirer of the King of Kabul, almost his alter-ego. The suggestion is very clear that Babur is someone the Rajputs would do well to emulate, for their own good. The Maharaj

Kumar perceives the deadly combination in Babur of unwavering religious zeal and shrewd political vision and strategy. This is what is sadly lacking among the Rajputs. The Prince provides profound insights into the multi-cultural and multi-religious nature of Indian society in the accounts of the war over Malwa, the war against Gujarat and the war council meetings. Indian society was already a mesh of Hindus, Jains and Muslims. The Jain moneylender, Adinathji, is Chancellor of Exchequer in the Rana's cabinet. Shafi is the Maharaj Kumar's main military strategist. The Muslim Prince of Gujarat, Bahadur Shah, seeks asylum in Mewar for some time. A Rajput, Medini Rai, is Prime Minister in the Muslim Kingdom of Malwa. In the latter part of the novel, there are also references to the Portuguese "governors" on the West Coast of India and their introduction of Christianity to the country. The Maharaj Kumar is placed by the author in a critical position, standing at the threshold of a new historical epoch. It is sad that he does not become empowered to carry out his vision, and it is Babur, who has the last laugh on the Rajputs because they did not heed the wise counsel of this remarkable Maharaj Kumar.

Cuckold is a profoundly serious novel of great range and depth which uses humour to question and re-examine traditionally held values and attitudes.

All the quotations from *Cuckold* is taken from Kiran Nagarkar. *Cuckold*. New Delhi: HarperCollins *Publishers*, 1997.

Mirth, Introspection and the Human Condition: Humour in Kiran Nagarkar's fiction

Shobha Viswanath

Analyzing humor is like dissecting a frog. Few people are interested and the frog dies of it – E.B. White

In my understanding, the literary experience is not dictated by the text, but is evoked by it. The words enter the reader's consciousness and awaken memories, associations, thoughts, and questions, all of which become part of the reader's experience of the text. Meaning, in this conception of the literary experience, is not resident in only the text. Rather, it also lies in the mind of the reader, created and shaped as she works with the words on the page. My attempt within this paper is to examine the play of humour in Kiran Nagarkar's fiction as a lay reader and hope in the process that I do not "kill the frog."

What struck me most about Nagarkar's work is the fact that the reader is unable to pin him down to a single style. The autobiographical and staccato tendency of his first novel *Seven Sixes are Forty-Three*, which moves between the past and present has little to compare with the breathless narrative of *Ravan and Eddie*. And in *Cuckold*, Nagarkar treads an entirely different ground, with a style that is so deft, defiant of tradition and so well able to capture the matter, that as the blurb rightly says, it "enlarges our notions of fiction." It does so to such an extent that it bears no apparent resemblance to his previous works, or for that matter any work of fiction that I have read.

The author himself, in the jacket cover of *Cuckold*, talks about the need for not keeping to a single style, as a successful style or technique runs the risk of becoming a rut and a formula. The temptation to try the same trick again and again, Nagarkar believes, spells death for a writer as for any artist. From his limited, yet varied oeuvre, it is amply clear that the author has not yielded to that temptation. However, even if there are no overt similarities in style, one cannot escape the play of humour that runs as a common thread in Nagarkar's works. It is a device that he employs with such craft and cunning, (although the work appears spontaneous, with no suggestion of deliberate crafting), that it complements the theme of the work and anchors the novel to the overall tone he intends it to have.

The humour assumes different shades, tones and textures, covering an entire gamut – from the black brooding humour in *Seven Sixes are Forty-Three*, to the bawdy, ribald, witty yet occasionally dark form it takes in *Ravan and Eddie*, to an ironic, self-deprecating tone in *Cuckold*. Despite the range of the humour, the underlying factor is the inescapable poignancy of life and the existence of humane values in face of all odds.

In my experience, there have not been many contemporary Indian writers in English who have used humour for self-analysis, reflection or critiques on society, culture and social mores. It has always been a secretly potent, delightfully dangerous, wonderfully seductive and, most importantly, a powerful way to make a statement, to tell our stories, to make sure *everyone's* voice is heard. Humour has seldom been used to correct, to restore, to define, to cope with situations, to mirror truths, to discern and therefore set a value on things, in Indian writing in English. When it comes to historical writing, the overwhelming use of chronicled material as the background for much recent Indian Fiction in English has in some way relegated humour to a subordinate, if not non-existent position.

Nagarkar in that sense is the exception. Humour requires a measure of emotional disengagement. And one reason that Nagarkar is so efficient at handling humour is that both his first person protagonists, whether it is Kushank, or the Maharaj Kumar possess this attitude.

With particular reference to *Cuckold*, one could say that the author's use of humour to negotiate, to ridicule, to rail, to banter, to discern, to criticise, to reflect, to mock, in fact the use of humour to either enhance or undercut every possible gamut of human emotion and condition, is nothing short of genius.

Although in both *Seven Sixes* to an extent, and *Ravan and Eddie* to a larger degree, the author makes apparent the use of humour as a mode of survival, and as an instrument to understand and empathise with human predicaments and frailties, with *Cuckold*, his adroitness and ingenuity in adopting humour subtly, suggestively and ironically in order to seriously examine many of life's shades of grey, makes the reader feel that one can indeed look to literature to offer us that rare insight and understanding into the human condition.

I

> *Humour is the only test of gravity, and gravity of humour; for a subject which will not bear raillery is suspicious, and a jest which will not bear serious examination is false wit* – Aristotle

Seven Sixes are Forty-Three (1980) translated from Nagarkar's Marathi *Saat Sakkam Trechalis* (1974), by Shubha Slee, is a story that disturbs and moves. It also has an unusual pace and narrative style.

The central consciousness in *Seven Sixes are Forty-Three* is that of Kushank Purandare, essentially a lonely man, whose actions and feelings are separated from each other. Through Kushank, the reader gets a peep into the complexity of his universe, as well as that of the author. Different experiences, each with its own drama, conflict and tension, assault the narrator, and he develops a highly individualistic attitude to life. In his characterisation of Kushank, Nagarkar has used a humour that is grim and dark, while highlighting some hard-hitting home truths. It is this detached humour with which Kushank makes his observations while in hospital,

> There are two kinds of people in the world – the sick and the not-sick. The sick person lives in a world of his own. The not-sick have a collective world of their own too. (9)

Nagarkar spares us no details: neither the ugliness and repulsion of vomit and sputum, nor the debasing and erasing of human values and hopes, nor yet the carelessness and heartlessness of those in charge of curing mankind's ills. Sickness affects every possible human relationship. Love? It is actually holding hands across a restaurant table, writing riddles in aerogrammes, sex (which sometimes transports him into another world), leads to abortion, bastards, bitterness.

This existence made soulless and complex, this wire-mesh cage of societal insensitiveness, this careering speed of urban living, this growing up in a diseased civilisation which is mangled by hate, despair, indifference: towards what end are we pushing forward? His despair is transparent through his grim description of Bombay.

> After years and years in Bombay, you stop seeing it. It's like someone with a permanently open mouth; you never know when it's swallowed you. If anyone asks you what Bombay's like, you don't recall those millions of other Bombays from your memory, and even if you did they wouldn't be the real Bombay. (170)

Yet, the gruesomeness of life is punctuated by situations of pure comedy as when Kushank's friend Raghu makes love to a village girl at the bottom of a half-dug well and Kushank has to think of ways to ward off the girl's suspicious father-in-law and a sniffing Alsatian; or an embarrassed Kushank meeting Chandani for the first time in an awkward situation. Rendered hilariously in the impeccable and racy translation – the comic episodes give the novel an extra dimension, steering it away from the bleakness which is always threatening to surface and take over.

In a review of *Seven Sixes are Forty-Three*, (*Indian Review of Books*, July '96) Jai Nimbkar writes, "From people who pay condolence visits and spout meaningless platitudes to the work of international do-gooding organisations, nothing escapes Nagarkar's satirical pen. He also has an uncanny skill in combining the bizarre with the mundane, the tragic with the ridiculous, so that you cannot help chuckling one moment and are chilled to the bone the next."

The book sets its tone by this juxtaposition in the opening episode itself. Pratibha, a woman who only wants to teach her husband a lesson in order to end his physical assaults, pours kerosene over herself, lights a match, and without intending to, burns herself to death. Kushank, the protagonist, is deputed to carry the news to the mother-in-law of the dying woman. The conversation that follows between him and the deaf old woman is at once hilarious and macabre.

> "Run away?"
>
> I repeated the message slowly and solemnly. In case she might faint at the sudden bad news.
>
> "Who do you think I am, your girlfriend? Stop whispering and mumbling. I can't hear you."
>
> "She burnt herself."
>
> "Run away? Was nobody home? What did she take with her?"
>
> The old hag was impossible.
>
> "Not run away, burnt herself," I yelled into her ear. "Poured kerosene over herself."
>
> "Good lord! And if the house had caught fire?" (3)

Underneath the hilarity, Nagarkar's subtext is transparent: Kushank's despondency and inability to deal with the illogical ways of life and death. Pratibha had wished to live but was dead. Whether it is this juxtaposition of the tragic with the ridiculous, or his description of the Mumbai suburban trains,

> If four million and sixty-seven thousand cobalt bombs were dropped on the earth, and if they killed all of humanity, the local trains of Bombay would still have people hanging on to people hanging out of doors and windows. (148)

Or when he talks of the beggars of India,

> The beggars are a race apart. They will digest anything. If the intestines of the beggars all over the world were to be dissected, the Indian beggars' intestines would emerge as the toughest. They eat everything, good, bad, poisonous, they assimilate it all. A beggar is like God – with an infinite capacity to absorb. (21)

Nagarkar's humour unsettles the reader and persuades him/her into the belief that it is never in the absoluteness of black and white but in the intermediate shades of grey that we exist and come to terms with life.

In the instance when Kushank makes fantastical plans with six-year-old Arshad and writes to Okhon of the "formation of the new Society to Spread happiness in the World," where it rains Coca-Cola and Gold Spot on birthdays and where a year comprises twelve days so that one can celebrate one birthday every 12 days, Okhon's father answers his letter thus:

> "Okhon is growing up in the Western world, in a society where people have realized the primacy of logic and of rational thought. In the circumstances, it is hardly surprising that Okhon finds your and Arshad's ideas nothing but patent nonsense." (101)

Nagarkar pauses here to reflect on the definition of "patent nonsense." With great astuteness, he writes bringing out the irony of how the absurdities and horrors of daily life are never looked upon as "patent nonsense" while the term is readily applied to a fantastical world, one of make-believe. He writes,

> When almost all our lives are patent nonsense, we can't identify what patent nonsense is. I was reminded of *The Bridge on the River Kwai.* Of the British colonel waving the Geneva convention in the face of the Japanese officer, protesting against the inhuman treatment meted out to his men. Pointing out that the Japanese had gone against the rules! I first saw that film when I was fourteen, and I couldn't make up my mind whether to laugh or cry. Germans, British, Japanese, and Americans, all hell bent on killing as many million people as they could, and this guy has the temerity to wave a piece of paper and demand justice ... Only human beings know the convention of killing their own kind. Raghu once told me of a group of twenty-one Adivasis in Bihar who had walked for thirteen

> days without food to reach a famine relief camp and gorged themselves immediately on arrival, despite advice to the contrary. Only three survived the meal. In Bergman's *Winter Light*, a fisherman wants to opt out of life. He sits in solitude for days and refuses to come to church because he had heard that the Chinese had invented a cobalt bomb capable of killing ten million people at once. What should one call patent nonsense? (101–02)

Religion is another experience that burns Kushank at every turn. He feels at home in no religion but speaks of it frequently. Nagarkar writes about believers and non-believers with a wry wisdom,

> Believer, non-believers, we all require an audience. The believer has someone up there who will listen to him. The non-believer flings a passionate glance at the sky and says, "I'm stoic." But for a human being stoicism is only an aspiration. He struggles hard to achieve it. (6)

and again, when he talks of God,

> If God is in every stone, then there is a saffron-painted stone in the heart of God. Nothing escapes God. Nothing slips out of his sack. He has no eyelids. He had them once, but they fell from disuse. They had no purpose, since he never closes his eyes. He is obsessively greedy, incurably so. (26)

Nagarkar's honesty sears and singes. His humour which unmasks social pretensions without distortion, and through Kushank's search for meaning in life, arrives upon a personal truth which is complex, perplexing, and paradoxical, and which is never as simple as seven sixes making up forty-two.

In reading the reviews of *Seven Sixes are Forty-Three*, it is surprising that almost every critic has misread the context, provenance and significance of the recurring line in the novel, "What difference does it make?" This favourite query of the character only referred to as "You"(and not Kushank) made in a derisive and resigned fashion, is not, as is often stated, reflective of Kushank's world-view, and by extension, the author's. Quite the contrary, despite his moments of deep despair, Kushank's quest is life-affirming and accepting. Notwithstanding all the pain and suffering he sees in life, he can't have enough of life, and again and again he protests that to him life *still* makes all the difference. This, even when faced with utter misery, whether it is of one's own making, or because of the hand of cards one is dealt with. Life is still worth living and celebrating. One doesn't throw up one's hands because the odds are against you but merely tries a little harder.

II

> *Humour is ... despair refusing to take itself seriously – Arland Ussher*

Ravan and Eddie (1995), which took ten years for Nagarkar to resurrect from a screenplay to a novel, a black comedy about two young boys growing up in a Bombay chawl, is full of strange twists and turns. Suffused with delightfully bawdy language and sarcasm, it, however, is also laced with a serious and dark edge

The novel named after the two boys, who are born and grow up in CWD *chawls* in Bombay, mirrors the heterogeneity that is India. The *chawl* houses people of different religions, languages and cultures. Though Ravan and Eddie seldom meet, accidents shape and reshape the contours of their lives, and the way they intersect with each other.

Ravan, originally named Ram, is born to Shankar and Parvati Pawar. With her heaving and inviting breasts, Parvati, unbeknown to herself has Victor Coutinho, another inhabitant of the chawl, under her spell. One day, when she is in the balcony with her son in her arms, Victor tries to draw her attention by calling out to him from the road. The baby topples out of Parvati's hands and while falling towards him, Victor sees a vision of the child Jesus hurtling towards him, the sun behind him forming a stellar halo. Wickedly, Nagarkar tarnishes this glittering vision,

> Nobody could have said with any certainty whether Victor's hands shot up for Parvati's foolish son, or for Parvati. (4)

The baby falls into Victor's arms, and Victor dies. On the day of his funeral, his pregnant wife Violet is removed to the hospital in the same van carrying his dead body, where she gives birth to Eddie.

In describing Parvati's recollection of the incident much later, Nagarkar uses a deadpan prose, (so akin to that of the Marx brothers) to convey the absolute hilarity of the situation.

> When she recalled the incident in the years to come, Parvati's comment had two words of English, as befitted the seriousness of the occasion. Heart and halt. Mazhe heart halt zale. But despite her cardiac arrest she had enough presence of mind to scream preternaturally. Even today people in the chawl across point to a break in the monumentally solid wall of their building and tell you it's Parvati's crack. (4)

After this, Parvati calls her son "Ravan," to save him from the evil eye or *nazar* of people. Her word prevails because her husband is no more than a useless fossil. The confrontation between them over the name "Ravan" is portrayed hilariously by Nagarkar.

> Shankar-rao was screaming by now. "Which mother will want her daughter married to a villain called Ravan?"
>
> "Makes no difference. From today his name's Ravan."
>
> "Wait till he grows up and tries to abduct every Sita in town. You'll regret it."
>
> "Mark my words. Every Sita will be chasing my Ravan."
>
> "Call him what you want, he'll always be Ram for me. The boy will curse you all his life." (11)

The two names are symbolic of the terrible divide in the young boy's soul. For the rest of his life he is plagued by the dilemma of whether he is Ravan or Ram. Good or Evil? A Murderer or a Victim? As they grow a little older, Ravan turns into a thief to see *Dil Deke Dekho*, a compulsive singer, and a great proponent of Tae kwan do; Eddie for a while into a blackmarketeer in order to be able to afford endless tickets to *Rock Around the Clock*, a fervent RSS member, with a natural flair for the wooden staff and lezhim exercises, and a fertile liar whenever it suits his purpose. He is forced into making several confessions to the priest, some of which are pure invention.

Tongue-in-cheek and with great sarcasm, Nagarkar writes about the business of confession as Eddie sits in the booth with Father Agnello,

> More? What more did Father Agnello want? Eddie had already ransacked his memory for plots from all the comic books he had read. Mutt and Jeff, Archie, Roy Rogers. He added whatever tit-bits he remembered from the conversations

> of older boys and his older friends but even that was not enough. He had to fall back on his own resources and imagination now and concoct his own masala. How many more terrible things could he have done in just one evening? But there was no end to Father Agnello's appetite. Nothing was going to satisfy him and Eddie feared he would still be here when the church reopened for six o'clock mass the next morning. (258)

And as if that wasn't enough to have the reader guffawing, Nagarkar continues mischievously,

> Oh, what a relief. Eddie's labours had finally borne fruit. Father Agnello was no longer asking for more details. Eddie's crimes had been identified and he was about to be punished. He was beside himself with joy. He could not believe his luck. He tore the dark velvet burgundy curtain behind the confessional and rolled at Father Agnello's feet. (260)

However, despite having laughed oneself into stitches over the description of the "sins" and Eddie's obvious joy that it was all over, the reader is stunned by the irony of the situation. The reader is able to share the secret knowledge of sin and all that society considers to be taboo that is deeply ingrained in a small child's mind, years before it actually takes place. Ravan and Eddie are unaffected by their abject poverty and deprivation. Not only do they not think that their lives are crippled by their disadvantage, but the resilience that they display to any failure to achieve their goals, and their zest for life, somehow seems to be the whole point of the novel. Interestingly, it is this life-affirming and inherently positive attitude that surfaces above all the injustice and the horror that we witness, the ability to laugh at life's seeming paradoxes, that makes Kushank, Ravan and Eddie cousins of a kind.

Notwithstanding the black detail in which he describes life in a chawl, the author's delineation of the Hindus and Catholics is witty and riotously funny. Hindus eat *paan*, "but do not think that spitting was peeing from the mouth. Catholics do" (173). While Hindus went to municipal schools and did not always go on to college, "Catholics went straight to Heaven or rather its equivalent on earth, St. Xavier's College" (173). Nagarkar's tone, although tongue-in-cheek and facetious, urges the reader to inquire into the dangers of subscribing to stereotypes.

Whether it is his enthusiastic description of Shammi Kapoor:

> "He could not say a simple 'yes' or 'no' without going into a series of contortions, raising and wrinkling his brows, pulling a face, dropping a shoulder, running up his hand over his slicked black hair ... his narrow mouth went all over his face, all in the course of one song." (188)

or the manner in which the Anglo Indians speak English,

> Chhya men, he's a dutty bugger. Tree times I told him don't climb the tree to look at my sas. Leave my sas alone, men. I asked him "gain and again but he din listen, so I gave him a hit, straight on the face like. De bugger began to cry like a baby men." (179)

or the part about the art of tying a *langotie* which is described with a serious deadpan humour.

> Putting on the white shirt and khaki-half-pants (never called shorts) was a ritual as complex as a samurai initiation. First, the loin cloth. You tie the string around the waist at the belly button while the tail of the loin cloth trails on the ground. Ensure that it's at the dead centre of the cleavage of the buttocks. Now pick it up,

> bring it forward between your legs and pass it under the knot at your navel. Heave. Tighter and tighter. Can't breathe? You're joking. Looks loose even from this distance. Haul, heave, pull and then pull some more till your testicles have ascended all the way into your brains. Now pass the band of cloth over your crotch once again and tuck in the remainder as tightly as you can at the back.
>
> Your balls may be pinched, smashed, squashed and crushed but this home-made jock strap will make sure that you'll never get hernia. (18)

or the short and humorous monographs, some of which provide a social commentary, Nagarkar's humour at once reveals that which is stereotypical and obvious but at the same time dares the reader to challenge it. Language, religion, dogma – any of these which assumes a custodial role to unite or to bridge differences is unceremoniously knocked down by Nagarkar's incisive wit, biting observations, and a scathing humour that slaughters the sacred cows of Indian society.

Finding humour in a situation is finding some incongruity, that is, some disparity between the way things are and the way they should be, and in discerning this, Nagarkar displays his keen critical mind. What Nagarkar is constantly asking the reader to do is to avoid taking anything on faith; neither gurus, teachers, parents, the author nor, most of all, themselves.

Beneath the sardonic treatise on Afghan Snow, or the Great Water Wars, or the Meditation on Neighbours, or his Harangue on Poverty, Nagarkar uses humour to express rage at the existing hypocrisy, pretension, injustice, inequality and wretchedness in the society we live in,

> To be fair is to be God's chosen. Fairness was more precious than immortality, nirvana or even

> moksha. It was on par with virginity. It was more desirable than all the treasures of the Moghul emperors and the inspiration of the poets. Admittedly, not more sought after than wealth and power, but just as potent and indispensable. For truly what are wealth and power without a fair skin? (84)

And even as this elicits a chuckle or two from the reader, the commonplace obsession with fair skin in Indian society that the author brings to light coaxes the reader to pause and reflect.

In the Great Water Wars, the author's frustration and anger are clear when he resorts to humour as a weapon to make his point: the absolute injustice of denying a basic amenity like water to the common man. Pointing an accusing finger at the political system of which the poor man is often the victim, Nagarkar writes,

> The nature of the municipal water tap is feudal and bureaucratic. It replicates and clones the Almighty's manners and moodiness but never his generosity since its power is entirely derivative. It is a middle-man, its patronage disburses what does not belong to it. The only way it can experience and feel power is to exert it erratically and often. Hence it is not enough that it calls the shots, it must perforce leave you in the dark. You are at its mercy. You are grateful for its seasons and droughts. (69-70)

In the short essay, A Harangue on Poverty, we again get to see Nagarkar's understanding of what can be considered "patent nonsense," the same concept as in *Seven Sixes,* this time in terms of the poverty line.

> As familiar as a clothes-line, most people in India spend their entire lives trying to reach out beyond

> it. It is their greatest aspiration. If you are fortunate, if the gods smile and you are lucky, you may get a glimpse of it. You can't see the line, you can't touch it and five hundred million people are trying to get at it. But if you brush against it, sink your teeth into it, grow your nails, scratch at it as if you were trying to gouge out the eyes of a man who had tried to rape you, take a breath, deep but quick and hoist your right leg. No toehold, no thin end of the wedge, no chink in the armour, just the transparent give of air, what patent nonsense.... (39)

Depicting Ravan's thoughts as he dwells on the discovery that he had murdered Eddie's father and then Gandhi, the father of the nation, Nagarkar poignantly shows the burden of an unknown guilt on the young boy's mind. While it may appear ludicrous to the adult reader, for Ravan it is truly shattering. His tortured mind asks,

> Was it possible to do something while one slept and not recall it? Then how come, Eddie who was younger than him, remembered something he did not? When had he killed Eddie's father? And how? And why? Was he leading two lives and did the one not know the other? Did his parents know that he was the murderer? Were they keeping mum because he was their son? He seemed to be adept at killing though he couldn't recall the second murder either. Mr. Dixit had very clear memories of his killing Gandhi. Did he kill Eddie's father first or Mahatma Gandhi? Or did he commit both crimes on the same day? They had hanged Godse. Would they be coming to get him one of these nights? Are you hanged twice if you commit two murders? (46-47)

While the author's double-edged humour brings us to

both tears and laughter, it also works to change the character of our thought. For even at his comic best, Nagarkar's irreverent humour has the capacity to engage those who take themselves a little too solemnly and over earnestly.

III

> *Humor is something that thrives between man's aspirations and his limitations. There is more logic in humour than in anything else. Because, you see, humour is truth. – Victor Borges.*

A book that we love haunts us forever: it will haunt us even when we can no longer find it on the shelf or wherever we have left it. *Cuckold* is one such book. It grips, engages, fascinates, enthralls, bewitches, overwhelms, and holds the reader so completely spell-bound that no sooner than one finishes the last page, one wants to return to the first.

Cuckold (1997) cannot be categorised as a "funny" book, the way *Ravan and Eddie* is. However, if one were to strip the novel of its humour and irony, it would rob it of a vital ingredient, an intrinsic fabric, which I suspect is the unique flavour of this brilliant book. *Cuckold*, bereft of its sardonic tone, its quiet irony, and the cool, detached attitude of mind, would diminish to a whining tale of a weak man, full of abject self-pity and self-loathing, winning neither the sympathy nor the admiration of the reader.

But with the infinite grace and sleight of hand of a gifted magician, Nagarkar does just the opposite. He uses humour at its ironical best, a humour that accentuates the incongruities and complexities of all experiences, and seduces the reader into love and admiration for the Maharaj Kumar, the narrator and central character of *Cuckold*.

In an incredibly probing portrayal of Bhoj Raj, the unfortunate husband of the saint Meera, Nagarkar has done the impossible. Taking this footnote character in history, the author has created a six hundred-page novel around him. His book is epic in its scope and sweep, yet, it is an intensely personal and introspective look at the people and times. The finely crafted language adds sheen to every page and the earthy humour humanises his characters. Maintaining the fine balance between history and fiction, between character and caricature, between the sublime and the ridiculous, Nagarkar brings an entire era to life.

So here we have our protagonist, the Crown Prince of Mewar, who unlike the archetypal macho Rajput prince, busy hunting and conquering lands and women, is a man full of contradictions, self-doubt and introspection. In the voice of the Maharaj Kumar, Nagarkar questions the Rajputs' code of honour, valour, loyalty, with a sense of what is right and wrong. His irony comes alive because of his observations on the jarring confrontation of incongruities,

> They paint a rosy picture, these tellers of tales and very sensibly, don't dwell too long or too often on the bad guys. That's not quite true. What they do is far more dangerous. They turn the fratricidal and bloody struggles that always preface the assumption of the throne after a king dies, into a hundred thousand pretty couplets about heroism and valour. They cannot see death's head above the crown of each king. And nobody calculates the cost of all this insane and internecine bloodshed to Mewar. We are our enemies' best friends. For what better chaos and anarchy can they wish upon Mewar than that which we wreak upon ourselves? (54)

This is our prince then, a man of tremendous vision, a pacifist given to continual introspection, a statesman, a music lover, and a Rajput prince, who above all else has the infinite capacity to laugh at himself, even while being made the butt of ridicule by those around him. Repulsed by his wife, who was later called "the Little Saint," ridiculed by his half-brother Vikramaditya and the society he lives in, termed a cuckold, it is this man, this lonely prince who right from the beginning wins the reader's heart, respect and allegiance.

Nagarkar's irony and self-deprecating humor are evident from the title of the novel itself. The *Webster's Dictionary* defines the word "cuckold" as a man whose wife commits adultery, and traces the etymology of the word to the female cuckoo bird which is prone to the habit of changing mates. There is an element of prurience also in the title that provokes the reader's curiosity: who is the wife sleeping with?

The self-proclaimed cuckold, the Maharaj Kumar, has none other than the Blue God, Lord Krishna, as his rival. One of the brilliant epigraphs to the third person chapters appears as if spoken by the Maharaj Kumar,

> We were that rarest of couples. Even after years of marriage we were madly in love. I with her and she with somebody else. (147)

The epigraphs that punctuate the chapters at frequent intervals are brilliant in the sagacity that hides behind the apparent wit. Whether it is the opening epigraph, which introduces the reader to the Maharaj Kumar's knowledge of his cuckolded position,

> Let nobody fool you, most couples are conjoined on earth. The mismatches, now are a different story. They are made in heaven. (40)

or, later after his discovery of the identity of his wife's lover,

> It was the stuff of nautanki plays. Man. Woman. And lover. Except that the last one was an almighty god. (89)

and much later of his helplessness as the cuckold,

> It was an unequal fight. No Armageddon this, just the sport of a god. (126)
>
> You can exorcise the devil. But how do you rid yourself of a god? (186)

Nagarkar's humour resembles Wilde's, in its sharp wit and perspicacity that is layered beneath what appears to be a frivolous and clever apothegm. And like Wilde, not only does he turn his wit on society, he argues through his characters that there is a need for a different kind of society, and a new kind of human personality. The Maharaj Kumar's tragedy as was Wilde's, was that he fought his battles within the very social institutions he despised. His observation of the Jains as moneylenders is astute and accurate bringing to light the hypocrisies of puritanical ideologies.

> You give alms, you earn merit. You feed the poor or the Digambaras, you collect some more merit. Pacifism is a capital investment of a high order. It's a kind of super-compound interest scheme with an eye on both heaven and earth. Extend the metaphor and it has a foot in the here and now, and the ever-after. Let's look at the latter first. The more merit you earn, the more you are likely to abridge the number of reincarnations you have to go through to reach the kind of enlightened state which gets you to moksha. In the meanwhile, just see how profitable the fruits of non-violence are in this life. You stay pure while someone else, someone like me and my Rajput clan, does the sinning and the killing. While you religiously refrain from bloodying your hands, you lend vast sums of money to finance the mightiest armies at miniscule decimal point percentages which add up to monstrous sums as interest. Whatever the outcome in the killing fields, we warriors protect

> you. We often die; you live unscathed to finance another war. And here's the best part: thanks to in-laws, nephews, cousins and the whole unbelievable complex of the extended family, your interests are safeguarded in every way, and you emerge substantially richer whoever wins, be it friend or foe. (5-6)

These observations and others that Nagarkar makes in the course of the book, cover a whole range of human experiences and principles, and are almost aphoristic in quality. The book, unfolds page after page with words that dance to the cadence of their own lyrical quality, revealing the limitless expanse of the human condition, making *Cuckold* one of the finest literary works of the 20th century.

Makarand Paranjape in his review of *Cuckold* in *The Pioneer,* rightly says, "It is a veritable manual on medieval warfare, armament technology, civic administration, government politics, social life, harem management, palace intrigues, sexuality, hunting, food, social stratification, caste and communal relations, and, besides, contains what might broadly be termed the underlying *webanschanung* to make all of this coherent and plausible. Nagarkar, then not only has all the talents of a novelist, but also a philosophy of history."

It is not the conscious use of contemporary language which gives the novel its immediacy. Nor the savage images of violence and disease which could be slices of life today. Or even the Maharaj Kumar's perception of life which is far ahead of the times. It is the cognitive irony which makes connections between seeming contraries, and develops insights that lend credibility to the experiences, and endears the Maharaj Kumar to the reader. Far from the boisterous, uproarious kind of fun and high spirits in *Ravan and Eddie*, the humour here, subtle and underplayed, heightens the subtext. Often, the reader is left gasping at an obvious truth that was always apparent but missed notice, until it falls under the sharp and penetrating inspection of the author's eye. With a thin veneer of words that appear funny, Nagarkar transparently coats an underlying, unmistakable reality.

The humour so often shows itself as the Maharaj Kumar's perception of his own vulnerability, seen time and again in the Maharaj Kumar's encounters with his wife. The instance when the Princess is in the throes of her frenzied chanting on Janmashtami day, crying out again and again to her Blue God, "Save my honour. Save my honour," Nagarkar's twisted irony, through the Maharaj Kumar's words, tugs at the reader's heart,

> There is some misunderstanding here, my dear wife, I believe it is my honour and the honour of Mewar which need safeguarding. (168)

Even in his description of the Princess playing a game of checkers, Nagarkar uses humour to pick holes in the monochrome saintly image that has been etched in our consciousness. Demystifying the whole idea of a sanitised woman and saint, the author shows Meera as having the additional qualities of a woman with human qualities: passionate, clever, conniving, not always likeable.

> She looked what she was, a little saint whose innocence shone through like burnished armour while she masterminded every devious scheme of self-advancement, buccaneering and profiteering known to man or woman and many unknown to both.
>
> [...]
>
> It was impossible to grasp the enormity of her mendacity, the subtlety of her finger-work and her sense of aggrieved outrage when she was caught red-handed. Her rapacity was as great as her inexhaustible charm. (351)

Nagarkar continues this description of the Princess much to the reader's delight,

> On the rare occasion when no ruse worked and all seemed lost, she would get an attack of hiccups and sneezes and accidentally scatter the coins on the cloth board. (351-52)

Or later still, when the Princess comes into the Maharaj Kumar's room to invite him to a race,

> I stopped short again. I had become a one-response man. Every time my wife suggested one of her impromptu projects, she didn't have any others, my reaction was to ask her whether she had gone mad. Didn't I know by now that she was born that way? She was certifiably insane. It was an infectious sort of craziness. Mangal, Mamta and I were also suffering from advanced symptoms. (355)

But again, at the end of the passage, the author provides nuances in the picture of the Princess and forces the reader to reassess her character. She "takes out the Maharaj Kumar's nazar" and exclaims that she would guard him against all evils and not let anyone come between him and his father, that she would vanquish all his enemies. The Maharaj Kumar reflects sardonically, "Dear God, did she not know who she would have to destroy first?" (356), referring to his rival, and her lover, Krishna.

To find humour in the most incongruous circumstances without reacting with fear or sorrow requires a certain playfulness, a certain irreverence. The Maharaj Kumar is able to disengage himself emotionally from the situations he finds himself in, and allow his critical mind to work on them. This disengaged attitude is best described by the author himself through the words of Kushank in *Seven Sixes are Forty-Three* as "a strange stillness that watches the world around it and its reactions with aloofness."

> It maybe time for me to take up a second career as seer, soothsayer, oracle and prophet but my clairvoyance is not yet foolproof. It had not taken into account a small twist of fate, or should I say foot. (As you can see I may criticize mediocre word play severely but catch me on a bad day and you'll find me indulging in the foulest and most revolting of puns) (284)

Nagarkar's physical description of his characters whether it is the one-eyed Rana Sànga, Adinathji, or Queen Karmavati, assumes a wicked, sometimes macabre image. In describing Rana Sanga, his father, the Maharaj Kumar says,

> "How can any woman bear to look at him, let alone make love to him? My wife fainted the first time she saw him. Father pretended that it was the heat or maybe the effect of one of those long and dire fasts young women undertake before marriage. But he is too shrewd not to know that the nightmares and the villains in Pataldesh look less terrifying than him. One eye he lost to his brother, an arm to the Lodi of Delhi, the drag in his right foot he owes to Muzaffar of Gujarat, and as to the cuts and nicks and wounds and slashes on his torso, the dummies and targets we use for target practice are more whole than him." (10)

Or when he portrays Queen Karmavati,

> "Queen Karmavati had a complicated network of spies and the most tortuous but fail-safe way of checking whether the information she received was a hundred percent reliable. Add to that her astounding arsenal of grilling techniques. She was single-minded, uncouth,

> and effective. She would stoop or rise to any means; tease, coax, cajole, threaten, blackmail, broker, barter, whatever it took to elicit some inane, nasty or critical tidbit." (8)

Her prowess at prying out information from whoever she wants is wickedly portrayed by Nagarkar in her confrontation with the Maharaj Kumar, late one night at the palace,

> "Surely you didn't come at this time of the night for this inconsequential tittle-tattle."
>
> "Let me be the judge of that. You may be heir apparent, but let me hasten to add, more apparent than heir, at least so far." (8-9)

The Maharaj Kumar's shyness and embarrassment in requesting the gardener to tend to the parijat tree which somehow doesn't seem to thrive under his own care, is tender and funny. It is a revealing incident, where the reader catches the prince's perennial difficulty in going after what he wants, whether it is the throne of Mewar, his own wife, or even something as simple as the welfare of the parijat tree. And even as he squirms with embarrassment and discomfiture, the reader's heart goes out to him.

> "The Prince would have liked to throttle the man. The gardener however had not finished with his homily. 'Learn to leave nature well enough alone with just the occasional nurturing. Perhaps it might take heart and rise from its ashes yet."
>
> The Maharaj Kumar expected that the gardener would at least now suggest that he would take over the task of rejuvenating the parijat. No such offer was forthcoming.
>
> "Would you be so kind to undertake the care of this plant for me?"
>
> "Certainly Sire, I believe that's what I'm paid for."

> "If only the parijat would die next week, the Prince thought, and I could with a clean conscience sack the swine or maybe have him beheaded in public." (411)

And even as this sensitive Maharaj Kumar showers his sleeping wife with the *parijat* flowers from a tree he loves, we are also struck by the unrequited love that tugs at both his heart and ours. It is largely in the description of his wife's activities that Nagarkar wields his sharp wit. For example, he describes her presence in Chittor as a tourist attraction and a financial gain for the province, and one can't help laughing at the absurdity of the situation:

> The pilgrim and tourist traffic in the citadel had gone up by a hundred and fifty percent since we got back from Kumbhalgarh and shows no sign of abating. Caravans of people from Chanderi, Champaneer, Jaipur, Delhi, Agra, Mathura, Ahmedabad, Raisen, Daulatabad, Pune, Vijaynagar, even the valley of Kashmir came by bullock and camel cart, by palanquin and on horseback. My wife, as the finance minister was discovering, is not just a rare and living treasure, she is Chittor's biggest economic asset. (394)

Even in inventing the Princess's songs in praise and longing for Krishna, the author has deconstructed the traditional and sacrosanct lyrics of Meerabai and irreverently, but to the utter enjoyment of the reader, given a new set of poems, tempting the reader to set them to melody. The use of contemporary language applied to a bygone era, especially in the poems of the Little Saint, is comical as well as delightful. She is shown as mischievous, passionate and conniving,

> Get him on the double
> Tell him it's an emergency

> The doctors have given up.
> I can't bear it
> I think I'm going to die
> It's a slipped disc
> A shooting pain up the spine
> A fire in the brain
> A comet bursting in the kidneys.
> Is he here? (91)

The author endears the Little Saint to the reader through this robust, lively, sometimes child-like image, fleshed out in blood and bones, so unlike the stereotypical white sari-clad, *ektara* strumming saintly Meera. And even as she reaches out and touches you with her playfulness, the heart also grieves for the Maharaj Kumar for whom she remains unreachable and unattainable.

Kausalya (the Maharaj Kumar's wet nurse, friend, lover and confidante) in her final letter to the Maharaj Kumar, writes with great foresight and perspicacity about how history will record her beloved Prince,

> "The legend of the Little Saint will become great with every passing year. The whole world loves a lover. Love and overheated poetry will make her immortal. As for you, Highness, if Queen Karmavati and Vikramaditya don't get you, the Princess and her lover will. Either way, they'll wipe out your memory." (599)

Indeed history has left no traces of the Maharaj Kumar. All we know of him is that he lived, married Meera and died before he could claim the throne of Mewar. However, through the ingenuity of Kiran Nagarkar's imagination and incredible talent, the reader is offered a glimpse into this rare individual. And even if it is fiction, one is left with the feeling that the Maharaj Kumar of the book could very well have been the historical Bhoj Raj, and that this story could really have happened the way it has been told.

In conclusion, all I can say is this. I do not know what it is that draws me to Kiran Nagarkar's work. And although, I have gone on endlessly about his humour, to say that it is just the humour in his work that captivates me would be doing the author a great injustice. Is it his style? Is it his wit? Is it his language? Is it his imagination? Is it his keen and critical mind? Is it his perceptions? Is it his wisdom?It is all these, and it is more.

I wonder, though, finally, if it is through the Maharaj Kumar's ironical view of life that we get a complete understanding of the Prince. It is through his humour that the reader experiences the Maharaj Kumar's understanding and acceptance of his enemies as much as of his friends, his compassion, his foresight, his love for several women with passion and tenderness, his generosity in the battlefield and his ability to come to terms with disillusionment (just like Kushank, Ravan and Eddie), his own introspective nature which is as deep and meditative as the Gambhiree river. It is because of the Maharaj Kumar's detached attitude, often laced with wry humour, that the reader sees a character of many dimensions. Finally, it is due to the mirth, which is simultaneously meditative and sheds light on the human condition with such poignancy that *Cuckold* wins its place among the classics.

Perhaps my sentiment is best expressed through J. D. Salinger's words in *The Catcher in the Rye*, "what really knocks me out is a book that, when you're all done reading it, you wish the author that wrote it was a terrific friend of yours." And after reading Nagarkar's books, especially *Cuckold*, I do not merely wish that the author was a terrific friend of mine, but I am also left with the haunting curiosity to know how much of the Maharaj Kumar is really Kiran Nagarkar.

Works Cited

Nagarkar, Kiran. *Seven Sixes are Forty-Three.* Heinemann Educational Books, 1995.

———. *Ravan and Eddie.* New Delhi: Viking, Penguin Books India, 1995.

———. *Cuckold.* New Delhi: HarperCollins *Publishers*, 1997.

Nimbkar, Jai. *Indian Review of Books.* 16 July 1996 –15 August 1996.

Paranjape, Makarand. *The Pioneer.* April 5, 1997.

Salinger, J. D. *The Catcher in the Rye.* New York: Penguin Books, 1958.

REALISM AND THE NON-RATIONAL IN *CUCKOLD*

Maria Luisa Parra

The notion of reality and what is not considered real has varied throughout the history of man. For primitive man, the idea of reality encompassed both the tangible world and the animistic or spiritual world. In ancient Greece, considered the cradle of Western thought, the gods were perceived as being just as real as ordinary people, and Homer took hold of history, mythology and everyday life to create his two great epics, the *Iliad* and the *Odyssey*. Plato, however, was the first to bring into question the notion of reality, with his theory of archetypal ideas. For Plato, the world we see is a world of appearances, and a mere reflection of the ultimate reality, and art, therefore, is only an imitation of an imitation. Aristotle's view that the artist, in fact, is able to perceive the universal truth behind everyday reality is seen as a reply to Plato's theory.

Since then, over the centuries, the relative importance of the world as perceived by the senses and monitored by reason, on the one hand, and the world as experienced by the spirit and by mystical vision on the other, has varied. For Medieval man, the material world and the world of the spirit were two equally valid realities. With the Renaissance came the beginning of the cleavage between these two worlds, which, reinforced by Descarte's dictum, "I think, therefore I am," widened during the Enlightenment, to give almost exclusive validity to the world of reason and the senses. However, it was not till the 19th century that the focus of the writer shifted almost exclusively to the reality of this world, and contemporary life began to be presented in both its beauty and its ugliness and horror. The novel as a form focused on human life in all its complexity.

Unlike Europe, in India (as in Mexico, and other Latin American countries, for that matter) a multidimensional sense of reality prevails. The divorce between reason and the supernatural world never took place. The animistic world of the dead and the miracles performed by holy men remain as much a part of everyday life as the results and findings provided by science. Traditions, local customs, religion and the world of the spirit are as valid as rational and scientific development.

Any generally accepted view of reality inevitably claims universality. A belief in an external reality implies the existence of other persons who can likewise approach the same reality. Furthermore, common sense is an element to be taken into account to validate that reality, so, we can conclude that anything that contradicts common sense or that cannot be attested to by other people, is non-rational.

The rational, physical world runs in an orderly manner, and this is generally held to be true. This belief is the outcome of culture, the result of education over centuries. Conversely, the subjective world of the mystical experience, the miraculous and the magical is considered illogical, even absurd, by many educated people. It obeys different laws, a different logic. It is the inner world of the individual. It does not follow reason, but intuition. The personal experience of the mystic is private, intimate and unshared; the miracle is inexplicable, the magic is unfathomable. Reason takes a long path, intuition and revelation just a leap.

In Kiran Nagarkar's *Cuckold*, the Maharaj Kumar, on the one hand, and his wife the Princess, who is sometimes referred to as Greeneyes, or the Little Saint, on the other, represent these two conflicting worlds. Through them, the reader is able to explore two modes of being: the rational dialectic one of the Maharaj Kumar and the imaginative, intuitive, spontaneous world of Greeneyes. Through them, the writer is able to create a fine tension between "reality" and "illusion."

Based on historical events in medieval India, the novel has multiple layers. The hero, the Maharaj Kumar, is struggling to retain his right to inherit the throne of Mewar from his father Rana Sanga. At the same time, he has to fight against other kingdoms in order to achieve territorial expansion or sway. At another level, his heart is troubled by his wife's "treason," and his love for other women is shadowed by misfortune. We witness battles in the open field, hate and intrigue among members of the same family and dynasty, and sorrow and grief in the Maharaj Kumar's soul.

Nagarkar portrays an extraordinarily rich tapestry of characters and events that depict with great immediacy the feudal world of 16th century India, the world of magic and religion as well as the world of everyday life, creating a sense of the mysterious, enigmatic India of the time.

The Maharaj Kumar is never divested of the intense sense of belonging to India, the sense of the continuity of his life with that of his predecessors. He says:

> We are a country of bards and minstrels and storytellers and troubadours. They never tire of telling stories of the heroic exploits of my ancestors ... I think we breathe in less air than we inhale these stories. Our anecdotes are all history. The bed-time stories of our children are about these larger-than-life monarchs and

> warriors from the past. Our arteries and veins are clogged with them. Sometimes I think we have no present, only past. (54)

Except for the chapters in the voice of the omniscient narrator, only the Maharaj Kumar's perspective prevails in the major part of the book, and although he is the sifter through whom the story is seen, his outlook is detached and objective. Through him, Nagarkar describes the atmosphere of the epoch, providing the reader with a realistic picture of everyday life, politics, tactics of war, engineering, love-making and music; he also reveals the whole spectrum of the Maharaj Kumar's life: his activities and duties as prince, his performance at court, at parties, in the temple; the reader has access to his immersions in the river Gambhiree and his conversations with her, has access even to his bedroom.

The immediacy of this world is enhanced by descriptions of gardens, palaces, cities that are so real that one can penetrate into even the tiniest detail. Their materials, shapes, colours, and smells strike the reader with their enormous beauty and sensuality, like on the occasion when the Prince is invited to dinner at Adinathji's house where the "*Daal bati*, *rotis* of cornflour, *khatti daal chawal, gatte ki sabji, kanji wadas and maal pohe*" are put together to form an inviting still-life painting. (4) Or, the wedding ceremony, where the ritual takes place with great glamour and splendour and where the writer's appetite for detail is also felt.

> He was suddenly at the threshold. He had alighted from the elephant. The priest had performed the puja and tied a string around his father's silk purse to make sure that the Rana didn't spend even a copper while he was a guest of Metra. The drums and the trumpets were still blaring ... He touched the toran on the lintel of

> the gate with his sword seven times to signify that he had fought and won his bride in battle ... His aunt made him sit on a low wooden bajot, and put a tilak on his forehead. "Open your mouth" she said and fed him curds and sweets. Then she took out a gold tanka from the purse at her waist and stuck it over the tilak ... He sat down on a carpet. His bride walked in. The chunni which covered her head fell over her face.... (44).

In the same way, when the Prince climbs up the Victory Tower, the view, as he himself says, is breathtaking. He shares it with us and we can face what Franz Roh called the new objectivity: reality and poetry are put together to convey an astonishing, amazing moment. The wild, natural elements like the animals, or the branch are mingled with the sophisticated, elaborate mastery of the artist. Roh says that happiness lies in the unexpected and insignificant moment.

> In the thick forests on the slopes of the hill on which Chittor stands, the lions and the tigers, the deer and the boar are calling it a day. I can see one of their watering holes from here. A male antelope with magnificent antlers drinks unhurriedly and then looks up. Was that a footfall or just a dry branch falling down? The muscles in his neck are taut. He looks around carefully just in case there is an unwelcome visitor. Everything seems to be all right. He calls his mate. She comes out shyly, rubs her flanks against his and drinks from the pool. A tribe of monkeys swings off the branches and lands at the opposite end. They are a noisy, cantankerous lot. Soon they settle down to remove lice from each other's hair. (48)

Or,

> ... Mewar is colour. There will be other answers ... But that's not a spontaneous, instant reaction. When I close my eyes I see colours leaping at me ... there's the sun in them and a rawness that's an open wound... Mewar is like a punch in the solar plexus. In the most ordinary and quotidian moments in life, my people rewrite the dynamics of colour every day. They are profligate and prodigal and yet so controlled, they re-invent colour every time they use it. (49)

Life in Mewar is sometimes marvellous, but not ideal. Financial problems, crime, sickness and other misfortunes take place and as the reader turns the pages he sees the image of a harsh and complex society which he is able to enter and experience. The atmosphere of beauty and enchantment is broken again and again by scenes of the sick, the wounded, abused women, dirty ditches and puddles, or cruel and devastating scenes of war. With naturalistic zeal (like Zolá or Balzac), Nagarkar describes the horrible sensations of festering, rotting flesh in a wounded leg or the sickening odour of infection and death, as well as the magical beauty of a moment of rapture.

The quality of realism is connected to the personality of the Maharaj Kumar as narrator. The writer has endowed the Prince with a brilliant intellect and a cool mind. The negative side of a scene is seen with the same objectivity as the positive side.

> Re-examine, question, doubt. And if need be, but only if the advantages more than outweigh the ill effects, don't hesitate to swim against the tide. (l09)

In the Maharaj Kumar we have a "hero" narrator who is critical of the world and of himself. He is objective even at his own cost as he sometimes is much harsher with himself than with anybody else. Unlike the traditional hero who wins the battles and the princess' heart, he is willing to accept failure in war and love affairs. His sometimes unorthodox ways arouse contempt in the traditionalist Rajputs, admiration in a few, and respect in all readers.

Like Hamlet, the Maharaj Kumar is always assessing circumstances. Like him, in a sort of detached way, he thinks and analyses, examines and ponders every situation in the light of reason, and like him, he meets with a dead end when it comes to trascendental issues.

> Everything is conjecture, speculation and suspicion. Droughts, famines, floods, epidemics, too much and too little, defeat, deprivation, whether it's personal or universal suffering, the explanation's always the same: we must have done something wrong, very wrong. (318)

But the answer does not satisfy the Prince. "Life is not explicable nor does it pass the test of reason," says the Maharaj Kumar in one of his soliloquies when he meditates on the death of his little sister and the sick people during the plague, but these could be the words of the Prince of Denmark as well. The same overwhelming sense of despondency that afflicts Hamlet strikes the Maharaj Kumar over and over again, with his inability to arrive at a definite answer to his questions. They search in their heads for answers, for solutions to the inexplicable, to the riddles and mysteries of life. They cannot go any further, hard as they try. They feel trapped. Doubt and question are at the centre of their lives as they both unsuccessfully try to adjust to reality.

The Prince is aware that his duty is to fight. As a prince and Rajput his participation in the war against the neighbouring kingdom of Gujarat is inevitable, but he wonders if it is reasonable or worthwhile. War decimates people, leaves them maimed, crippled and disfigured. He finds war within his family as insane and irrational as war against other people, furthermore, he is convinced that after the war one returns to the starting point so the struggle, the loss, the suffering turn out to be worthless, if not foolish.

> Our greatest call to war is the *Bhagavad Gita*. And what does the *Gita* say? Fight the war and perform the duties of your vocation whatever they may be, but without thinking of the fruits and consequences of your actions. (208)

As a clear parallel with Arjuna in the *Bhagwad Gita*, the Maharaj Kumar is reluctant to participate in war. Like him, he has had Krishna as tutor and guide, and like him he has to go to war in order to follow his *dharma*.

For Arjuna the dilemma is resolved when he learns from Krishna that even when he had to kill people he was not destroying anything, because what is cannot cease to be. The *Atman*, the Supreme Soul which dwells in every person is the ultimate reality and is indestructible and immortal. For the Maharaj Kumar, the justification for war is its likely outcome: he wants to win the crown, because it is his birthright (he might not have been ambitious otherwise), he wants security and power for Mewar, and for that he is prepared to engage in warfare.

The existentialist question of Hamlet and the ethical conflict of Arjuna are shared by the Maharaj Kumar, but his choice, as usual, stems from his mind and is made on the basis of practical considerations. He goes to war, but does not hesitate to withdraw his men from the battlefield in order to save their lives (even at the cost of being considered a coward). He agonises about the people he has to kill, but once in the battle he is detached and ruthless and contradicts the codes and conventions of the feudal world, a world in which political and personal conduct are dictated by ideals of courage, valour, and courtesy, and death is preferable to dishonour. Unlike the traditional Rajput or medieval knight who had a strong concept of honour and would choose to have a glorious death, he is willing to use unconventional and non-heroic methods to win the war. He has his eyes on the ground, is realistic and rational about the value of human life and the need to avoid death if at all possible, as against what is seen as the non-rationalist view of the Rajputs towards warfare – fighting to the death even if the battle is already lost.

The "easy colloquial currency of language" in the book serves Nagarkar's intention of building up a sense of realism. This, together with the chronological order of events, creates a sense of actual reality. One is not just reading, but living the experiences of the characters. Part of this effect is due to the highly objective, logical character of the Maharaj Kumar as narrator. But his logic again and again clashes with the "non-rational" events revealed before his eyes. The book has scope for other "realities" beyond the Prince's world and comprehension.

The Maharaj Kumar's striking intelligence is balanced by Greeneyes' dazzling personality. Her beauty, her talent for singing and dancing, her poetry, and above all, her passion for Krishna, make her an enigmatic character. The Prince is intrigued, then infuriated, and finally completely obssessed by his wife. The moment he meets Greeneyes, which is on his wedding day, his hitherto orderly vision of life is overturned. The Princess is not able to perform her duties as a wife because, as she herself confesses, she is betrothed to another (which does not prevent her from being practically raped by her husband). This other man, he later discovers, is no other than the god Krishna.

After the shock of this revelation, the Prince's conflict starts: he is unable to understand his wife; he is unable to participate in her world or introduce her to his; he is unable to recognise his feelings or find solutions to his situation. Jealous and critical of his wife's passion and mystical devotion, he becomes bitter and violent towards her. She bears his aggression with dignity, but when he is not at home, she dedicates her life to the writing of passionately devotional poetry and the adoration of Krishna.

The Maharaj Kumar has also had a personal relationship with Krishna and his actions are, in many cases, inspired by the god. But the official god that he worships is Eklingji and this faith stems from his heritage or culture, not from first-hand experience. In the Maharaj Kumar's presence, offerings are made to invisible powers, formidable blessings are pronounced, and all kinds of solemn rites are performed that go beyond the rational, tangible world, but when he speaks to the god, his discourse is intellectual rather than emotional. The Prince does not understand that religion cannot be disposed of with rationalistic "enlightened" criticism; that it depends on an authority which is not of this world and that it has other sources, other dynamics, other ends. For Greeneyes this is clear. She does not ever question herself (or, at least the reader does not know about her questioning). She surrenders herself completely to her god, Krishna and what she feels goes beyond any human bondage. Her submission, her obedience have nothing to do with any intellectual attitude. Her faith and her love are indestructible. Her heart rules her actions and holiness and love are the result.

The mystic experience of the ultimate reality is perceived as a private gift and Greeneyes is aware of that. Her love for Krishna is portrayed in a way very similar to the most intense human passion, and there's no doubt about it, she will surrender to whatever he wants. She admires her husband and tries to please him, but her priority is her love for the god.

Being something beyond holiness, mysticism is not a

state chosen by the individual. It is said that the person is chosen by the God. A saint is a spiritual model, whereas the mystic is possessed in flesh and soul by the divinity. Greeneyes becomes a saint and as that she's worshipped by the people, but it is not her holiness that strikes the reader, it is the ardour of her poems, the vehemence of her desire for Krishna that fascinates and intrigues us.

Get him on the double
Tell him it's an emergency
The doctors have given up
I can't bear it
I think I'm going to die
It's a slipped disc
A shooting pain up the spine
A fire in the brain
A comet bursting in the kidneys.
Is he here? (91-92)

says Greeneyes in a fragment of a poem written to Krishna. In it she tells us about her urgent need, and continues:

Ask him to come fast
I'm about to breath my last
Nothing serious really
Just a routine heart attack
Tell him I die ... (91-92)

One wonders if it is possible for anybody to be in love with the divinity to such an extent. Is it really love, or passion, or faith? Or is it that the person is possessed by a strange force that compells her to act this way and her will has no power to stop her?

Two remarkable Spanish poets of the 16th century, Saint John of the Cross and Saint Teresa of Avila, have also provided examples of this kind of expression. Their poems seem to be written by a lover, the sensual content and daring language making us doubt that they were addressed to God.

In this fragment, Saint John of the Cross[1] reveals how desolate he is without the pesence of God:

> Niña que la presencia del amor
> que no se cura sino con la presencia
> del amor y la figura ...
> (This love cannot be calmed, but by the person
> and the presence)

St. Teresa of Avila[2] as well, in this famous poem talks about her great love for God and her rejection of life. Her desire for her reunion with Him makes this life unbearable.

> Vivo sin vivir en mi
> y de tal manera espero
> que muero porque no muero.
> (I live without truly living. In the same way I
> hope to die, because in dying I do not die.)

The two poets resort to erotic images, to voluptuous language to express their yearning for their Lover and their expectation of meetimg Him after death.

In his realistic novel, *The End of the Affair*, Graham Greene's subject is also this unbelievable love for the divinity. Bendrix, the hero and narrator of the book, is tortured by jealousy because he feels betrayed by the woman he loves, Sarah, only to find that his rival was God himself and that she had offered to stop seeing him in order to save his life. Bendrix's feelings of defeat, disappointment, and impotence are very similar to those of the Prince. Like Bendrix, at some

---

[1] St. John of the Cross (1542-1591). One of the greatest Christian mystics and Spanish poets, doctor of the church, cofounder of the contemplative order of Discalced Carmelites. John schematized the steps of mystical ascent. John combines a poetic sensitivity for the nuances of mystical experience with a theological and philosophical precision guided by his study of St. Thomas Aquinas, expressing the mystical union between the soul and Christ.

[2] Teresa of Avila, Saint (1515-1582) Spanish nun. One of the great mystics and religious women of the Roman Catholic church, and author of spiritual classics. She was elevated to doctor of the church in 1970.

point in the novel, the Maharaj Kumar is unable to sustain his position of indifference to Greeneyes and has to recognise that he is obssessed by her. Like Bendrix, his jealousy leads him almost to the brink of insanity. To ransack her writings, to rage at her or slap her provides no satisfaction. He wants to possess her and he is willing to resort to any means – force, spying, impersonation – to obtain her love. The desperate Prince turns to a witch, a supernaturnal creature in the cast of a woman called Bhootani Mata for help. This peculiar and interesting character corresponds to the shaman figure of many early communities.

Like the shaman, Bhootani Mata through a trance or a dream is possessed by spirits and foretells the future or answers the questions of people. Verrier Elwin, in his article on shamanism says: "The spirits speak through him and the person can encarnate a woman, a man, old or young and behave like one. The picture that emerges is a curious one: on the one hand, we discern traces of kindness and amiability, even of love, a willingness to help, a concern for human welfare. On the other, there is greed, temper, selfishness and an extraordinary lack of dignity. Sometimes they begin to joke, often obscenely; they show a keen ear for gossip; they themselves let out scandals at which no one living has yet dared to hint. For his work, a shaman must not only have a good grasp of general knowledge; he must be acquainted with the circumstances and geneologies of every family in his circuit, and he must also be well aware of village gossip" (265).

It is Bhootani Mata (who lives some distance from the city, and has the power to transform herself into anything she wants – a witch, an old woman, or a young and beautiful girl – or be in any place at any time she pleases) who confronts the Prince with himself for the first time. Is Greeneyes possessed by a strange force or is it he, the Maharaj Kumar, who is possessed by the Princess?

The moment the Prince enters the cave where the witch

lives, his sense of realit) and reason fades away. He enters another form of reality as if he had come down to the underworld, to hell, to another dimension, to the world of the unconscious where time and space vanish.

The Prince is sceptical of the supernatural and aware of the insanity of his behaviour, but cannot stop himself. He needs to know why his wife cannot belong to him; he needs to know the name of his rival, furthermore, he needs her above anything else in the world, and is willing to do everything in his power to get her.

> Bhootani Mata was not the kind of person he would have turned to, ever. But "ever" is a flexible and finite word. Whether he knew it or not, he had crossed the shifting line that separates the sane from the unbalanced. Anything, he was willing to do anything, to retrieve his wife from the forces that had robbed her of her will and set her on a path of collision with the whole of Mewar. (l49)

The Prince is mocked at by Bhootani Mata and after some moments of confusion and bewilderment when he sees the unbelievable visions, he is asked the fatal question: "How far are you willing to go to get what you want?"

"Pretty far I would think," is his answer, but does not know yet how far he will go. He is not aware that he, like Faustus, will be willing to bargain with the dark forces. "I will make a covenant with the gods and the devils. Anyone you say ..." he says to Bhootani Mata. "I will embrace evil and the black arts. I will blacken my heart and of a dark night open the gates and invite a black pestilence upon her and her kind ..." (l69).

He tries to fool himself into thinking that if he harms Greeneyes, he would be rid of his obssession, but he is mistaken. Greeneyes is a complete person without her husband. Her love for the god is much more than duty: it is life itself. Her body, her soul, her heart are involved in it.

> "Body on body, breast on breast, tongue coiled
> with tongue.
> We'll tie a knot that can never be untied
> We'll intertwine into a double helix.
> Weave vein, artery and capillary into an
> inseparable plait ..." (130)

says the Princess in her song. For the Maharaj Kumar, on the other hand, religion is a matter of duty and reason. Hard as he tries, the world of his wife is alien to him, for his reason is always in the way to stop his attempts to enter it.

Kausalya tells her: "... I don't know what black magic you have worked upon him.... Whatever your devious designs, and however subtle, I'll get you" (75). But Greeneyes succeeds in everything she wants to achieve. Indeed she has an extraordinary force, an imperturbable dignity, an incredible allure.

The fascination the Prince feels for Greeneyes implies the great attraction he feels for this other world, alien to him and represented by her. Thus, instead of ignoring or rejecting her, he takes the risk (though unconsciously) of falling in love with her and through his attempts to conquer her, he is willing to open his mind to other possibilities, to other perspectives beyond his reason and senses. At the end of the novel, when the Prince is defeated and alone, when his intelligence and common sense finally could not lead him to peace or success, and when he turns his heart however inversely to the god, he merges with Krishna symbolising the reunion of the two worlds, of the two opposite perspectives that have been confronting each other throughout the book.

The fact that the personal, subjective story is subordinated to the realistic narrative thread of external action, or that the metaphysical world of religion and magic is subordinated, at least during most of the novel, to that of reason and logic, indicates that the novel is planned on mainly realistic lines. In the same way, Epic, one of the dominant genres chosen by the writer (though several other genres are used as well) is a male vision of the world in which the masculine Animus, representing Logos, predominates over the feminine Anima, representing Eros.

Furthermore, the main story progresses in the traditional, chronological order, whereas the other story (the personal one) shifts back and forth in time. From a flashback when the Maharaj Kumar starts telling us about his wedding (which is when he first meets Greeneyes) to the moment when Krishna and the Prince become one, the chronological concept of time is disrupted. (In the scenes where the Maharaj Kumar meets Bhootani Mata, time does not exist. In fact it is as if he has lost consciousness of reality – time and place vanish – as if he were dwelling in another dimension).

Some cultures are able to hold both modes of perceiving reality – the rational and the intuitive – simultaneously. Kiran Nagarkar merges these two "realities" in the final fusion of the Maharaj Kumar and Lord Krishna. The startling conclusion of the novel (the fourth ending) symbolises the reunion of the two worlds, of two opposing perspectives that have confronted each other throughout the novel. The absolute values of Greeneyes and the relativism of the Maharaj Kumar have allowed the reader to dwell in and compare the two main trends of Indian, (and for that matter, universal, thought) – the material and the spiritual – which the book puts face to face, and then, at the end, unites.

Works Cited

Elwin, Verrier. "Saora Shamans and Shamanins." *Religion in India*. Ed. T. N. Madan. UK: Oxford UP, 1993.

Nagarkar, Kiran. *Cuckold*. New Delhi: HarperCollins, 1997.

Cracks In The State: Morality and Tradition In 16th Century Mewar

Usha Hemmady

The advent of the Bhakti cult in the early 16th century signalled a sharp severance from the hegemony and totalitarian control of God and ritual by the Brahmins. It emphasised that any man be he cobbler or king, from any *varna*, had direct access to God. In Maharashtra, Dnyaneshwar was the first to break from the old ways. Persecuted and reviled, he still dared to translate the sacred texts into Marathi, allowing access to the common man. All that was needed, said Dnyaneshwar, was an intense devotion to God. Those who followed him agreed whole-heartedly and attempted this repeatedly in their work.

A peculiar feature of this very personal and intimate rapport with God was that Bhakti mystics all over India felt an almost compelling need to converse with the Lord in poetry. They adopted different styles – abstruse, intellectual, colloquial, lyrical, romantic, passionate, playful – but their subject was always the same – God. He was father, friend, lover, companion, soulmate. They did not seat him on a pedestal or shut him off in a temple, but teased him, ordered him and were playfully familiar in their attitude. They were able to do these things because of their belief that there was no dividing line between God and man. He could send you calamity, but he could also comfort you with great love. In fact, love was the bonding factor at all times.

Despite the robustness of their poetry, the Bhakti mystics who followed Dnyaneshwar – Namdev, Eknath, Tukaram, Krishna Chaitanya, and in later years, Thyagaraja, Swami Tirunal, Muthuswami Dikshitar and Papanasam Sivan were well known, though mainly regionally. The 16th century Meera of Chittor on the other hand enjoyed a wider reknown. A princess by birth, she was married much against her wishes to Bhojraj, the Maharaj Kumar of Mewar, the most eligible bachelor prince of the time in all Rajasthan. The Indian imagination has responded wholeheartedly to her total absorption in Krishna, the Blue God. "The legend of the Little Saint will become greater with every passing year," says Kausalya, near the end of Kiran Nagarkar's novel *Cuckold*, reflecting history accurately. "The whole world loves a lover. Love and overheated poetry will make her immortal" (599). The lyrics in the novel have been written by Nagarkar and are more "overheated" than Meerabai's own, because the character of the Princess is different from that of Meerabai. Meera's lyrics are sung not just in India but in many foreign countries: in the 1980s, she even became a feminist icon and inspired plays, paintings, dance and poetry. It is an irony of history that while she is celebrated for her devotion to Krishna, her husband has been totally forgotten – or if remembered at all – he is thought of as someone who jealously persecuted her.

Both Meera and Bhojraj are never named in *Cuckold*. The lyrics Nagarkar gives to the Princess are passionate, even frenzied: the language of love-making is used most uninhibitedly. To begin with, she is reviled, given appellations such as "nautanki" or "nautch-girl" because she quite innocently dances to her own singing. This of course allows Vikramaditya, the Maharaj Kumar's brother who lusts after the throne, to build up a scandal to ruin his elder brother so that he may stand ridiculed in his father's eyes. In a letter of which every word is insidious and treasonable, Vikramaditya writes to Prince Bahadur of Gujarat, offering him a valuable stolen horse in return for military help in overthrowing the Rana. One of the reasons he puts forward for doing this is that his brother, the Maharaj Kumar, regent of Chittor, is weak and unassertive, his wife is a national scandal and while she leads him a song and dance, he broods and vacillates and is, even after so many years of marriage, without issue (36). Mewar watches in fascinated agony as this court drama of the Maharaj Kumar and the Princess unfolds. (The Maharaj Kumar is a great favourite but if he cannot subdue his wife, how will he rule the state?)

Since the Princess is based on the real life character of Meera, there are a great many myths and legends ascribed to her; making it impossible to separate biographical detail from the apocryphal history that grew around her. History tells us that she was a prolific writer, a superb musician and dancer. In the novel, however, she is a different type of character, not as sanitised as the Meera of tradition. In the novel, the Princess gradually gets a following and people forget their earlier distaste of her ways, and she succeeds in enthralling them with her devotion to Krishna. People begin to attend her sessions and even ask for her blessings when faced with calamity.

The story of the Maharaj Kumar is a different one altogether. History has mainly ignored him, if not presented him in an unkind light. Kiran Nagarkar in his superb novel has taken up the challenge of filling in this gap in history in his usual intrepid way, and attempted to make the Maharaj Kumar a man who was truly remarkable.

At the very beginning of *Cuckold*, the Maharaj Kumar links himself to the river Gambhiree: "The Gambhiree is my mother and my memory.... She is privy to all my doings, my innocent thoughts and the dilemma that wracks my soul" (13). Like the Gambhiree, the Prince is sober, meditative and deep, given to long sessions of introspection. He is also practical, well-versed in warfare, an intrepid soldier as well as an accomplished musician. Loving peace better than war, he knows that playing at soldiers drains the state's resources:

> We fought endless wars so that our enemies would sue for peace and fill our coffers, and immediately emptied them to pay back the interest ... to our gracious financiers, the Mehtas, and borrowed from them on the instant to finance further wars, ... till the vicious circle had become the web at the centre of which we were stuck like flies.... (3)

In sharp contrast to the pugnacious Rajputs, Adinath Mehta, who is also the Finance Minister, is a Jain who may finance wars but not fight them himself. The Mehtas were moneylenders to the kings on both sides. While moneylenders stay pure, the Rajputs do the sinning and the killing, the Prince muses ironically. "Whatever the outcome in the killing fields, we warriors protect you" (5). If the Jains stay safely out of the battlefield, the Rajputs love going to war: dying for Mewar is the greatest honour they seek. When they die in thousands, tortured, maimed, killed if they are lucky, their widows throw themselves gladly onto their funeral pyres. It is a tough if honourable tradition, except that the Maharaj Kumar has his own ideas on preventing war, not encouraging it.

This rare creature, in energetic pursuit of a better life not just for himself, but for his people, is also interested in civic welfare. His ancestors have always ascribed the drop in population to the wars they were forever fighting, whereas he feels:

> War certainly decimates us (the dead are nothing compared to the maimed, crippled and disfigured in every warrior family, not to mention the hundreds begging for alms ...) but it is endemic and epidemic disease which wipes out a quarter or a half of our population every few years. (20)

Instead of building victory towers and palaces (which he claims you find every ten yards in Rajasthan), the Maharaj Kumar of the novel is determined to use the exchequer for more mundane matters like funding discharge and outlet systems. If they don't pay heed today and bring the weight of both technology and the royal imprimatur to bear upon the problem, "we are all going to be awash in our excrement and sewage" (20).

If the Maharaj Kumar prefers peace to war, he is not allowed to enjoy working for the welfare of his people for too long. The Sultans of Malwa, Gujarat and even Delhi are watching Mewar closely, eager for battle and annexation. In such a situation, the Maharaj Kumar has to keep his ear close to the ground, for not only are there enemies outside Mewar, but also within the royal palaces. Vikramaditya his younger brother, who has already made the treacherous offer to Prince Bahadur of Gujarat, has his eye firmly on the throne, and will do anything to unseat his brother from his father's favour. The Rana himself has come to his throne after having waded through oceans of blood: "Blood. Will we ever be able to stanch the rivers of blood?" How often, wonders the Maharaj Kumar, has he pleaded with his father to issue a royal proclamation, once and for all, "that anybody but the heir apparent, who has designs upon the crown will be put instantaneously to death" (68). The Rana knows how many lives this will save. He himself has become the most powerful and feared of the Rajput princes, but only after having been through violent confrontations with his brothers and having suffered great indignities. Despite this, he will not put a seal to such a decree because Queen Karmavati, Vikramaditya's mother and the Rana's favourite Queen, stands over his shoulder. Echoes of a similar situation in the *Ramayana* tend to trouble the reader's memory. For Karmavati read Kaikeyi, who wanted the throne taken away from Rama, the heir-apparent, and given to her own son.

There is therefore no support for the Maharaj Kumar from that quarter. When Prince Bahadur of Gujarat, or the Shehzada, as he is known, rides into Mewar praying for asylum, the Maharaj Kumar knows that for him, this will be a test case. Instead of killing the Gujarat Prince, or at least imprisoning him, he installs him in the Royal Guest House, replacing the servants with intelligence men who are also excellent cooks and personal valets. The Maharaj Kumar can only conjecture as to the character of the Shehzada, knowing this to be a highly unreliable business, "If I am often a good judge of people it is because I go by my instincts while simultaneously distrusting them" (51). The Maharaj Kumar's penchant for rational analysis tells him that even if there were a hundred per cent guarantee of Bahadur winning the Gujarat throne, it would not alter two facts: "One, his father the legitimate king is alive and two, he is number two in the line of succession" (53).

Bahadur touches a particularly raw spot. The Prince is a loner and a self-conscious man. He is also an honest self-analyst, aware of his ambition, "Ambitious enough to want to be king today. In matters of policy and state I have few scruples ..." (54).

Vikramaditya is a malcontent, spoilt disastrously by his mother, whose all-consuming desire is for the throne of Mewar. Once a favourite playmate of his elder brother, he has now become a ruthless enemy. He feels that all things can be gained by theft, force, even murder. He steals a beautiful horse, Kali Bijlee, from Jai Simha Balech, a senior

Rajput noble, in order to bribe the Gujarat prince to bring a force against Mewar. When accused by the Cabinet of alienating Balech and his clan for a mere horse, he does not seem to care about the political repercussions. The Maharaj Kumar realises that reasoning will not work when Vikramaditya says to him, "The horse is mine. And even if it wasn't, no Rao, Rawat or Raja for that matter could take it from me. Pusillanimity is your second name, brother, but I am the King's son. I will take what I want" (24).

Vikramaditya's theft of the horse, serious enough in itself, is a test case. The Security Council, summoned by the Maharaj Kumar watches his every move. "If I did not wrest the initiative now, Adinathji and Pradhan Pooranmal would leave me holding the bag" (28). The Maharaj Kumar who is totally unlike the normal Rajput in that he can see all sides, understands the sense of guilt in the aggrieved party, Jaisimha Balech: "When you deal with naked power from an inferior position, perspectives get distorted" (28). The danger confronting the Maharaj Kumar is that, "I would overstep myself and move beyond the rigorous prosecution of the case into personal hostilities" (29).

At every stage, he is aware that he has merely to place one foot wrong and he would be disgraced. Given to introspection at all times, he knows: "Of course there would be consequences, maybe there would be hell to pay but such is the nature of action and authority and responsibility ... Cast a stone in the pond, there were bound to be ripples" (31). Vikramaditya, not one to pass up an occasion for heaping insult on his brother, describes the court convened to try him for the theft of the horse as a "sad circus with three superannuated clowns and a spineless prince whose wife is a common *nautanki* girl" (32). A master of vituperation, he can zero in on friend and foe alike when their guard is down and they least expect it.

Wondering whether Vikramaditya's subsequent

imprisonment (though well deserved) was not a political error, the Maharaj Kumar once again ponders on the dividing line between morality and political expediency. "Perhaps we should have treated him exactly like other commoners and noblemen who had committed treason and paid for it with their lives" (37). This is just one of the several incidents in the novel which Nagarkar uses to comment on the nature of power. The mind must have the final say in the matter and sway over the body, so the Prince's yoga instructor has taught him, yet it is the mind that reminds him of the consequences of any action he may take against Vikramaditya. The fact is that Vikramaditya is a prince, and the Rana's favourite son. Guilty he may be, but the Maharaj Kumar will perforce have to leave his ultimate punishment to his father. Perhaps, thinks the Prince, if Vikramaditya had been treated like a commoner, the fate of Mewar might have run differently.

So much for political treachery at home. While the Sultans of Malwa, Delhi and Gujarat are waiting to make their strike at Mewar and the smell of war is in everyone's nostrils, there looms at first shadowily, then more clearly, the age-old triangle of man, woman and lover, except that the lover is Krishna, the Blue God, or the Flautist as the Maharaj Kumar calls him. The Maharaj Kumar with his ability to look at problems through others' eyes had, when on the brink of the marriage ceremony, empathised with his wife-to-be: "In one stroke her past would be severed from her and turned into the ashes of memory" (43-44). An intrepid fighter in the battlefield, the Prince has a tender protective side, too. However, as the narrative proceeds, the situation becomes impossible, even absurd. The Princess maintains that though she will not sleep with him, being espoused to another, she still loves her husband as a human being and is ready to serve him in every other way. This is a difficult, almost impossible facet of characterisation for any novelist to attempt. Yet Nagarkar carries this off so successfully that his readers willy-nilly find their sympathies divided between the Prince and his adamant wife. We see the Maharaj Kumar constantly torn between his ego which demands that his wife belong to him, and the myriad demands made on his time and conscience. And at the end of the novel, Nagarkar has his reader accept the Princess as real, not just as a creature of legend.

Kausalya, the Maharaj Kumar's devoted wet-nurse, companion, friend and lover, watches over him jealously. Who is this Princess who can reduce her beloved Prince to such a state? But the Princess is aware of the suffering she is causing. "There was a tightness to his mouth, and his eyes were the water at the bottom of the hundred-foot well in her home" (73). If he held himself erect, it was something his body would not unlearn after so many years of military training. "But it was an empty shell that managed to be at work at six, ... talked business, assisted his father in formulating strategy, ... played cards ..." (73). But "there was no person there, only the pain of not knowing and the fear of discovering the truth" (73). Realising how deeply the Maharaj Kumar is hurt by his rejection, Kausalya confronts the Princess, tries at first by gentle means to discover the cause of her rejection of her husband and then threatens to kill her if anything were to happen to the Maharaj Kumar. There is no resistance in the Princess, "just the despair of the cornered animal" (75).

Desperate to find some way of alleviating her nurseling's misery, Kausalya steals some of the Princess's poetry to show him. The writing is frenzied, disconnected and disjointed. The delirious ravings are all addressed to the same person. They constitute a mad outpouring of passion and plaint, changes of mood ranging from abject grovelling to temper tantrums. There is too, naked eroticism, begging her lover to visit her, asking him "what was she to make of him and her unrequited love" (79)? Meanwhile, she has started singing and dancing so openly that both the inmates of the palace and the townspeople can witness it. No Rajput princess has ever dared to do what she is doing. Confronted by her husband, she admits: "I didn't know I was going to sing. I sit down to pray and I lose consciousness of my surroundings. When it's all over I discover that I have once again disobeyed your injunctions" (148).

His wife's rejection drives him to brooding and self-examination. Rajput princes are brought up to be fearless. The title of "Simha" for instance, is added to a prince's name after he has proved himself. From childhood, personal courage is taken for granted amongst the Rajputs. "No one in Mewar brainwashes children or stresses the importance of courage. It is all in a day's work" (57). To the modern mind, the story of the Maharaj Kumar, aged fourteen, made to stand in a circular enclosure to confront a tiger, is, to put it quite simply, alarming. The tiger has been starved for a week. When he kills the tiger at the second attempt, his father the Rana observes: "There, you are a real lion now, just like your name says"(58). The options of doubt and fear are sealed off in a Rajput's mind: there is no question of choice or will in Rajput valour – it is blind, headlong and unflinching, because it is the only known way of reacting in a confrontation.

The Prince may be remarkably brave, but unlike the unthinking warriors of Rajput fame, he broods over the moral implications of valour. "Being in the right has nothing to do with courage or exceptional bravery" (57). He has noticed too that fighting is an addiction: "The unmentionable truth was simple. They enjoyed it. Mauling each other had become an end in itself; it gave purpose to their lives" (64). When it comes to war, internal strife, bloodshed etc., the Maharaj Kumar has the intellectual capacity to stand back, to distance himself. But what price objectivity, when it comes to personal love. Here, he is helpless. "What was this arrow stuck in the soul? Where was this wound that bled day and night and yet had no mouth?" This is true too, when his young sister Sumitra who hero-worships him dies of gangrene after a fall. Tradition denies her amputation, which could have saved her. Apart from Kausalya, she is the one human being he has been close to and her death brings in his first tragedy. "There are some people you can afford to lose only by your own death" (100).

The Maharaj Kumar has always been a loner. His father, the Rana, is constantly at war, his mother who loves him dearly, can express her love only through the food she plans to serve him. The Rana loves him too, but has been traumatised into suspicion by the memory of how his brothers had tried to kill him when he was a young man. The Prince yearns to be close to his father, but is aware of the nightmares that usurp the Rana's living moments. "Does he worry every night that I will raise the flag of rebellion and usurp his throne?" (121) Besides patricides and fratricides are not a Rajput monopoly. The aspiration of Prince Bahadur for the crown of Gujarat (despite his being a younger son) is example enough. No wonder then, that the Rana cannot think sanely, nor accept his first-born with the love and understanding he deserves.

If his family doesn't believe in the kind of warm closeness he wants, the Prince naturally turns to his Kausalya. It is she who provides love, sanity, warmth, and a willing audience for his agonised outpourings. He owes her a great deal: "... If one day I do become king, something of her slant and colouring and world-view would affect a whole people ... I think she gave me a sense of perspective" (136). There is right and wrong in the world and there is, as the Prince knows, always an ethical choice involved. The art of statesmanship is knowing, "how far you can side with the right and when to abandon it in the interest of policy" (136). Kausalya has taught him that ruthlessness which has nothing to do with cruelty or torture is merely the habit of paring down issues to their essence, "so that you did not get caught or influenced by the abracadabra and the side-shows of life" (136). But for Kausalya, the Maharaj Kumar might have had the same contempt for pursuits of the mind as the rest of the men in his family have. "Intellectuals are never at a premium among my fellow Rajputs ... A life of action for them is the one and only goal of life" (136).

Kausalya, despite being illiterate, has total recall. Going to temples and *kirtans* regularly, she has heard the Brahmins and *charans* quoting from all kinds of sources, mythological, historical and secular. One work they have quoted most is Kautilya's *Arthashastra*. She makes the Prince borrow it from the palace library and read it every day. As a supplement, he says, she "demonstrated Kautilya's teachings to me with the real-life situations and crises from Mewar's own political events" (137). If Kausalya supplies the Maharaj Kumar with mental sustenance, she also initiates him into sex. As a bewildered adolescent who cannot handle his erotic feelings, he turns to her for comfort.

After the Maharaj Kumar's marriage, when his wife rejects him, he needs Kausalya desperately. "I wanted to cling to her and bash my head against her breasts till they burst and my head cracked open and I couldn't feel anything anymore" (140). But he is unable to go to her, pride, humiliation, a damaged and traumatised ego standing in his way, making him almost shun her company. It may not have resolved anything, but talking about his bizarre relationship with the Princess "to someone who had made my life her mission" (140) would have eased him considerably. Perhaps she could have even found out who the Princess's secret and nameless lover was.

The Prince's relationship with Kausalya curdles further

after the advent of Bahadur. Despite the high intrigue in the kingdom, the Maharaj Kumar's perverse silence separates them. "In the past, I would have bounced ideas off her or at least divided my cussed silence between us" (141). The last straw comes when Bahadur demands her, his sexual appetite for her having been whetted by her devoted nursing during his illness. The Prince refuses to be drawn into whether she should or shouldn't go to him – he is too obsessed by his own pain and yearning for his wife. However, now, another man's desire rekindles his passion, but his pride prevents him from expressing it: "Something that I had killed deliberately ... was rising phantom-like and haunting me. I gritted my teeth and put Kausalya away" (142). Then the unexpected happens. "My tortured and ravaged mind which had been run over, usurped and vandalized by that woman at home, the one they called my wife had now, however fleetingly, room for somebody else, Kausalya" (143). The Prince could have turned down Bahadur's request, quoting one of a thousand reasons. But he was so busy playing a role, – "I don't give a damn, do what you please, what's it to me" (143) – that he has not bothered to ask himself what she means to him.

Nagarkar's skilful use of epigraphs for the third person chapters is both pertinent and revealing. Chapter 14, for instance, is preceded by: "We were that rarest of couples. Even after years of marriage we were madly in love. I with her and she with somebody else" (147). Desperately needing to do something about the Princess's being possessed by Krishna, the Maharaj Kumar pays a visit to the dreaded Bhootani Mata. When he finally reaches her, the Mata is painfully direct, "Is she possessed or are you possessed by her? ... I would say that it's you who needs to be exorcised. We are always trying to cure other people when we ourselves need the cure most" (152). She offers to free him, but doubts whether he really wants to be free of his wife. "He wanted to say yes, every bone and pore in his body said yes, but he couldn't bring himself to utter the word" (152). The Mata's response is a sardonic cackle: "Who wants freedom when you can have perpetual bondage" (152)?

Janmashtami, the festival celebrating the birth of Krishna, brings with it an intensification of the crisis in the Prince's life. Riding back to Chittor after his frustrating visit to Bhootani Mata, he hears his wife's voice singing her lyrics as usual, more frenzied than ever. Isn't it the day reserved by the whole of India for her lover? The Prince cannot understand what she could be doing in that part of town, into which no Rajput Princess would normally venture. Since he and his wife have led separate lives, he could be excused for not knowing exactly where the Princess might be. But even to his ears this sounds like a lame excuse. "If the Maharaj Kumar of the realm was going to be in the dark about his wife's movements, he had better become a hermit and go into the mountains" (166-67). If he couldn't take care of his wife, how was he going to be a future king? Given to such self-examination on every occasion, the Prince feels bitterly that he has no one to blame but himself. If Vikramaditya hadn't already helped him become the subject of gossip in the town, he was about to make himself, "the cuckold, jester and fool in every *bhavai*, *nautanki* and farce in Mewar"(167). As the Princess pleads with Krishna: "Save my honour, beloved, save my honour" (168), the Maharaj Kumar comments sardonically to himself, that it is in fact his honour and the honour of Mewar which need safeguarding. The Princess dances in full public view at the temple, with a *nautch* girl's band of bells around her ankles, provoking an onlooker to shake his head sadly, "Princess, part company with the saints. Your own Merta is ashamed of you, and so is Chittor" (169). From commoner to royalty, the townspeople are willing to condemn the Princess. Queen Karmavati, who like her son, is never one to pass up a chance to revile the heir-apparent, screams at him to have her trampled upon by the royal elephant. "How will we ever survive this shame? How will His Majesty the Rana, your Father, hold his head up again ... Get up you pansy and drag her home" (170). Driven beyond endurance, the Maharaj Kumar is filled with loathing for Krishna : "I wanted to strangle him till the last breath had gone out of him and then snap his neck" (171).

Yet, the Blue God had once been very dear to the Prince. If only his wife had chosen any other god from the Hindu pantheon. But fate has willed that she choose Krishna. Suspicion creeps into his mind that the Princess has deliberately chosen Krishna to torture him. "Whoever had heard of falling in love with a god, for God's sake? Gods were for worshipping, praying, interceding, invoking in times of distress and calamity, begging favours" (103). Krishna the most loveable of the gods, had always had a myriad women in love with him; "Apart from his wives, he had a seraglio bigger than those of all the other gods" (104). But then they saw him in the flesh. "That's the only way you can fall in love, not by seeing a carving or a statue or a painting" (104). As a child, the Maharaj Kumar has had many heroes, but whether they were his own kin, or from the epics, he found that they did not change at all, they were the same at the end as when they began. The one exception was Krishna. "He was protean and he changed his role according to the circumstances in which he found himself. He defied definition. You could never predict how he was going to act or react"(106). In many ways he was the exact opposite of the Maharaj Kumar, "the ultimate brat, mischievous, obstinate, disarming, cocky, exasperating, loveable and gregarious" (107). Does the Maharaj Kumar feel that Krishna and he are two halves of one whole?

The Prince does not forget Krishna as he grows up and his own personality is moulded on his. Certain sections of the *Mahabharata*, presenting the mature Krishna puzzle and intrigue him. What impresses him most is that Krishna, unlike the Prince's ancestors and other Rajputs, loathes heroics. "If his statesmanship did not work, he became wily and devious. War was never an alternative, it was always the extreme resort when every other means of persuasion had failed" (108). Unlike Krishna, the Rajputs, despite their valour, needed to convince themselves almost on a daily basis that they had not lost their spirit. Why, asks the Prince of himself, did the Rajput code of honour and chivalry always devolve upon the sacrifice of their own lives? He realises that this foolish, attitude, however brave it might be, left no room for manouvering, a concept which, he feels, the world owes to Krishna.

"Perhaps," comments Nagarkar in a third person chapter, "what the Maharaj Kumar owed most to Krishna was a habit of mind: don't take anything on authority" (109). Received wisdom is good, but requires to be sifted, analysed, examined. The Prince always refers to Krishna's precepts and actions when planning strategy, and in times of crisis, draws out their meaning and their implications. And now his wife has come along to form the destructive third in their friendship. They are now, "Two mortal enemies. Correction. One mortal and the other divine and immortal" (171). His frustration is naturally aggravated because he has no physical access to the Blue God who has cuckolded him and become an enemy. As he watches his wife muttering love epithets to Krishna in her sleep, he realises that she and the Flautist have formed a complete circle in which he has no place. "It was impossible to break in. He was excluded. Out" (189).

The idea of being cuckolded drives the Prince not merely to frustrated frenzy, but to petty strategy: painting himself blue in an attempt to impersonate Krishna and gain his wife's love. Success only leaves him bitter, since now, more than ever, it proves her involvement with the Blue God.

Indeed, one of Kiran Nagarkar's triumphs in this novel is that he positions the reader into looking at the legend of Meerabai from an unusual and unexpected angle. Some critics have taken exception to the sexual imagery in the novel. If explicit sexual images are used, they are not meant to titillate, or to raise the sales, but to provide important clues to Meera's frenzy, drawing the almost imperceptible line between the physical and metaphysical.

The Maharaj Kumar becomes a cuckold all over again, when he is persuaded to marry a second time, to provide a male heir to the royal line of Mewar. His new wife, Sugandha, totally unlike the Merta Princess, has no inner resources to sustain her when rejected by her husband. She is hurt by his inability to consummate their marriage, and bored to death by idleness, riven by palace intrigues, easily falls prey to the wiles of the unscrupulous Vikramaditya. When he is through with her, he returns her, bruised and tortured, to the Prince. Pity for her overcomes the Maharaj Kumar's impotency (impotency strikes only when confronted by Sugandha) and Sugandha becomes pregnant. At this point in the story, Nagarkar introduces a puzzling development. The saintly Princess, who conjugally would have nothing to do with her husband, suddenly demonstrates flickers of jealousy: "Greeneyes," as the Prince sometimes calls her, is tormented by the green-eyed monster.

During the Janmashtami celebrations, the Prince's cousin Rajendra provokes Bahadur, taunting him by presenting high born women captured in war from Gujarat as dancers. Bahadur, always impulsive, takes grave offence and stabs Rajendra to death. The entire court falls upon him with murderous intent but the Prince whose guest he is, steps in and saves him, despite his having dishonoured his own hospitality and that of Mewar. Aware that his interference is not looked upon kindly, the Maharaj Kumar broods: "Perhaps Mewar and its people will never forgive me for not avenging Rajendra's death. Had I too just sealed my fate?"(185)

Rajendra's murder at the hands of Bahadur creates further havoc and upheaval. Mewar has spent months negotiating and forging ties with Bahadur, even as it was fighting his father and the Gujarat armies. Why go to war with one's neighbours is a question that often troubles the Prince. "It makes better economic, political and military sense to make peace with your neighbours and live amicably with them." (190). This hope has been shattered by recent events. The honour of Mewar's venerable elders is deeply wounded, and as the Prince remarks, "if they could, they would be happy to have my head along with Bahadur's" (190). The Prince questions this concept of honour: "Surely Mewar is larger and more important than a personal slight delivered many moons ago by a Prince and guest who had imbibed too much" (190).

If Bahadur, son of the Sultan of Gujarat, were to be put to death in Chittor, "The inexorable logic of retribution and national pride will demand satisfaction and roll its armies towards Mewar" (191). This will put the economy in shambles, lead to loss of life on a gigantic scale, with people maimed and helpless. Meanwhile, the Rana has ordained his eldest son commander-in-chief of the armed forces and ordered him to conquer the neighbouring state of Idar. Prince Bahadur, as much an enemy of Mewar's as of his father's, is escorted under guard to the border, leaving for an unknown future.

The too-serious and intellectual Maharaj Kumar has never, even in childhood been one for pranks, even dampening the spirits of his cousins when they were indulging in high-spirited fun and revelling. His mindset is so totally at variance with the average Rajput's, that it sets him apart, isolates him. For instance, war is not his pastime. "I would resort to it only under exceptional provocation, or if, after thorough planning, I was going for the big kill" (199). He is painfully aware that most wars lead nowhere but back to where you started. When he goes into battle, the Prince requires to get into the mind of his enemy, discover what he wears and eats, his sleeping habits, in fact all the trivia that will help him to understand what he is going to be up against. He knows too, that collecting information of this kind is a bore and could take years. "Imagine studying the enemy's economic, political and military abilities for months, sometimes for years, when all that the decisive battle itself will take is three, five or seven hours at the most" (200). Riding with the forces towards Idar, "a ball in perpetual motion between Gujarat and Mewar" (200), the Prince is a little disturbed that he has had no time or opportunity to make the necessary strategic preparations. At the border, Bahadur seeks audience with the Prince. His comments are startlingly revealing for one who is almost an enemy : "You are the loneliest man I know. No slander nor ridicule can touch you because you do not let the personal affect your professional life, ... I doubt you'll ever be a popular king when it is time for you to ascend the throne because you do not know how to make unpopular measures palatable" (201).

In sharp contrast to his brave but essentially pacifist son, the Rana, so muses the Prince, is always afraid of being considered a coward: "Somewhere deep in his heart Father subscribes blindly to the Rajput code of heroism and honour and is ashamed that he did not die an utterly pointless death" (203). As the Prince begins to persuade his father to abandon a fruitless confrontation with the Sultan of Gujarat, he knows in his heart that it is a losing game. When he advocates the idea that it would be more profitable to attack the decadent and rotting state of Ibrahim Lodi's Delhi, rather than Gujarat, the Rana is sharp with him. Nevertheless, he realises his worth: "I had forgotten how deep still waters run, son. I had not realized that your ambition had taken the form of such clear long-term planning" (205). To which the Prince though taken aback, answers quite directly, "We are kings before we are warriors, which is why it is our task to have a vision first and then a policy to translate that vision into reality. Whatever ambitions I have, your Majesty, are for Mewar" (205). The Rana is not open to persuasion, so without encouraging any further discussion, he blesses his son, demanding that he take back Idar.

Just before the Prince goes into battle, the reader finds him musing on the contrasting mindsets of Hindu and Muslims, where war is concerned. The motivation and power of Islam is a potent call to arms: "We too, could and do fight holy wars but there's no mechanism for conversion in our religion" (208), whereas the urge to convert is definitely, one of the driving forces of Islam. The greatest call to war in Hinduism is in the *Bhagavad Gita*. Yet what the *Gita* really says is, "fight the war or perform the duties of your vocation, ... but without thinking of the fruits and consequences of your actions." If a Muslim fights, he does so for God and goes directly to heaven and a very pleasurable after-life. "It is a wonder then that the Hindus win as many wars as they do" (208), thinks the Prince. Where the Rajputs have been trained to fight fairly and justly, to behave like gentlemen soldiers, the Prince is way ahead of his times, preferring guerilla tactics and waging a war of nerves. Such behaviour is considered unseemly and disgraceful in battle, especially for a Prince of the Royal House of Chittor. As he orders his troops to raise the white flag, in a pretence of surrender, the Mewar troops wonder: "What kind of signal was the Rana's eldest son sending to our armies, and more importantly, to the enemy?" (214-15) The Rana had spent a lifetime building a reputation which was the envy and awe of the most powerful kingdoms in the country. And now, "With one thoughtless gesture, the heir apparent had brought down this carefully wrought edifice of determination and deterrence" (215).

War is a strange thing, comments Nagarkar. Feuds and rivalries between two villages, two royal houses, or religious groups are invariably transferred and carried on to the battlefield regardless of who the common enemy is. Cleverly revealing an absolute in the Rajput tradition of valour, Nagarkar sets it off against the flexibility embodied in the Maharaj Kumar. Using the strategy of retreat proves very successful in the battle for Idar. Yet right through, the Prince is aware of the consequences. "The two thousand seven hundred and ninety four of us would never be able to join the mass of humanity again. We would be bonded together by the unspeakable deeds we were going to commit the next morning" (226-27). "Deception, diplomacy, intrigue ... all these and many small and great things the Flautist had taught me were the tricks of a king's dharma and trade. But where had I inherited this wanton cruelty from? No amount of culture and civilization can subdue or hide the wanton violence in man" (232-33). As the Prince's sword comes down on the Sultan of Malwa's neck, he hesitates for a significant second at the very last moment, reminding the reader (for such is literary memory), of Hamlet's hesitation in killing Claudius at his prayers. But where Shakespeare's Christian beliefs spare Claudius, the Rajput spares the Sultan only because he is under orders not to annihilate, nor to annex his state. Angry with himself, emotions churning, he thinks ruefully: "Perhaps it is time I gave up being a prince and took up my true vocation: become a court chronicler or *charan* turning defeats and stalemates into triumphs" (451).

The Maharaj Kumar uses the ruse of surrender followed by surprise, through a calculated attack scheduled for a time when the two opposing generals were to discuss the terms of surrender. This was a strategy which was as devious as it was repugnant to the Rajput sense of honour and valour in warfare. He is poignantly conscious of this and knows that if at this moment his troops admire his new approach to warfare and adore him for his heroism, the unscrupulous Vikramaditya, waiting for such an opportunity, would soon win them over, turn them against him and urge them to go back to their time-honoured ways of fighting. He is quite right about Vikramaditya who has been busy stirring up the populace. As the victorious army reaches Suraj Pol, the threshold of Chittor, it is greeted not by the Rana and his queens and cabinet ministers, but by a black flag demonstration, and the shout of, "We are Rajputs here, not cowards" (271). This attack finds its way unerringly to the most vulnerable spot in the Prince's strategy of war. The chant takes up the central theme of cowardice with several variations. As the mob frenzy increases and it seems as if the Prince is about to be lynched, the crowd is suddenly silenced by the entry of the Princess with an *aarti* tray. Her popularity as the "Little Saint" saves her husband. With the usual dip and sway of mob feeling, cries of adoration now rend the air, though for the Princess, not the conquering Prince.

Though the Prince refuses to come right out and say it, he suspects quite rightly Vikramaditya's hand in the day's events, but he is also sure that "today's fiasco could not have taken place without Father's tacit consent" (273). The Rana has deftly underscored the Maharaj Kumar's fall from grace and demoted him to a mere Prince. "Butcher" his people have screamed at him, and try as he might, he knows that this honorific will stick to him for life. Swimming in his beloved Gambhiree, he muses :

> War was a Rajput's dharma. When they disowned me, were they simultaneously disowning war? War is about power and supremacy. It is territorial ambition and greed. You cannot fight a war without killing. I did

> not invent war. I had merely extended its scope and taken it to its logical extreme. (277)

Now, more than ever, is the Maharaj Kumar alone. Atlas-like he carries his misery around with him, forgetting what the *dhobi's* wife Sunheria had once told him: "Let go, Prince, let go of so much unhappiness" (123). He is accused by his own people of "Conspiracy and treason against the crown: ... Egregious and criminal defiance of the most revered traditions of Rajput honour and valour, ... the list goes on" (305). The Rana brings out a document for him to sign, a paper which says that the Prince willingly relinquishes the title of Maharaj Kumar and all claims to the crown. He promises his son that he will be signing the paper only as a "temporary measure." The son refuses, the Rana is disappointed, but is secretly proud of him: "You are a prophet who's come before his time" (307). The people of Chittor use him as a scapegoat till the time of the terrible cholera, which as a last chastisement, visits Chittor. The royal family leaves, but not the Prince or the Princess. "Someone of the royal family," says the Maharaj Kumar, "must be in Chittor if our people are not to feel abandoned and lose morale and heart altogether" (313).

The Princess prays for succour day and night in the Brindabani temple. Her songs underscore what has now become the logo of *bhakti*, treating the sensual and the spiritual as one and the same. If the Princess sings her heart out to Krishna to save them, the priests hold a *Sankat-vighna Yagnya* for thirty days where thousands of tons of milk, ghee, fruit and food, and firewood, are sacrificed in the fire. To the Maharaj Kumar, the notion that the gods can be bought over to provide favours has always seemed dubious and abhorrent. However, this continues to be done on a large scale. The people of Chittor come to listen to the Princess, but to doubly insure themselves, they attend the

Yagnya. In due time, the fury of the cholera abates. Whoever was responsible, the Prince is thankful that the nightmare visiting his people is over.

Cuckold is a first person narrative for the greater part. The remarkable dexterity with which Nagarkar moves from first person to third person narration creates the right kind of distancing, as in the instance when right at the end of the cholera epidemic the Princess too is infected. In the third person account (Chapter 25), we are told that the Maharaj Kumar at first doesn't worry too much. After all, "The Flautist didn't turn up to rescue Draupadi till the Kauravas were well into disrobing her" (320). Her saviour would arrive, but only in the nick of time. However, the Prince's indifference is assumed: he is still carrying the weight of his hurt on him. The dying Princess mutters, "No man and no god has your fortitude or your dignity. You did not deserve someone as cold and ungrateful as I ... I have loved you. A strange love, but love nevertheless. Thank you" (321-22). The Flautist still does not appear. The Prince is appalled:

> "... however great your grievance you don't abandon the people who are yours" (322).

So he sets out to meet challenge once again, nursing her selflessly day and night and ultimately managing to save her. The whole of Chittor celebrates her recovery. But the Prince and his wife are exiled to Kumbhalgarh, ostensibly to supervise repairs to the fort, which is clearly in perfectly fine condition. Obviously, the jealous Karmavati has learnt of the change in the status of the now adored Princess. The Prince can be slandered, even murdered. But touch the Little Saint, and she would become a beloved martyr: so she has to be exiled. At Kumbhalgarh, the Prince has all the time in the world to think about life, even to write about it. One of the most significant conclusions he comes to (and this is closely linked to the way his own end is projected), is the profound Upanishadic concept of interchangeability, or "the oneness that the individual living creature shares with the cosmos and the Almighty" (342).

He also starts to write two books – his autobiography (is this Nagarkar's way of giving credence to his novel?), on odd dates, and the massive introduction to Shafi's book on *The Art and Science of Retreat* on even dates. His first task would be to remove the stigma from the notion of "flight" in warfare, and to educate his countrymen in the art of hurrying slowly towards change, in accordance with circumstances. Rajputs do not entertain the possibility that they have to pay for their grandiose views of warfare and honour, and seem to consider that the past was never their responsibility. The Prince, on the other hand, thinks of personal history as an inheritance, so that posterity will learn from its mistakes.

Soon enough, the Prince and his wife are called back to Chittor. The Sultan of Delhi has engaged the Mewar forces and been routed once again. The Rana has been badly wounded, but dauntless as ever, has called for an audience in the victory hall. He has decided to abdicate; his announcement being greeted with noisy consternation. Where Vikramaditya is among the first and the loudest to display his protest, the Prince has pushed himself into a corner. "Why was I tongue-tied, why couldn't I compete with the rest of them and tell Father that I wouldn't permit him to retire from kingship when that was the truth and nothing but?" (370) This Cordelia-like silence is not going to profit him, as he knows, but he refuses to get carried away by mere words. But that old fox, the Rana, is still to spring his last surprise. He appoints the Maharaj Kumar governor of Chittor and asks for his assistance in the War Council.

In a recent essay in *Outlook*, Amitav Ghosh referring to the aftermath of the 1857 Mutiny in India and the punitive measures taken by the British, asks: "Do such exercises of power really work? ... Those who are accustomed to the exercise of power know that power can sometimes be used to redirect the forces of resistance." He goes on to observe that defeat itself is a transaction and can be negotiated in many different ways.

Nagarkar's 16th century Maharaj Kumar has realised this, as he goes about his duties, drawing up battle plans for confrontation with Babur. Fed on scraps from Babur's diaries by the faithful Mangal, the Prince ruminates on the exact nature of the Padshah's character. The man has crossed the river Indus, and having tested the waters of Hindustan and found them inviting, he has now made a second incursion from his base in Kabul. The Prince feels great kinship with Babur. The scraps from the diary show many aspects of Babur which are to be found in the Maharaj Kumar as well: swimming across rivers, affection for his father, (though he is not always complimentary in his remarks about him); but when he commits mass murder, unlike the Maharaj Kumar, he conveniently leaves his conscience and sentiments out of the picture. Babur's extreme faith in his God, too is different from that of the Prince. The Prince's religion consists of worship of the family deity, Eklingji, in which he establishes a relationship which is distant, formal, more in the nature of protocol and habit, while his other god Krishna and he share a relationship which is highly personalized.

The Prince tries to enter Babur's mind and occupy it in order to plan for Babur's defeat. Yet, the more he gets to know of Babur, the more he wants to know of him : "Why must religion be such an unbridgeable divide? I would have liked to meet him, perhaps, even be friends with him" (421). Lonelier than ever before, his days filled with war plans, the Prince asks himself why he is incapable of making friends. "Perhaps my state of almost total friendlessness is good training for kingship ... Friendship and favoritism go hand in hand" (418). This then leaves him with only Mangal, Kausalya's son.

Using excerpts from Annette Susannah Beveridge's translation of the *Baburnamah*, Nagarkar weaves these into his story to reveal the first Moghul's determination to be the Emperor of Hindustan. These excerpts are skillfully deployed at critical moments in the narrative to point to the inexorable movement of history, and to make for a really sharp contrast between Moghul ambition and the over-played and effete chivalric Rajput code. Through all this telling, the narrator often pauses to comment on the conflict between the personal and the public in life. War is not something the Maharaj Kumar has ever liked, and now that he is so close to it once again, he thinks of the hundreds of women in the palace waiting for their husbands or lovers. "Who would scotch their loneliness?" he asks (393).

Even as the Maharaj Kumar tries hard to persuade the Rana to move against Delhi, before Babur can step in and conquer it, while he and his units marched on to Gujarat and Malwa, the narrative moves relentlessly towards confrontation with Babur. While the Prince advocates waiting for at least half a year, so as to acquire foreign cannons and other effective weaponry to use against Babur, the Rana wants none of this. He is adamant, will not fight on two fronts simultaneously, and will wait for the "right moment" to attack Babur. Immediate glory is all he seems to desire. Meanwhile, the King of Kabul, Zahiru'd-din Muhammed Babur is riding hard towards Hindustan. Where Timur the brave had been more of a whirlwind dacoit than a king, Babur's eye is firmly on the Delhi throne. Once the Rana has decided to ignore his son's advice on strategy, the narrative gathers great momentum and moves inexorably towards a predictable end. Simultaneously, and parallel with the narrative thread, the introspections on conscience versus power are evocative and effective.

Delhi falls like a ripe plum to Babur. "Not Babur, but we, Father, should have fought Sultan Ibrahim Lodi and taken Delhi," thinks the Prince. The Rana again makes a tactical mistake: he not only offers Babur's puppet Mahmud Lodi asylum, but strikes an alliance with him to drive out Babur. Intoxicated with his recent victories, his misplaced haste and enthusiasm drive him into helping himself to territories that once belonged to Lodi, but are now Babur's. Babur meanwhile has begun to cast himself in the role of a Ghazi or Avenger. The Prince realises that the simplest explanation is the naked assertion of brute power. "The victor is signaling that the old order is dead and letting his new subjects know who the new master is" (489).

The narrative moves to its logical conclusion, with the Rana losing in the confrontatiion with the formidable Moghul. Nagarkar has focused the reader's attention not on the famous defeat at Panipat, so much the subject of history text books (the battle between the Lodi King and Babur in 1526), but on the far more fateful battle of Khanua where the united might of the shaky Rajput confederacy was crushed, resulting in the establishment of what was to be the Moghul Empire.

The vast canvas of the novel mirrors the two-fold defeat of the Maharaj Kumar. On the battlefield he loses because, for all his pleas for strategic warfare, his father has insisted on direct confrontation. One is reminded of Hamlet's famous words: "The time is out of joint, oh cursed spite ..." At the personal level too, the Maharaj Kumar suffers a defeat because he must now admit the power of his personal vanquisher, the Flautist. After the disastrous episode of Khanua, the Prince escapes to the temple at Baswa, determined to confront the Blue One. The prince raises his double-edged sword (are we once more reading Nagarkar's symbolism into this?) to strike the beatifically smiling face of the marble Flautist. Just inches behind him are his enemies, six swords drawn for the kill. "It was then that the Flautist embraced the Maharaj Kumar," says Nagarkar (602), "taking him into himself, leaving visible just the end of the *Kesariya Bana*, the turban of the final confrontation" (601). Is this dramatic, almost theatrical ending a ploy, one wonders. Then it comes back, memory flooding one as it were. One remembers an equally dramatic and climactic scene in Nagarkar's earlier novel, *Ravan and Eddie*, where the protagonists fall on each other, and the burden of sin is metaphorically transferred from one to the other. Nagarkar's use of climaxes for thematic conclusions is extremely effective. Krishna, God of dalliance and the eternal lover, has merged with the Krishna of the *Mahabharata*, redeemer and guru, as the Prince once regarded him.

One of the most significant chapters in this epic novel is the debate between Bruhannada, Queen Karmavati's eunuch and master spy, and the Maharaj Kumar. In a statement just before a near fatal attempt on his life, the eunuch extols the virtues of Bhishma, one of the great characters of the *Mahabharata*. Bruhannada chooses Bhishma, the greatest celibate in the epic, as the symbol of an abstemiousness that is not of one's own choosing. Without putting it in so many words, Bruhannada seems to suggest parallels between Bhishma and the eunuchs of the Court: he hints that they shared a common fate. But what is significant in his analysis is that it is what you make of this imposed condition that brings in the question of moral choice. You could rail against your misfortune, of course. But the better option is to rise against your neutered fate, internalise your calamity and give it a heroic dimension as Bhishma did. The Prince challenges this, observing that had Bhishma been courageous enough to throw in his lot with what was right rather than uphold tradition blindly, he would have displayed greater moral fibre. Significantly, the Maharaj Kumar insists that we owe our loyalty not to people and institutions but to values. When

Bruhannada counters this by saying that Bhishma's life expresses the highest integrity, the Prince makes a revealing statement about his own ideals, "Integrity, I'm afraid, is not enough, Bruhannada. Only when it is in the right cause, is it worthwhile" (533). At the end of this mental exercise, the Prince asks: "Have you ever tried exercising your right to make a moral choice, Bruhannada? You'll be amazed, truth too, has its lures and gratifications. More to the point, probity needs a Bhishma" (534).

Bhishma was Bruhannada's ideal in life. There is little doubt, thinks the Prince, as he lights Bruhannada's funeral pyre, after he has been fatally poisoned in the open Court, that Bhishma's patience, self control and abstinence were tried as no man's were. Yet, in his funeral address, he points out that Bruhannada was tested far more harshly than Bhishma ever was. He had at the end been able to question the very principles which had been the polestar of his life. Not because those he was loyal to those who let him down, but because he perceived "the possibility of a more honourable and meaningful loyalty than the one he had been practicing: a faith in just causes and the value of right over wrong" (546).

This section is perhaps the moral core of Nagarkar's novel, for the debate covers the issues of right and wrong, loyalty and treason, honour and selfishness, power, and human pain. Nagarkar's treatment of these eternal polarities acquires the sophistication of a Socratic debate. Confrontation of oneself, knowledge of one's innermost motives is seen to be crucial. In the ultimate analysis, human aspirations, pride, vanity, all must die before the soul can acquire meaning. The Prince quotes the *Gita* over Bruhannada's funeral pyre and a verse from it is most apt here :

Death comes to all who are born
The dead too cannot escape birth

> If both birth and death are inevitable,
> Wherefore wilt thou mourn? (547)

Epics are, therefore, not tragedies. They are meant to reveal the true moral fibre of mankind, with a little help from the gods. And this is what Nagarkar's *Cuckold* does. It leaves behind, not sorrow, but a whole host of philosophical questions prompting the reader to look into himself, and at the world, making *Cuckold* an intensely thought-provoking novel.

Works Cited

Ghosh, Amitav. "Nana Saheb and the Texas Detour." *Outlook*. New Delhi, 21 April 2003. 30-31.

Nagarkar, Kiran. *Cuckold*. New Delhi: HarperCollins *Publishers*, 1997.

Purdeh Ke Peeche[1]:

Historically revisionary readings of women characters in *Cuckold*

V. Padma

The problematics of historical representation and the deliberate deployment of the modes of historiography have become major concerns in literary and cultural studies in recent years. Traditional modes of presenting historical events seem to presuppose certain notions of gender and ethnic superiority. With changing moral and social perspectives, much of what was previously read as historically objective and "correct" is now being challenged, along with the methodology employed for establishing an accurate historical picture. A great deal of effort is being put into rewriting history in order to fill in the gaps left by traditional, perhaps biased, writing. Some of the newer

[1] The Hindi title, literally translated, means "Behind the Veil." The metaphorical and connotative meanings it carries are many. It signifies exoticism and beauty (mostly of the woman) hidden behind the veil. It also carries connotations of the moment of unveiling when the onlookers are dazzled by the beauty of the figure within. Mostly, it carries the implications of expectation, surprise and suspense.

histories purport to tell a different story from the traditional version, deliberately using a previously marginalised perspective such as that of the Dalits or women. This paper will look at how Kiran Nagarkar's novel *Cuckold*, which deals with 16th century Rajput – and to some extent Indian – history, presents a revisionary picture of the life of that period, which is perhaps even more convincing because it is not limited by a particular social perspective. The focus in this paper will be primarily on the treatment of the women characters in the novel, situated as they were in that period. The contention is that the way the women characters have been depicted in the novel, and the roles they play, challenge the modes and assumptions of traditional historiography as well as the more recent attempts at reworking these representations.

The novel also portrays a variety of different ways in which the women characters attempt to move out of the social and sexual confines set on them. Not all the women in the novel are concerned with the political life of the time, but insofar as they impinge in some way on the life of the Maharaj Kumar, the heir apparent and the narrator, they can be said to play a role.

I

As *Cuckold* is basically a historical work and this is one of the important aspects under consideration here, it is necessary to analyse the dimensions of the term "history." The *New Penguin English Dictionary* defines it as the "branch of knowledge that records and interprets past events" (660) while the *Little Oxford Dictionary* defines it as a "continuous record of (esp. public) events; study of past events; total accumulation of these" (298). Taken together, these two definitions bring out the principal issues and assumptions concerned with history, the important among them being the act of *interpretation* and the recording of *events*.

Current trends in history do not deal only with political events and the lives of rulers. Elements of "popular" culture such as mass movements, means of entertainment, saints and villains are now all seen as part of the history of a place or an age. Of course, individual life stories and biographies or autobiographies also act as histories of an era. Harivanshrai Bachhan's autobiography *Dashdwar Se Sopan Tak* for instance, has been lauded as a history of Hindi literature at the moment of its transition from Chhayavad or romanticism to Modernism.

Cuckold can be considered "history" in precisely this sense. It includes not merely a list of the wars that the Maharaj Kumar fought, or the treaties that Mewar signed with other kingdoms. Presented mainly in the guise of the memoirs of the Maharaj Kumar, the novel also deals with a number of other behind-the-scenes activities. What this essay will look at is the role of women. These include the manner in which the royal Princess (based on the character of Meerabai) rose to sainthood, which could be considered one of the major cultural events in the entire history of Mewar; the machinations of Queen Karmavati to get the Crown for her son – a political event with wide-ranging implications; and the various relationships that the Maharaj Kumar has with different types of women ranging from his wife, whom he sometimes refers to as Greeneyes or the Little Saint (the Meera of legend) the washerwoman Sunheria, Kausalya his wet-nurse and Leelawati, the child who matures into a woman – all part of his personal history. It is when all these aspects of the Maharaj Kumar's life are taken as parts of a whole that the picture of his life and of an era can emerge.

All historical writing involves some amount of interpretation, and the act of interpreting anything implies the use of certain paradigms. Much of the controversy surrounding historiography in recent times is actually a controversy regarding the use and validity of these paradigms. Its supposed "objectivity" provided the basis for the belief in the universality of history, implying the essential truth of a historical account.

The reaction to the awareness of these frameworks has led to many kinds of rewriting and re-appropriation of the past or of received tradition. At a very basic level, the hierarchies implicit in colonial historiographies were turned on their head. For instance, while colonial historiography liked to posit the coloniser as some kind of a messiah come to save the subjects from political and spiritual ruin, the new historiographies show the coming of the coloniser as a means of destroying the edenic pristine lifestyles of the colonies. Poems like Gabriel Okara's "Piano and Drums" show how the virility and purity of the native African had been curbed and destroyed by the coming of the British. Many Indian histories and novels too depict the coming of the British as having created more problems than solutions for the Indian communities.

The other very popular kind of rewriting is to fill in the gaps or silences in traditional histories. This is based primarily on the realisation that the writing of history involves narrative strategies like the choice of incidents to deal with, involving rigorous selection and rejection. The decision regarding which events will be left out or interpreted in what light will depend upon the point of view or ideological stance of the historian. This stance may be (and often is) unconscious and such ideological underpinnings are rarely overtly visible. It is only in the process of rewriting, that they are made explicit.

The critiques of historical positions traditionally generated from the centres of power in society, being challenged now from the margins, give voice to the people of that period who had previously been "silenced." In Ki Rajanarayanan's Tamil novel *Gopallapurathu Makkal* (1993), the moment of India's freedom is narrated through the description of the naval mutiny that occurred, not through the depiction of the celebrations at the Red Fort. The story focuses on the sailors' sense of betrayal at the hands of the Indian National Congress when leaders like Nehru and Patel forgot their promise of retaining them. This shows the achievement of Independence itself in a slightly dubious light, identifying deceit as the foundation – an idea reinforced by the three separate celebrations of Independence in Gopallapuram village, one each by the Congress Party sympathisers, the Marxists and adherents of the Dravidian ideology. Such a reworking of a historical situation shows familiar situations and events in a different, sometimes antithetical light.

The same process operates when the focus is not on an event, but on significant individuals. This has relevance to *Cuckold*. Reworkings of history often show known personalities in a different light, thereby giving events another interpretation. This again is not a new idea. Michael Madhusudan Dutt's *Meghanadbadhkabya* in Bengali, written in the mid 19th century, turned the *Ramayana* on its head by positing Meghnad, Ravana's son as the hero. More recently, Sunil Gangopadhyay's *First Light* (1996) and *Those Days* (1981) depict the human, de-glorified lives of people like Iswar Chandra Vidyasagar, Michael Madhusudan Dutt, Rabindranath Tagore and of saints like Ramakrishna Paramahamsa and Swami Vivekananda. The various reworkings of the *Mahabharata* and the *Ramayana*, each one focussing on characters marginalised in other versions are another instance of this. Pratibha Ray's Oriya novel *Yajnaseni* (translation, 1995) tells the story from Draupadi's point of view, while M. T. Vasudevan Nair's Malayalam novel *Randamoozham* (1977) centres around

Bhima. Although the *Ramayana* and the *Mahabharata* are not histories, these retellings point to a critique and reinterpretation of received tradition. To read Rama from Sita's point of view was one way of re-reading the *Ramayana*. But centering Sita also marginalises the sufferings of other women who are not given much voice either in the "original" or in the reworkings. Hence, the focus may be shifted to Urmila or even more interestingly, Shurpanakha.

The Bhakti movement has been one of the most fertile areas in India's cultural history by itself and in the number of reinterpretations that it has allowed. Essentialist, almost ahistorical, readings of the songs of many Bhakti poets have been soon replaced by a notion of the movement itself as a form of widespread social rebellion. Hence, many of the poets were seen as victims of society either of its caste system or gender politics. Kabir has today been appropriated by the Dalit movement just as Meera and Andal have been seen as victims who raised their voice against the oppression of women. *Cuckold*, however, moves even beyond this kind of a re-appropriation of the past. As the paper hopes to show, the novel in depicting Meera not merely in her role as saint, but also as a Rajput Princess who had the potential to affect political decisions and personal actions, reads her as a woman character who influences both the Maharaj Kumar as a man and Mewar as a nation.

This itself is only part of a larger design that runs through the novel, much like the underground drainage system that the Maharaj Kumar dreams of. The novelistic design is different from a historical account in that it concentrates not on the events themselves but on the silent machinery that subtly gives rise to these events. Much of this silent machinery is in the form of the women in Mewar – especially Queen Karmavati and Greeneyes who operate more in the public sphere, while other women such as Leelawati,

Bhootani Mata and Kausalya act on the personal plane. The position of Bhootani Mata, of course, is somewhat ambivalent. Is she a figment of the imagination, a psychological manifestation of the Maharaj Kumar's fears and hopes, or does she have some foundation in material reality? Certainly, she doesn't exist on the same plane of existence as the other women.

II

This brings us to the second aspect of traditional historiography that we had identified – the concentration on *events*. Events are the raw material of history. It is in the series of events-as-cause and events-as-consequence that we have what we metaphorically call the flow of history. For instance, if the First World War was a consequence of a certain set of events that went before it, by the late '30s it had turned into the cause of another gory World War. In other words, events-as-consequence in their turn become events-as-causes and it is partly this transition that is called history. However, events need human agency to occur and the intricacies of characters or the subtleties of human relationships that cause these events are not given much importance in traditional histories.

Traditional historiography looks at individuals as merely agents of history: they are seen in their official capacity, in the political roles they play, in the major philosophies they propagate or the decisions they take. Insofar as this is true, history *is* impersonal, for it does depersonalise the subject. Even histories about a country at the time of a single ruler would confine his individual contribution to his political decisions. A history of India during Akbar's time would at the most describe Akbar's various policies that made him a different ruler or made him India's first national Emperor.

The dimension of Akbar as a person with likes and dislikes, superstitions, perfections and imperfections is mostly confined to a few anecdotes.

It is here that novels like *Cuckold* set in historical periods have an advantage, because they deal with historical events as well as the personalities of the characters. *Cuckold*, on the one hand, is based on solid historical facts that, for the most part, cannot be disputed. On the other hand, Nagarkar invents the character of the Maharaj Kumar, for hardly any evidence exists about the historical figure of Bhojraj. The Maharaj Kumar's wife who represents the saint Meerabai, is very different in character from the Meera of legend. The focus in this paper is not on the events alone, but on the silent figures, in this case behind the purdah, who influence in subtle, and not so subtle ways, the people who act and make events happen. One may remember the television series *Yes, Minister,* also remade in Hindi as *Ji, Mantriji.* The series showed in its inimitably humorous way the Chief General Secretary to the Minister insidiously shaping the decisions that the Minister took.

Cuckold brings out this behind-the-scenes machinery of history. In doing this, it deals with yet another area about which histories are often relatively silent – the role of women.

III

While women would appear to be marginalised in nearly all societies, this is certainly true of India where the space for a woman is clearly demarcated and restricted. In the traditional family, she is to stay largely within the house or within the *zenana* quarters. But always away from the larger concerns of society and from public events – away, in other words, from all that constitutes history. To reinforce their isolation, the system (shall we call this patriarchy?) opposes all deviations from the norm. Queen Karmavati in *Cuckold* refers to the Maharaj Kumar's wife as a "nautch girl" (9), cleverly using all preconceived public assumptions about feminine decorum as ploys in getting the crown for her son Vikramaditya. She subtly turns public opinion against the Maharaj Kumar by imaging his wife as a prostitute because she sings and dances, and for coming out of the seclusion of the *zenana* quarters. In effect, Queen Karmavati is using all available discourses about what constitutes masculinity and femininity as her ammunition. A man who cannot control his wife is traditionally seen as weak and "unmanly." Patriarchal discourse does not give a man space to indulge in compassion or the "softer" emotions – certainly not Rajput men. For women, it also defines boundaries and limits, outside which lie freedom of choice, singing and dancing, and other such activities.

It is noteworthy that only deviant women are considered suitable material for history to record, particularly if their behaviour adversely affects the lives of their menfolk. The adage, "Caesar's wife must be above reproach" is rigorously applied, for the actions of the wife can be used against a man in public life. Attacking the women to get at the men is a common enough practice in every sphere. The raping of women and the unspeakable horrors perpetrated against them during times of riots or crises is very often an attempt to engender a sense of moral defeat, a sense that the men are incapable of protecting their women.

However, patriarchal values cannot be associated with men alone. In India especially, the norms of patriarchy are so deeply ingrained in the religious and social codes stamped in the general psyche that often women as well as men practice them. This is hardly surprising, as the overriding belief structure also implies that maintaining these ideas assures one of immortality. The Tamil classic *Thirukkural* has a famous couplet that says that a woman who worships her husband before God can bring down rain as she wishes (56). In other words, adoration of husband as *pati-parameshwar* gives woman supreme power. Often, the attraction of patriarchal discourse is the promise of special powers for women.

On the other hand, flouting the norms of feminine behavioural ideals is seen as a mark of faithlessness and this, Queen Karmavati uses for the benefit of her own son. Unable to rule as an individual, she aspires to rule by proxy – by making her son the king. In many ways, she reminds one of Tughlaq's stepmother in Girish Karnad's eponymous play. The *Ramayana* contains Kaikeyi's maternal aspiration to rule through her son, combined of course with genuine ambition for her son Bharata. Queen Karmavati is Kaikeyi incarnate, but since she also combines the traits of Manthara, she becomes doubly cunning and more dangerous for the heir apparent in *Cuckold*, the Maharaj Kumar.

Karmavati like many other women in the novel, makes use of her position to deftly guide the course of events to her advantage. From within the *zenana* quarters, Karmavati, with the help of her excellent espionage system, gets news about everybody at all times – "Queen Karmavati had a complicated network of spies and the most tortuous but fail-safe way of checking whether the information she received was a hundred percent reliable" (8).

It is not only in her use of her spy network and her aspirations to make Vikramaditya king that Queen Karmavati shows her intelligence and prowess. She is also one of the important advisors to the King and many of the King's moves – military and political – are brought about through her subtle coercion. For instance, the King's decision to send the Maharaj Kumar as the commander-in-chief of the Mewar forces in the battle against Gujarat appears to be the result of, as the Maharaj Kumar puts it in his typically ironic way, "Mother Karmavati's good offices" (161). Indeed, the decision to appoint one son as heir apparent or to remove the existing heir apparent from his place – decisions that actually turn the "course of history" – are heavily influenced by the roles that the mothers of the princes play. When, after his ignominious victory in the Gujarat war, the Maharaj Kumar is faced with the question of what is to happen to him, his thoughts immediately turn to the women in the house who can plead his cause for him. His mother's pleadings would not be taken seriously for the Maharaj Kumar feels that if she does broach the subject, "Father will look quizzically at her and point out that she must be more watchful for she has just dropped a stitch in the nine hundred and seventy-seventh sweater she is knitting for him" (253). The other possibility – his wife Greeneyes – was out of favour because of her singing and dancing. Finally, it is Queen Karmavati and the influence she wields over her husband that will matter and make Vikramaditya the favourite.

What we have then, is a set of women apparently without any scope for public activity, devoid of "freedom"; but nevertheless, a set of women who play a role in the course that history takes. Inside the supposed seclusion of the *zenana* quarters, schemes are hatched to make one's own son the King's favourite so that he may become ruler. Counter schemes attempt to remove the present favourite from his privileged position. This planning is put into action in such subtle ways that the subjects of history – the royal men – often give the impression of individual decision and action. One of the best instances of this can be seen when Greeneyes subtly plays upon the King's feelings to get the Maharaj Kumar sent as the leader of the Mewar armies against Malwa. Although the narrative voice says, that "as usual His Majesty had already made up his mind" (423), the impression we get is of another behind-the *purdah* mind conflicting with that of Queen Karmavati. The Maharaj Kumar's earlier notion of Greeneyes that, "it would not occur to her to stay in Father's orbit, cultivate him and insinuate herself into his inner circle" (253) is soon proven false as he realises that his wife knows his Father much better than he does and that she can use this to his and her advantage.

The colourful name of Greeneyes conjures up the picture of a shrewd, calculating, stubborn woman, rather different from the woman who gets into history under the name of Meerabai. Part of *Cuckold* is, as already mentioned, hagiography turned on its head – again part of the trend that sees historical and mythical figures as human beings, desacralising them, bringing them down from their inaccessible pedestal to look at the historical, cultural and personal forces that shaped them.

Hagiography traditionally refers to the glorified story of a saint or a well-known person. However, recent accounts of saints and historical characters, do not seem to go in for glorification. *First Light* by Sunil Gangopadhyay, for example, is partly the story of Ramakrishna Paramahamsa and Swami Vivekananda, both of who are presented in very human and accessible terms. The latter's addiction to tobacco and spicy food as well as his relationship with Sister Nivedita show him not as a glorified human-demi-god, but as an ordinary human being, as susceptible to love and hate as anybody else. Indira Parthasarathy's Tamil play *Nandan Kathai* shows the Saivite saint, Nandan, not in glorified terms, but as a victim of his times. In fact, the play portrays *bhakti* itself as something that is used to victimise and silence Nandan. The recent film *Joan of Arc* (directed by Luc Besson) portrayed the eponymous saint as a woman who, as her mysterious confessor says towards the end, saw what she wanted to see in her visions, not what was; a very human error. Nagarkar's depiction of Meera as Greeneyes or the Little Saint is partly to create a credible woman out of Meera lore, and partly a tribute to a highly individual woman who knew her own mind.

The development of the Princess from being denigrated as a nautch girl and *tawaif* to receiving accolades of acclaim as the Little Saint is a journey in which she herself has played no role. Blissfully and deeply in love with Krishna, she is depicted as a highly self-willed girl who while being aware of her role in the royal family and her potential power over others, openly flouts the restrictive rules and norms of the palace. Simultaneously, she also plays the typical *pativrata* to the Maharaj Kumar, washing his feet and putting them to her eyes even when he hits her. After the first half of the novel when we are imbued with the picture of Greeneyes, we begin to wonder whether the legendary Meera could have been as other-worldly as traditional accounts make her out to be, or even as much a victim as feminist accounts make her out to be. One has a strong feeling that Greeneyes enjoys the emotional power she has over the Maharaj Kumar. And she is perhaps clever enough never to let that power wane by giving in to him. This difference in the depiction of Meera – from both hagiographic and feminist accounts – is reinforced by the fact that her name is never once used in the entire novel. She is called "Greeneyes" or "Little Princess" or "Little Saint," but never "Meera." The difference in name reflects the difference in the way she is depicted.

The Little Saint's sainthood is seen through a perspective not uncommon in re-writings of hagiographies. To look at *wives* of male saints and see them as *victims* of their husbands' sainthood is part of the feminist agenda. *Cuckold* plays quite a dangerous game here, for the saint involved has already been appropriated by this marginal discourse and made into a victim. To show her husband – the usual *victimiser* figure – as a victim of a different kind requires great artistic confidence.

Both Queen Karmavati and Greeneyes use their sexual power over their husbands. While the former does it to win the crown for her son, the latter does it simply because she seems to enjoy it. Greeneyes' influence over the King too is a subtle use of gender politics as she plays the role of the ideal daughter-in-law to him. The portrayal of Greeneyes is especially striking as she is shown as a woman of extraordinary sexual power and of great shrewdness. She is shown as a woman who cheats with great élan at cards, a woman who can bandy words with the King and promise to take back all the money she lost to him. She is a woman who simply cannot be contained within the ordinary round of conventions. Her father-in-law understands her well (as also does her husband) and sees many sides of her, including her more earthly aspects, which he reveals when he says, "She's no saint, this woman. She has a moneylender's heart, mind and soul" (423).

The Little Saint and all the other women in the novel are depicted as belonging to their times. The Little Saint, for one, is a consummate archer and this is much in keeping with the historical tradition where Rajput princesses had to be taught certain martial arts. Similarly, she also knows how to read and write – again something she would have been taught as a Rajput Princess. In fact, throughout the novel, Greeneyes the Rajput Princess, and the Little Saint, vie for supremacy. Her threat that she would break off the legs of the Maharaj Kumar's second wife, Sugandha, if she tried to meet her paramour might appear ironic as Greeneyes herself has a paramour. However, her attitude also shows her as keenly aware of the political role that the Maharaj Kumar has to play as heir apparent to Mewar, even though she herself rarely considered the impact of her own behaviour on his career. Similarly, her jealousy at the entry of Sugandha portrays Greeneyes as having surfaced for a while from the stronger personality of the Little Saint. Her relationship with her husband is especially interesting, for while she does like him immensely, she is unable to be a wife to him.

Greeneyes' rise in popularity at once redeems and

condemns the Maharaj Kumar, while she herself remains absolutely inaccessible to him. Part of the success of the book lies in not denying the Little Saint's saintliness while also asserting her humanness. Saints are rarely judged by ordinary social rules. As Leelawati perceptively says in her letter to the Maharaj Kumar, "No living creature can be more self-centred than saints. They are self-sufficient. There is no life beyond themselves. When they need you, they use you. There is no malice in them, nor is there memory" (563).

What is most striking about her, however, is the absolute abandon with which she flaunts herself in public, immersed in singing and dancing to the Blue God. In fact, we might even conjecture that she successfully breaks the barrier between what could be considered "good" and "bad" arts for women. Her singing may have initially been viewed in the same light as that of the courtesan Rasikabai who ended all her programmes with a *bhajan*. But by the end of the novel, nearly all the women in Mewar hang on her lips and are singing her songs.

Greeneyes flouts social norms by her singing and dancing, but what is worse is that she does this in public view, thus becoming the object of male gaze. From a feminist angle one could consider that a dancer is available as the object of attention for many men and this prevents her from being considered as the "property" of any one man. For this reason, singing and dancing are denigrated as "bad" arts. Greeneyes' songs and dances also carry undertones of sexual release. Her assertion that there is just one male (Krishna) while everybody else is female in relation to him is yet another instance of just such a denial of socio-sexual norms. Then, of course, there is her sexual ecstasy with the invisible Flautist that completes the Maharaj Kumar's cuckoldry.

Unlike Queen Karmavati, Greeneyes has no political ambitions for herself. Perhaps this is why Queen Karmavati is more overt in her designs than Greeneyes and uses already ingrained social notions of "good" and "bad" to win her battles. It is tempting to see her as having fully internalised all the assumptions of patriarchal discourse. Greeneyes, on the other hand, does not appear to lay any store by society's notions of good and bad. Insofar as this is true, she is "otherworldly." She openly and boldly breaks all restrictive rules and appears to feel neither joy nor regret over this. It is almost as if these rules never really mattered to her in the first place.

Very often, the use of the female body to achieve certain ends has been projected as an abuse and as a commodification of the feminine. The advertisement and fashion industries have often come under attack for this. Certain feminist groups have accused advertisers of "using" women when the projected linkage between the product and the beauty of the female body has been unnecessary and irrelevant. However, this practice can also be seen as the wielding of a powerful weapon on the part of the women. Groups of men ogling at semi-clad women in fashion-shows may be an instance of the much-maligned male gaze. From this perspective it is the men who are the victims. The female models who get paid much more than any male administrator or manager can be seen as using their sexuality to great advantage in a capitalist society. This is often the case with prostitutes. Not all prostitutes are necessarily victims. Behind the backs of glib men, a hundred jokes are likely to be made about the male inability to satisfy women, and thousands of comparisons between men. Ultimately, it could be argued that it is the men who are more victimised, as once their attention is held, they can be easily manipulated. The Maharaj Kumar shrewdly says, "It's not the person who tells tales who is the culprit, it is the one who listens to them" (162).

In *Cuckold*, however, the recurrent projection of the female body is not in order to dehumanise woman by using her as an object of lust (though there is a strong indication that Queen Karmavati does use her femininity to influence the King). This contributes in a large way to keeping *Cuckold* free from both feminist and anti-feminist attack. Decentring the historical Meera's character from the victim position given her by the feminists, and by more daringly re-centring the male (who cannot even claim to be a victim of class or caste oppression, unlike, for example, Kabir) runs the danger of reverting to a pre-feminist depiction of Meera and her milieu. But *Cuckold* deftly manages to steer clear of this, largely because of the personality of the Maharaj Kumar who is so outstandingly considerate and non-judgmental. Although he seeks his pleasure with Sunheria and Kausalya, and can enjoy Leelawati's company, he never once berates them or treats them as "objects" meant for entertainment. Sexuality is portrayed as a strong force in the novel: the flaunting of sexuality is seen as an assertion and an awareness of this force within oneself.

IV

Deviance from accepted sexual and marital norms applies to several of the women characters. Greeneyes is presented on several occasions quite explicitly in the act of love-making with the Lord Krishna (though here the line between sexual and mystical ecstasy is blurred), while at the same time, her flouting of marital norms is regarded as a disgrace, till the time she is recognised as a saint. Three other women in the novel – none of who actually affect the historical events described – also use their sexuality with pride. Sunheria, the washer-woman who initiates an affair with the Maharaj Kumar, is already married to a very old man. Right at the beginning, when her husband accuses her of loose living, the Maharaj Kumar, as judge of the small causes court, asks her whether she is having an affair with someone else. Her answer is disarming: "Ask him if he has performed his husbandly duties to me even once after my father got me married to him two years ago" (2). She retains this freshness of outlook throughout the novel, but ultimately falls a victim to her husband's jealousy and suspicion. She responds by fatally attacking him. The murder, and later, when imprisoned, her suicide, is possibly one more instance of a wife forced into violence to escape from the marital violence which is socially condoned, and then killing herself, to escape penal and judicial violence. This is the victim-as-aggressor syndrome. Sunheria, far more than other women in the novel, is seen as trapped with little or no possibility of escape except through destructive action. While both Greeneyes and Leelawati fall in love outside marriage, one with a god, and the other with the Maharaj Kumar (an unconsummated passion) neither of them faces the penalty of death. On the contrary, Greeneyes gets the standing of a saint, by which she is effectively removed from the bonds of socio-cultural norms. Her marital infidelity is no longer judged by standards of normal behaviour, but at the same time she is increasingly removed from being able to influence the course of events. A saint's impact is relegated to the realm of the mystical and not the lived social reality.

Leelawati probably tires of waiting for the Maharaj Kumar. She is not a saint – nor would she deem it a privilege to be one. Like Sunheria, she also carries her sexuality with pride and dignity. The difference in the story of Sunheria, on the one hand, and of Leelawati and the Little Saint, on the other, is class-based.

Leelawati is suddenly escalated into womanhood because of Vikramaditya's malicious words suggesting that she had been having an affair with the Maharaj Kumar. In a telling insight into the workings of society, the Maharaj Kumar reacts to this by conceding that "an aspersion, however false or jocular, does not make a girl-woman suspect in Mewar, it proves her guilt beyond any doubt and condemns her" (287). It is interesting to watch the little girl's playful pretence of the Maharaj Kumar being her husband turn into a semblance of reality (at least in Leelawati's eyes), and embodies some kind of a reflection of the Krishna-Greeneyes love story. Leelawati, like Greeneyes is married to somebody else and both of them consider themselves married to their paramours. If Greeneyes has cuckolded the Maharaj Kumar, he in his turn has unwittingly caused Leelawati's husband to be cuckolded, in a manner of speaking. The difference between their two lovers, of course is that the Maharaj Kumar is made of flesh and blood while the Flautist has many images. Again, the King's laughing comment that the Little Saint has the heart and soul of a moneylender brings out another resemblance between her and Leelawati. Leelawati is the granddaughter of the financer to the royal family, a mathematical wizard in her own right, and of enormous help to her husband in his business. The Maharaj Kumar and Leelawati's absent husband both seem to take their wives' infidelities with great compassion.

However, the two women are very different in their views. Leelawati's ideas about the role of the Rajput clan in that milieu show up the Little Saint in a very negative light:

> There are, you used to tell me, two Flautists. The warrior and the lover. We need to study the warrior. Instead the Princess's pursuit of her paramour has made the philanderer Blue God the paradigm of Mewar. This is sad. We are a warrior race, not a tribe of adulterers and gay blades dallying with maids in our sylvan dales. (563)

Leelawati is keenly aware of and rooted in her socio-cultural milieu, while the Princess escapes to the god within her. But Leelawati does not allow her milieu, however repressive to women, to subdue her spirit – either as a child or after she becomes a woman. Like Sunheria and Greeneyes, she too follows the dictates of her heart against socially imposed sexual norms. How far she is able to break free of them is, however, not known, as her story, just like the last moments of the Little Saint and Kausalya is left ambiguous.

The breaking of sexual norms in the novel is not confined to extra-marital affairs. The Maharaj Kumar's relationships with Leelawati and Kausalya border on incest. Leelawati's transition from a girl to a woman is also a transition from her role as the Maharaj Kumar's proxy-sister to his "proxy-lover." Kausalya, more daringly, was his *dai* or wet nurse and hence occupies the place of his mother. The strong Oedipal relationship between the two cannot be ignored, but both the Maharaj Kumar and Kausalya are totally unperturbed by it. Both of them, just like Leelawati, take this as just another natural phase in their relationship. What is interesting is that it is the women who make the first sexual overtures. For a community where the sexual desires of "good" women were not supposed to be made explicit, these overtures point to a willingness to move beyond narrow sexual norms. Kausalya sees it as her duty towards the heir apparent to introduce him into matters of sexuality. She also sees it as her duty to "save" him from the malevolent influence of his wife and even threatens to kill her should her behaviour have a dangerous effect on the Maharaj Kumar. Indeed, she remains protective towards the Maharaj Kumar throughout, even preferring him to her own son, in a Pannadai-like way. In many ways, she is the antithesis to Queen Karmavati. While the Queen is power-hungry, either directly or indirectly, Kausalya is self-sacrificing. Of course, Kausalya does not have a crown at stake, but she never uses her influence over the Maharaj Kumar to get anything done for herself or her son Mangal. If anything, it appears that she has passed on her sense of protectiveness about him to

Mangal too, who both as head of Intelligence and as a close friend, is fiercely watchful over the Maharaj Kumar.

Kausalya's individuality comes across very strongly in the novel. Without ever disobeying the Maharaj Kumar, she does only what she deems to be correct or in the best interests of the Maharaj Kumat and Mewar. In many ways, she is the quintessential Rajput woman for whom the son's valour and courage are all-important. One may remember the film *Mughal-e-Azam* where Akbar reprimands Jodhabai, his Rajput wife, for making their son Salim weak by drowning him in maternal affection. Kausalya's relationship with the Maharaj Kumar is singularly devoid of any overt display of emotion, but the undercurrent of affection and love is very strong. Her son Mangal points out once to the Maharaj Kumar that Kausalya was an independent woman fully capable of taking her own decisions, besides being economically independent. The idea of a woman being dependent upon her father in childhood, husband in youth and son in her old age is proven false by the women in the novel, especially Kausalya.

V

While Queen Karmavati and Greeneyes are presented as active behind-the-scene agents of history, the roles of Leelawati, Sunheria and Kausalya are confined to their relationship with the Maharaj Kumar. Of course, as the Prince says on one occasion, he feels Kausalya has invested her mind and soul so deeply in him because by grooming him with appropriate ideas, she could have an effect on the development of an entire nation. As protagonist and part-narrator, the Maharaj Kumar is at the centre of all events, and as heir apparent, is in a position to make history. It is therefore, through their relationship with him that Leelawati, Sunheria and Kausalya play their roles in the history of Mewar.

A novel, unlike a historical account has the scope to

present history as a series of human relationships. The novel form allows for lengthy presentations/analyses of character and relationship; it provides space to understand the way these relationships affect others, and the manner in which social and political life (the stuff of history) changes as a result of personal factors.

In the figures of the various women in the novel, we are shown the silent machinery that operates the wheels of history, sometimes wittingly, sometimes unwittingly; sometimes successfully, at other times in vain. Interestingly, while Queen Karmavati is by far the most powerful woman politically, she appears the most trapped and confined. Perhaps this is because she, alone of all the women dealt with in some detail in the novel, has fully internalised all the socio-sexual norms of femininity and masculinity and uses these to the advantage of her son. She is not a free woman, however strong and active she might be, but a reflection of social mores. Women like Kausalya and Sunheria who have a strong emotional hold over the Maharaj Kumar do not use their influence to political ends. They appear as individual women taking individual decisions. None of the women in the novel allow others to take their decisions for them. More importantly, they appear as women who are capable of taking full responsibility for the outcome of these decisions. Karmavati can be considered to be trapped perhaps because she identifies herself and her power only with her son. She is caught in this vicious circle which allows her no scope to change and develop. The other women, however, do not project themselves or their ambitions on to anybody else. Even Leelawati, just graduated into womanhood, is realistic enough to point out to the Maharaj Kumar that her patience in waiting for him is not infinite, and that her life is not entirely dependent on him.

It is not that there are no women victims in the novel – Leelawati's is one obvious case. The Maharaj Kumar's sister who dies because of an infection in her leg is another. While an amputation would have saved her, it would have made her un-marriageable and hence the infection is allowed to grow. The Maharaj Kumar's second wife, Sugandha, is one more victim, first to Queen Karmavati's designs against the Maharaj Kumar, and then to childbirth. Even these women affect to some extent the history of Mewar.

The one female character who does not fit into any of the above moulds is Bhootani Mata. As a priestess or at the best, a deputy of the all pervasive Devi, she appears as at once a malevolent and benevolent figure, out to fulfil the Maharaj Kumar's initial desire to kill Greeneyes. In fact, he attributes all the misfortunes of Mewar to her – the outbreak of cholera, the fire in which Kumkum Kanwar is killed, the attempted poisoning of the Princess, and so on. Both Bhootani Mata and Greeneyes are votaries of the gods, the one in the Tantric mode, the other in a spiritual, mystical form. Bhootani Mata openly claims to affect the course of events, while Greeneyes seems to do this unwittingly. Bhootani Mata appears also to be Kausalya's alter ego as she attempts to fulfil Kausalya's desire to get rid of the Princess. Of course, the Maharaj Kumar defeats them both at this attempt. His victory is actually the victory of the Princess, for who else could even claim that the heir apparent of Mewar not only tended to, but also washed and bathed his unfaithful wife during her attack of cholera?

VI

Cuckold is not merely the story of the Maharaj Kumar and his exploits. It is also a depiction of the social, cultural, political and sexual climate of the times. Within that climate, the women achieve some kind of satisfaction and self-awareness. The fusion of historical content and the novel form makes it possible for the text to look into aspects of human relationships and the impact of these all-too-human feelings on public events. Historical novels like those of Scott, Dumas, Bankimchandra and Kalki used history as a background for dealing with the private lives and aspirations of the makers of history. With the more recent interest in alternate modes of historiography, the focus in novels like *Cuckold* is on the invisible but strong forces that subtly work these histories – not merely in political terms but also in social, cultural and religious terms. It is this that gives the novel so much space to look at the women characters and the ways in which they move out of or get further trapped in the socially generated confines of the age.

Works Cited

Carr, E. H. *What is History?* Middlesex: Penguin, 1961.

Gangopadhyay, Sunil. *First Light*. Trans. Aruna Chakravarti. (*Pratham Alo* in Bengali, 1996). New Delhi: Penguin Books, 2001.

———. *Those Days*. Trans. Aruna Chakravarti. (*Sei Samay* in Bengali, 1981). New Delhi: Penguin Books, 1987.

Nagarkar, Kiran. *Cuckold*. New Delhi: HarperCollins, 1997.

Nair, Vasudevan M. T. *Second Turn*. Trans. P. K. Ravindranath. (*Randamoozham* in Malayalam, 1977). Madras: Macmillan (Modern Indian Novels in Translation Series), 1997.

Rajanarayanan, Ki. *Gopallapurathu Makkal*. 1990. 2nd ed. Sivagangai: Selma, 1993.

Ray, Pratibha. *Yajnaseni: The Story of Draupadi*. Trans. Pradeep Bhattacharya. (*Yajnaseni* in Oriya nd). New Delhi: Rupa, 1995.

Cuckold: A Different Paradigm Of Romance?

Manjula Padmanabhan

My aim, in this paper, will be to (a) examine the romantic relationships described in Kiran Nagarkar's historical epic novel *Cuckold*, (b) present my claim that the author uses a different paradigm for romance from the one typically favoured in modern novels and finally, (c) to make a connection between romantic paradigms and religious faith. My aim will be to describe what I call the monotheist ideal of romance and to suggest that Nagarkar's *Cuckold* represents a heresy within that belief-system.

This first section of this paper presents a few general observations about romance. What I present here will be my personal observations rather than an overview of the opinions that have already been expressed on this subject. The second section deals with romance as it appears in *Cuckold*, keeping in mind the observations made in the first section.

A Few General Observations Regarding the Element of Romance in Novels

Let us look beyond the etymology of the word "romance" – which will only reveal that its root lies in the French word for "novel" – to ask ourselves what our instant associations are when we hear the word spoken today. There will be few speakers of English for whom the image of a couple, preferably young and heterosexual, will not be the first one to appear. More precisely the word refers to a fanciful rather than a strictly factual record of reality. If we accept the source of the French word as being a reference to Rome, then there is certainly a shade of derision, a sly political comment and a lack of seriousness tucked into the word's meaning.

For the purpose of this paper, however, I am going to use this word to mean specifically the liaisons between people, most often men and women, most often aimed in the direction of sexual conjunctions of one sort or another, that are so frequently to be found in novels. There are many excellent novels in which the element of romance is missing or relegated to such a minor role as to be inconsequential: *Hunger*, *Travels with My Aunt*, *Midnight's Children*, *The Trotternama*, *Catch-22* to name just a few. But the number of those that use romance as a binding cord snaking in and out of all the other elements that make up the substance of a novel is so much larger that an exhaustive demonstration is not really necessary. I will refer only to three well known examples.

In *Anna Karenina*, for instance, the delicate courtship flickering between Leo and Kitty performs this function in the background of the tragic romance that is the subject of the novel. In my view it is especially bold that a novel which focuses so acutely upon one romance should use another romance as its binding cord – and in such a way that we are soothed by the sweet wholesomeness of the one as it winds its way around the dark surging mass of the other.

In Mervyn Peake's *Gormenghast* trilogy, the affair between Steerpike and Lady Fuchsia, so attenuated that it frequently vanishes altogether from sight, nevertheless provides a continuous element between the sudden shifts of time and scale in the tremendous first two books. The removal of Fuchsia from the narrative at the end of the second book blocks the momentum of the series to the extent that the third book functions less as a sequel to its predecessors than as a long-drawn-out epilogue to the whole story. In John Fowles' *The Magus*, the relentlessness with which the protagonist's lady tormentors alternately pursue and abandon him is the blood and guts of the tale, as we – and the protagonist – try to understand the reasons why he has been so strangely and repeatedly duped in love.

In these three novels, as in countless others, even though the romance is not the main focus of the narrative, it acts as an interior light within the complex construction of the plot. We are given little bobbing reminders of its presence and prevented from forgetting that it's there as, all the while, we are drawn through the twists and turns and ante-rooms of the main story.

It is not hard to see how romance maintains this position of eminence. One obvious reason is that it is an element about which even the most mundane reader can be expected to have some first-hand knowledge.

An author may refer to many worlds of experience of which the reader might know nothing, and in which the author might take the lead in providing views and expositions. A reader may allow herself to be beguiled by what she does not know or repelled by what she may not want to know or feel excluded by cultural inputs that she cannot have knowledge of. But in the matter of romance, the reader and the author are on par. No author can have an absolute knowledge that she is more skilled or experienced in love than her audience. No reader can be presumed to be so ignorant as to know nothing of love.

The reader enters the world of an author's perceptions like a tourist in a foreign land, with his ability to read as his only passport. If he finds nothing recognisable or familiar, there is certainly a great chance that he will not settle anywhere within that other country. However, if a reader begins to trust an author's romantic intuition, the chances are, he will be much more inclined to accept whatever else that author wishes to reveal.

Familiarity alone, however, would not explain the pleasure with which most readers pursue the romantic element in a novel. From the moment that two characters who are of an eligible age and configuration to enter into a romantic partnership are introduced, a certain pleasurable tension is set up in the reader. The fact that the pattern is predictable is a part of its charm: it is like a favourite melody that can be listened to repeatedly, with variations.

The foundation of a reader's pleasure is, in my belief, the reader's own knowledge of love and romance. If so – that is, if readers tend to enjoy the romantic themes in a novel exactly because they present a dim mirror, perhaps with lively embellishments, of their own internal world – then it may explain why there is a certain limit upon the extent to which variations are attractive. A reader needs to feel included in the world-picture of the novel – because this is the domain of the familiar. If even in this area she feels excluded, then there is a risk that she will not accept the novelist as her guide through the rest of the narrative, for fear that she will be led into places she may not wish to visit.

In this context it may be worth noting the importance of the theme of monogamous love in literature. Whatever its importance in human social arrangements may be, it appeals to readers of literature in part because it offers a comforting and perhaps unconscious back-reference to the One True God. Those who would believe there is a single divine entity who rules over the heavens and the earth can be easily impressed by the notion that there is a reflection of this unity in the lives of mortals, in the form of the One True Lover. In my opinion, the fervor with which lovers pursue their romantic goal, the intensity of their devotions, the worshipful form their love takes – all of these are indications that there is a considerable mapping of reference points between religious experience and definitions of romance.

There can be few authors who do not know that readers look forward to the love element in a novel with enjoyment. Nevertheless, a love story within a larger narrative can have the effect of reducing all other elements to insignificant details along the path of describing how character A manages to wrestle character B into bed. An example of such a novel, in my opinion, is *The English Patient*. The entire panorama of World War II is revealed in the end to have served merely as a backdrop to the cosmic forces released by the romantic conjunction of the two primary characters. In my view, this use of the horror of war reduces the scale of reality to a type of bedroom farce played out across deserts and battlefields rather than drawing rooms and boudoirs. By contrast, in *Cuckold*, the love story forms a vital component of the plot and metaphysics of the novel, without dominating or trivialising the narrative as a whole.

In the books of many male authors, romance or its more prosaic cousin, sex, is often the only heading under which women enter a narrative. This trend may be changing as more women writers enter the field, but I think I am on reasonably firm ground when I claim that it is rare for a young female character to appear within the pages of a novel without acting as a herald for romance. Male characters are permitted to fall in love now and then, but their trajectory across the field of love is accorded less direct attention than that of the female lead in a romance. Female characters will often define their entire existence in a novel by the manner in which they resolve the romantic tensions of their fictional lives. Rumer Godden is one of the few authors who has memorably used female characters as the lead elements in situations which are not strictly romantic – *Black Narcissus* is one example, *Kingfishers Catch Fire* is another. One reason that she is able to depart from the norms is that she uses convents as the locale of her stories. In a sense, in her novels, her female characters aim their potential for romance towards something other than sex.

Sex may be fundamental to romance but the two are by no means Siamese twins in literature. Those authors who weave a sexual theme through their books are often careful to make their separations: sexual activity is intensely physical, while romance can transcend the typical boundaries of time and space to create immortals of anyone who presumes to scale its loftier peaks. Though none of us is immortal, true lovers can use their hearts as reference points to triangulate infinity.

THE ROMANTIC ELEMENT IN *CUCKOLD*

From the title alone we know that this novel defines itself around the bonds of marriage and fidelity. We are presented with the following situation: a man, the Maharaj Kumar, is married to a woman, the Princess, who loves Another. Such a situation has its typical outcomes – either the man will forsake the woman or the woman will forsake the lover, or she and the lover will both forsake the man. Usually, such situations are not conducive to strict romance: a man is called a cuckold specifically because of his wife's sexual infidelity. Once a situation has been defined in such earth-bound terms, it is unusual for it to pass out of the loop of the physical and up into the metaphysical. Most often in stories about sexual infidelity, there is little momentum beyond that of retribution, revenge, atonement and perhaps a renewal of conjugal vows.

In all these particulars, *Cuckold* is very unusual. Not

only is the narrative, which is intensely romantic, experienced through the perceptions of a man rather than a woman, but from the very outset, it is clear that he defines his entire being through several different channels of love not just the one. It also becomes clear that despite the title of the novel, his wife's infidelity will by no means remain coarsely material. The crux of the story is startling: the Princess's lover is divine. Thus, the entire plane of the narrative is elevated beyond the mortal, and the Maharaj Kumar's jealousy operates on an unexpected dimension. Instead of being a pathetic figure, fit only for ridicule, he acquires a heroic-tragic aura: his becomes a fate shared only by mythological figures. He cannot hope to succeed against a god and yet his love, his forbearance, his struggle to keep his pride intact – all acquire a grandeur that necessarily surpasses the human sphere.

Even before we are introduced to the wife, however, we meet the young girl, Leelawati. As she is just a nine-year-old child when she makes her first appearance (6) and as the Maharaj Kumar does not have the persona of a villain, we cannot suspect that he has designs on her and yet ... the faint musk of romance is evident from the first moment of her introduction. The familiarity with which she addresses the Prince, the way she "jumps straight into (his) lap" (6), and the tenderness with which he regards her – all these are the signs of a precursor to love which, in literary terms, is unlikely to go unexamined.

Then again, two pages after we are introduced to the Maharaj Kumar's faithless wife, we see him bulding up a relationship with Sunheria, the *dhobi*'s wife (13). One page later, he trysts with the river Gambhiree, whom he addresses as he would a lover. A hundred and twenty-six pages later, we know that he was introduced to sex by his dai, Kausalya. These women (if I can be permitted to include the river under that heading) remain at the romantic focus of the prince's life all through the book. His second wife, Sugandha, appears only on page 460 and she does not offer the others much competition.

The Maharaj Kumar lives in an era when no relationship can exist without its trailing strings of social class, of clan allegiance, of history. Yet, as he shows us, repeatedly, there is one level of emotions reserved for form and another given over to feeling. He is the hero of this book and yet, for all his introspection, his gaze is ever elsewhere – unlike other heroes, in other books, who rarely attend to the needs and passions of others with any degree of involvement, so tender is their involvement with their own needs.

ROMANCE IN *CUCKOLD* COMPARED WITH ROMANCE IN OTHER NOVELS

Fictional heroes, unlike fictional heroines, are often indulged if they have more than one beloved – but not if they have them simultaneously. A man who has sex with more than one woman at a time or who professes his love for more than one woman at a time is considered, both in fiction and in real life, to be a cad or a playboy or a gigolo – depending on the scale of his indiscretions and the type of material benefit he may get from them. But the Maharaj Kumar in no way resembles these characters. We are never given an opportunity to dislike him: he is presented not only as a hero but an extremely likeable one.

One of the sources of his charm is that he is permitted to express a feminine dimension in his personality, without ever relinquishing his claim to masculinity. In this, he is utterly different to the typical or even atypical Western hero, who can rarely let his guard down without in some way being harmed – the Biblical example of Samson and Delilah is echoed in countless stories where a man is undone by his weakness towards a woman. By contrast, here we see the Maharaj Kumar, a warrior, a ruler, a manipulator of the affairs of state yet willing to acknowledge without the least blush, his dependence upon the women in his life. His love for them does not incapacitate him nor does he feel the need to defend his love of several women with arguments – indeed, he does not acknowledge that he is unusual in having several lovers. His world does not know of another way to be – or so we are led to understand, from his lack of guile or guilt.

In his pleasure in women, he shows too, that he can express characteristics which are typically associated with femininity. He is vulnerable; he is sentimental; he is loyal – though he clearly loves more than one woman, he loves each one in her own special niche and to each one, in her niche, his love is precise and faithful. He is moved by music, he enjoys good food and he has a fine and discerning eye for beauty, evidenced by the quality of attention he pays to every detail of his environment, from the fine texture of a Dhaka muslin to an antelope as it drinks unhurriedly at sunset. He is even given an opportunity to see himself in the guise of a woman when, at Holi, he and the Princess exchange clothes. Briefly, he even turns into a woman:

> His feet had begun to shrink and worse, he no longer minded the bangles on his arms. He had the distinct feeling that he had grown small and delicate. If he had been horrified at the thought of masquerading as a transvestite, why was he not incensed that his step had become light and his torso lissom? Or were the reasons for this quite simple and banal? That at heart he was a woman or perhaps all human beings are really bisexual? What was the source of a person's sex? Did clothes play a role in it? Could he really get under a woman's skin merely by wearing a *ghaghra* and *choli*? All these years he had believed that the only difference between men

> and women was their bodies. But were their minds made differently too? What does it mean to be a woman? Is it long, flowing hair tied in a plait or knot, is it the fullness in the breasts, is it patience and nurturing as much as strength and intelligence? What is the most complete and sufficient idea that mankind has had? God. And yet if you assign sex to God, then he or she too becomes finite and incomplete. (495-96)

In this passage, Nagarkar has looked straight into the heart of the difference between Western and Eastern modes of sexuality: whereas the Western insists on a strict distinction being maintained between male and female, in the Eastern, a blurred line is understood to be a sign of spiritual transcendence. Not only that: the Maharaj Kumar does not attempt to unseat his rival in love. The best he can do is to pretend to be the rival, for however long he can succeed in his deception, at least in terms of what his wife believes. For himself, he knows that he will never win against the divinity who occupies the central position in his wife's heart and soul. And he accepts this fact, while continuing to offer his devotion to his wife, alongside the devotions he offers to other women.

In the plurality of his favours, it seems to me he offers a vision of romance that is rarely seen, that of a range of loves available to the human type. For who can deny that there are different registers of love? The insistence upon the One True Love – how many human beings can sincerely maintain that they have encountered this ideal in their lives? And to what extent ought they to try?

It seems to me that in offering a vision of love as a quality that can be portioned out in more than one direction at the same time, Nagarkar is hinting at a completely different concept to the one that is ordinarily met with in literature. I need only refer back to the three novels mentioned at the beginning of this paper, *The Gormenghast Trilogy*, *Anna Karenina* and *The Magus*, to show how important the idea of the One True Love is. In each of these three very different novels, each belonging to different periods and styles of literature, the thread of romance that winds around the narratives in each is obsessed with fidelity.

In the trilogy, Steerpike's ambition conflicts with his love for the Lady Fuchsia – in that sense, his ambition plays the role of a jealous rival for his heart's attention. When it prevails, he loses his One True Love as well as, ultimately, his own life. In *The Magus* the entire plot turns on the axis of the hero's fickle heart and makes it, in one sense, the instrument of his torment. Even though, in the end, we are introduced to what appears to be a sect of people who embrace the concept of multiple relationships, still, the novel is centred around the punishment that might be meted out to a lover who is careless with another person's heart.

In *Anna Karenina*, poor Anna is consumed by the heat of her passion; her suicide in the end is only a kindness she does to herself and to her readers, who would, I suspect, much rather see her dead than living under the shade of her lost love. It would be unthinkable to suggest that Anna might do well to divert her devotion in several different directions. She would surely have been incensed and insulted! It is not regarded appropriate to the station of lovers to have place for any number greater than one, within their hearts.

Yet in *Cuckold*, for all that transpires, for all the calamities, catastrophes and tragedies, the tale is essentially one of great joy in the bonds of love. Instead of being undone by his passions, or having regrets for his choice of paramour, the Maharaj Kumar seeks them out, finds succour and comfort, finds a meaning for life through the women whom he loves.

In this, Nagarkar shows himself to be far more bold and more innovative than many other authors writing today. For instance, unlike even the more forward-thinking women writing today, he creates a lead female character who is presented as a traditional Rajput princess yet does not show the least inclination to bear children. She does not so much as suffer the slightest pang of guilt or desire: she loves on a plane beyond reproduction. And in this, she is all but unique in the annals of literature, because Eastern or Western, a heroine is expected to find, in motherhood, her One True Vocation. Women in fiction who do not bear children, or desert their children, tend to be expendable or mysterious – Lady Fuchsia and Anna Karenina both die young and in *The Magus*, the beguiling twins who lead the hero on to his distraction are never quite real: we do not see them in the context of time, only as exquisite sexual foils for the hero. Few heroines are ever permitted to vocalise anti-child sentiments. The very least that is expected of a woman character in a novel is that she provide proof of a maternal instinct, even if she has no children of her own.

The Maharaj Kumar's Princess is, in this context of other heroines, almost masculine in the purity of her devotion to her divine lover. Against her example, other female characters seem curiously uni-dimensional and materialistic: all the lights and sounds of their love-making can be revealed, in the long run, to be features of their campaign to secure reliable mates for their nests. For the Princess, by contrast, there is only the lover. She has no ambition beyond her yearning to be joined with him.

NAGARKAR'S USE OF ROMANCE IN *CUCKOLD*

Nagarkar's use of romance in *Cuckold* is unique. It is not, for instance, the single hook which keeps us following the course of the story, because there are several potential romances to distract the Prince. At the same time, since the entire book is filled with the aura of love, there is a sense of intoxication awaiting, just around the next corner of the plot ... all the way through the book. So it offers the reader a continuous banquet of sensations and emotions. It addresses love in its familiar guise, in ways that any reader may have experience of – by referring to the yearning of a man for a particular woman's attention, to the fever of jealousy, to the pleasure of conquest by stealth, to the pleasure of being pleasured by women who give of themselves with generosity – and yet it also offers up all of this in a curiously semi-divine context. We are mortals, all of us: but through the Prince's reflections we become privy to the movements of a god in our midst. Whether we believe what the Maharaj Kumar tells us is left entirely upto the reader's own beliefs and own religious convictions. But the telling itself has tremendous warmth and power, because it is clear that the Prince believes in its utter veracity.

THE ONE TRUE LOVER COMPARED WITH THE ONE TRUE GOD

As already stated earlier, the insistence in romantic novels upon the ideal of the One True Lover represents a straying of the ideal of monotheism into the path of romance. Let me put this differently: the belief in One True God colours the perceptions of those who are brought up within monotheist cultures, so that they accept the concept of One True Lover more easily. The countless examples of monotheists who stray from the path of strict monogamy are only a sign of the obsession with monogamous relationships: in the errors of the many, the rectitude of the few is made all the more remarkable.

This is not to say that it isn't immensely comforting

and stabilising to think that there is only ever one source and object of love in a person's life, just as it is comforting and stabilising to think that there is only one divine sovereign over all the estates of reality. It may even be the truth – and yet, the fact that there are other paradigms of religious belief, as there are other paradigms of love, leads to the conclusion that however satisfying monotheism or monogamy may be, they are not the only ways to be.

Cuckold, I believe, offers a fascinating glimpse into the mindset of a man who belongs to a world that has not yet understood the power of monotheist ideals. The Maharaj Kumar witnesses the dawn of the Moghul era in India but his world is still intact, with its many gods and its multiple channels of reality. He has only the faintest inkling of the changes that his world is about to face – it isn't just an issue of thrones and power, it isn't just a matter of different names of god – it is a change of fundamental perceptions of reality. From the many names of god, his world is going to encounter the One Name of Allah. From multiple births and reincarnations, the concept of a single heaven and a single life are going to be introduced and enforced. The flexible, mutable universe of a faith which has no single source, prophet or text-book, is about to be challenged by the power of a unified purpose and a single written code of rules.

For better or for worse, this is the ethos that we in India, five centuries later, continue to live within. We are bound by written rulebooks and constitutions, and we know their worth from the point of view of international treaties and courts of law. But we are also aware, many of us, that these rules and regulations, however useful, do not hold sway over the vastness of reality. At the heart of all reality, there is an awesome Uncertainty which no textbook physics or handbook of rules can set aside. It is to this heart that *Cuckold* makes its appeal: to all that cannot be explained or rationalised, to all that is outside the power of mere laws and convenience.

Cuckold disturbs the universe that we are used to, by reminding us that there are other systems of accounting for reality than just the one. But it is not malicious or destructive in its purpose, in the same way that we can understand the binary system of counting numbers, which uses an utterly different notation to the familiar decimal system, without undermining mathematics as we know it.

Cuckold points our minds towards a more refined and complex understanding of reality, by reminding us that there can be beauty in diversity – and beauty in knowing that we make choices between the options offered to us. The very last pronouncement the Prince makes at the end of the book is to tell the reader that his heart has always belonged wholly – he makes the point of telling us that he includes all the worlds of reality – to the Princess. He makes this statement rather in the way of a Catholic, who has wandered far from the faith of his origin but permits himself to receive Extreme Unction on his death-bed, renouncing all other faiths and gods in that final moment.

Is this because in death we do return from the multiplicity of all our moments of Being to the final, singular moment that precedes the beginning of the infinity of un-Being? Is it because Indian philosophical thought has always recognised the One behind the many? Is it because the world of the future has already caught up with the Prince, always a forward-thinking and exceptionally precocious man? Is it because it somehow deeply satisfies all of us to believe that there is after all, only one anchor that really matters in life, despite the many that we may use while drifting abroad the ocean of reality, and that is the anchor of our own breath? Is singularity the final rule, only because there is only one beginning and one end for each of us?

Cuckold is a novel that invites us to ask these questions, while showing us that we need not be distracted by the answers we might find for them. It is a book intensely of the present but set in the past, a book that inhabits the eternal NOW! of historical truth. It presents a vision of romance that we are rarely permitted to savour, and it does so without threatening damnation and retribution as a consequence. It offers many possibilities within the pages of one book: infinity trapped on the surface of a single sphere.

The Local and the Universal in the Novels of Kiran Nagarkar

George Dardess and Peggy Rosenthal

The way we have approached the question of the local and the universal in Nagarkar's novels has been by asking why and how they speak powerfully to us, North American literary scholars as we are. The danger of this approach is that it risks literary hegemonism of a blatant kind, implying that the "North American" and the "universal" are synonymous. Such is not our intention! Yet, we can't presume to answer for readers beyond our own locality. If we can explain the capacity of Nagarkar's novels to extend their meanings from the locally Indian to the locally North American, we will have come as close to indicating their universal dimension as is perhaps possible. Such an outcome would please us very much.The question of universality in Nagarkar's fiction arises in the first place only because his novels seem to lack those narrative "hooks" by which Indian novels typically grab North American readers. Unlike Salman Rushdie, for example, Nagarkar doesn't focus on the plight of emigres from the subcontinent. And while he often, especially in his earlier novels, *Seven Sixes are Forty-Three* and *Ravan & Eddie*, employs modernist and postmodernist narrative devices (narrative instability and fragmentation in the first, comic extravagance and mixing of genres in the second), he does so with restraint; his novels never become theoretical or self-referential. Nor, on the other hand, does Nagarkar adopt more conservative novelistic practices, as Vikram Seth does, for example, in *A Suitable Boy*, which relies on Jane Austen's comedy of manners approach. It is true that Nagarkar's third and by far most mature novel, *Cuckold*, suggests, to North American ears, a blending of Western prototypes: the self-conscious playfulness of *Tristam Shandy*, for example, and the epic range and even something of the historical outlook of *War and Peace*; yet these resemblances seem adventitious, so strongly centred is this novel on specifically Indian cultural concerns. In short, the novels seem about and for Indians. Why then have they drawn us North Americans in?

The answer has to do, first, with the attractiveness of the narrative voice in the novels, and especially in Nagarkar's most recent novel, *Cuckold*. The voice of *Cuckold* is that of the first-person narrator, the Maharaj Kumar of the Rajput kingdom of Mewar. This voice reflects the partly comic, partly tragic frustrations of the Maharaj Kumar's role as heir-apparent. But it is also the voice of the third-person intercalated chapters where the subject is the stormy love triangle among the Maharaj Kumar, the Little Saint (his wife), and the "cuckolding" god, Krishna. The third-person voice is so close to the Maharaj Kumar's as almost to be his, but the distance suggests, though it never asserts, an omniscience outside his own – so is this Krishna speaking? True to the novel's playfulness, a playfulness whose hidden source and model is Krishna himself, we never know for sure. Yet, "playfulness" does justice neither to Krishna's devastating elusiveness in the intercalated chapters (if that is Krishna who speaks to us there!) nor to the Maharaj Kumar's growing complexity, resourcefulness, and self-understanding as we hear those qualities develop through the course of the novel. Whatever the voice's source, in the Maharaj Kumar himself or in the god, the voice itself is marvellously sensitive to physical and psychological detail, and especially to incongruity. It is nimble and self-aware and poised. It does not indulge in cleverness or self-consciousness for its own sake. It is too alive to the Maharaj Kumar's developing moral sense for that, too alertly engaged in both diagnosing and correcting the self-destructiveness of the wider political world where the Maharaj Kumar finds himself precariously placed in a position both of great power and of great weakness. What might seem "playfulness" for a god is deadly business for the ambivalent devotee. From what we've just said, it's apparent that the attractiveness of *Cuckold's* narrative voice can't be accounted for by its verbal qualities alone. The attractiveness is derived also from the voice's capacity to challenge us to imagine and embrace a significant, perhaps even a "universal," thematic. This thematic has to do with Nagarkar's effort to depict for us a culture afflicted by violence and manipulativeness, in tension with a yearning to discover an alternative.The self-destructive side of the dilemma emerges in Nagarkar's earliest fiction, in the very first scene of *Seven Sixes are Forty-Three*. As we open the novel, it immediately hits us in the face with a brutal wife-beating that we learn is the domestic ritual of this married pair. But this time the ritual takes a fatal turn. The wife threatens to set fire to herself. Her drunken husband goads her on:

> "So who's stopping you, you stupid bitch? Go on and do it if you have the fucking guts. What are you waiting for?" he sneered.He stared vaguely at her. She poured a bottle of kerosene over herself, muttering, "I'll teach you a lesson, just wait, you'll be sorry."She shuddered as the cold kerosene seeped through the folds of cloth and touched her skin. She lit a match and held

> it to a corner of her sari. Yellow flames sprang up. Some red, some orange, blue at the edges .... She had begun to scream. At the top of her voice. Scream and run from wall to wall. Round the room. And the flames went round and round too, like a whirlwind. She tried to embrace him. Then he moved. Ran. "Get off me, you bitch. Don't come near me ..."(2)

He escapes the fiery whirlwind of her embrace, and permanently, too, as she dies of her burns. But the scene doesn't die from our minds or from Nagarkar's fiction. That image of a pair of lover-enemies locked ritually in a reach toward self-destructive embrace will, as we'll see, be replayed.

In *Seven Sixes*, the violence we witness is domestic, shocking because it takes over and consumes the relationship that should be most tender, that between husband and wife. Nagarkar gradually enlarges the scope or site of the self-destructiveness in *Ravan & Eddie*, moving here from the domestic battleground to conflict between generations and social groups. In *Cuckold* he enlarges the perspective even further, situating the problem of violence in political, historical, and spiritual spheres. Interestingly, this enlargement does not lead to a diffusion of narrative focus but to an even firmer concentration and integration, as Nagarkar finds forms increasingly well-suited to express the full breadth of his engagement with his developing moral questions: What is the nature of this violence? and, how may it be transformed? These questions are implicit in the textures of each one of his novels. They are not framed and addressed directly. That is because Nagarkar, like any genuine artist (*pace* postmodernist claims to the contrary), has not a theoretical bone in his body. Theory is left to Nagarkar's readers, those of us who toss in the broad, turbulent wake of his novels, doing our best to examine the design of the froth of each novel's passage by one light or another. An especially helpful light, we've found, is the analysis of the dynamics of violence offered by the French literary critic and anthropologist Rene Girard. (And yes, this counts for us as a "universalising" tendency in Nagarkar's art, that it lends itself to Western anthropological insight.) [We draw on all of Girard's work, but particularly *Deceit, Desire and the Novel* (1961), *Violence and the Sacred* (1972), and *Things Hidden since the Foundation of the World* (1978).]

According to Girard, all human cultures require violence in the form of scapegoating in order to channel and sacralise the "imitative desire" that otherwise threatens to tear those cultures apart – or that never allows the cultures to be formed in the first place. "Imitative desire" is not desire for an object as such (i.e. a necessity of life). It is instead a desire aroused and inflamed by rivalry alone. It issues in mutual annihilation unless a scapegoat can be found upon which – or upon whom – the violence of rivalrous antagonism can be vented. Violence, focused and exhausted upon an appropriate victim, is thus a precondition of culture. What begins as a frenzy of mutual resentment is transformed by victimage of the "other" into the camaraderie of the lynch mob. Appeased and unified, the mob venerates the murdered victim as a god for its peace-bringing efficacy, a ritualised act that permits the mob's return to a "civilised" stability. When this stability is shaken, as it inevitably will be, by subsequent spasms of imitative desire, the mob forms again, cloaking itself in its sacrificial religious rituals, so as to be able to vent the renewed violence on new victims without compunction or self-doubt. And the cycle continues under the guidance of powerful myths which explain and justify the bloodletting as what is due to the gods. Yet, Girard points out the special agony of modern cultures which have lost or are in the process of losing faith in the controlling and sacralising myths. Such myths protect the cultures from seeing their own actions through the eyes of their victims. For as soon as they see themselves through their victims' eyes, the entire sacralising system crumbles. The culture is delivered back to the chaos from which the sacralising system was meant to rescue it. In Girard's view, there is for modern cultures only one way out of this hopelessly self-destructive regression, and that is through the cross of Christ. This is because only here is the sacralising system exposed for the horror that it is; the crucifixion accounts make starkly clear the utter injustice of such victimage. The crucified Christ becomes "sacred," not by means of the scapegoating logic of the chief priest Caiaphas (who said, "It is expedient for us that one man should die for the people"), but by means of his resurrection. Yet, it is not just the victim himself who is freed from the sacrificial machinery by this divine intervention. The entire human race is offered this freedom as well, by identification through baptism in the new Christic humanity. Such, according to Girard, is the alternative that Christianity proposes. Nevertheless, this alternative is apparently not available for Indian culture. At least this is what is suggested at the conclusion of *Ravan & Eddie*, in a powerful passage that uncannily dramatises exactly what Girard means by "imitative desire." The passage describes the moment towards the end of the novel when the two boys, now nearly grown up and ready at last to wreak havoc beyond the confines of the world of the chawl (the "public housing" in which they have come of age), immediately lock together in eternal combat, mirroring a desire for nothing so much as the obliteration of the other in a paroxysm of unquenchable rivalry. All that will save them from murdering each other is the bonding that would occur if they could locate in time a suitable surrogate for their rage. Yet, so tightly woven are the strands of "imitative desire" around them that distraction from their goal of mutual annihilation seems impossible. The "circle" is complete.

We see how the reach for mutually self-destructive embrace has enlarged the compass of its significance in Nagarkar's imagination since that fiery whirlwind at the opening of *Seven Sixes*. Nagarkar's language in this passage from *Ravan & Eddie* is wonderfully evocative of the immediate situation. We are certainly imagining the furious flailing of two adolescent males at a particular time and place. But coming as it does nearly at the end of *Ravan & Eddie*, the passage gathers up into one almost comic symbol (we can see the cyclone of cartoon dirt with arms, heads, and fists protruding from it at intervals) the way of life exemplified by almost every other resident of the chawl. (The one exception is a club-footed girl whose tender offers of disinterested friendship Ravan ignores.) But the narrator also indicates, though with restraint, the broader applicability of the symbol (viz. "They had become the double helix that entwines the very essence of our lives.") For our purposes, however, the most interesting ramification of this testosterone-soaked pas de deux is its twisting of the Christian Gospel: "Perhaps this is what it means to be born again or twice-born." The reference, of course, is to the Gospel of John, where Jesus tells Nicodemus that "unless a person is born again, he or she cannot see the reign of God." But "the reign of God" is not simply the reverse of the world of imitative desire into which *Ravan and Eddie* have been baptised or "initiated." It is the complete transformation of that world. Tragically, – for *Ravan & Eddie*, though fiercely comic, hints constantly and darkly at human limitation and entrapment – the possibility of such transformation does not exist in this world, nominally Christian though Eddie's half of it is. We could say that the possibility does not exist because Nagarkar does not seriously engage it. The language from John is evoked only to be turned on its head. Evidently that language never did provide a serious challenge to Ravan and Eddie's world, for the narrator can reverse its meaning without a qualm. So when the narrator asserts, "The bonding of fear is greater than the throb and embrace of sex, illicit passion or love," the Christian alternative – "love" – has shrunk to one of a group of desperate illusions, along with "sex" and "illicit passion." Yet, if the Christian alternative to the problem of imitative desire isn't available – isn't even seriously to be considered, – what is left? For clearly *Ravan & Eddie* cries out for an escape from the *cul-du-sac* to which it leads. Put another way, Nagarkar must have felt that the circularity of Ravan's and Eddie's fate was intolerable: not only artistically so (since characters locked in syndromes of imitative desire cannot develop), but morally and spiritually as well. Ravan and Eddie, and their creator too, needed to break the grip of a "completeness that would not brook intrusion or interruption." The problem of imitative desire had to be re-imagined. Now, we are not claiming that Nagarkar phrased his problem in Girardian terms. What we do claim about Nagarkar is that, independently, in his own sphere as novelist, and from within an Indian context, he seized on the same issue perceived by Girard in the West: an issue that concerns us all, yes, "universally." Between the writing of *Ravan & Eddie* and *Cuckold*, the need to expand the range of the novel form forced itself upon Nagarkar as a moral, historical, and, ultimately, a spiritual challenge, since only through such an expansion could the central issue – what to say and do about imitative desire and its release in sacrificial violence – be addressed. The challenge was met by constructing a novel along what might seem at first old-fashioned lines: a novel emphasising moral development within a world-historical setting. The main character must be placed high enough within that setting to be effective within it; his decisions must have large effects. The character cannot belong to our era, not because people in earlier eras were less dominated than we are by the sorts of self-destructive appetites dramatised in *Ravan & Eddie*, but because (presumably) they were less sceptical of transcendental meaning, less hemmed in by post-modernist self-enclosure. Yet, though separated from our era by time and history, the character must sound like us, not using archaic language and other forms of distancing. He must be the sort of person we would have been, had we lived in his era. In that sense, *Cuckold* is anachronistic, but necessarily so. In this world, the character confronts structures of imitative desire that form the basis of the very kingdom he is next in line to inherit. He struggles against these structures, striving (ultimately unsuccessfully) to correct them. This struggle is carried out not only in the discharge of his duties as the Maharaj Kumar and in the conduct of his personal affairs, but also in his own heart, afflicted as it is by the enviousness that consumes the rest of the kingdom. The character's distinguishing feature is that he is lucidly conscious of this struggle even as he is victimised by it.

This consciousness is not merely a private attribute, as if the Maharaj Kumar were simply a more mature version of Ravan (or, Eddie). His victimage is transformed by an energy that comes from outside his and the novel's world: an energy that only one other character besides himself – his wife, the Little Saint – is capable, not simply of noting, but of (literally) embracing. It is the energy of Krishna. So here we have what we can call the spiritual answer to the problem of imitative desire which Nagarkar is posing in *Cuckold*. It is, of course, an eminently Hindu answer. But like all good answers, it serves to provoke further questions: First, What kind of answer is this? How persuasive is it, as "answer," within the context of the novel? Second, and more pointedly, for Westerners like us: How "universal" is the answer? Is it one that we can in some way embrace as well? Can people like us imagine what it means to have a god as a lover, and especially this god, Krishna? Does such a relationship offer even us hope in our dilemma – the dilemma of finding ourselves trapped, like Ravan and Eddie, within ever more tightly woven cycles of violent rivalry? Does Krishna offer an escape that transcends the age-old solution, the lynching of the "holy" victim? The genius of *Cuckold*, it seems to us, is to say, Yes, there is the possibility of an escape for all of you here, but this escape is no bail-out. It demands mortal risk and painful moral effort and an infinite love of play. It is an escape which more than tolerates, even invites rejection and active revolt. What it cannot tolerate is complacency, "business as usual." It demands a courtship of the most dramatically spontaneous kind, ranging over the gamut of human emotions, involving also the most ingenious exercises of reason, the boldest exhibitions of valour, the craftiest embrace of subterfuge, the most lavish outpourings of sexual and aesthetic desire, the greatest possible reticence, the deepest hiddenness, the most traceless invisibility. The escape is Krishna himself, whoever Krishna is, whoever he is not. Krishna is the loved one and the lover at the same time, as well as the song that is sung by the one to the other. Krishna is a desire for transcendence carnalised, flesh made and then unmade, as children play dress-up with their parents' clothing. Krishna is hide-and-seek with the forms of time. Krishna is the constant translation of what is into what appears to be. Krishna is an orgiastic instability evoked and governed by the god according to his own inscrutable laws: inscrutable only because our languages lack the suppleness to translate them. Within this world of fiercest play, which is the god himself, all human roles are relativised, turned into game. So powerful is this relativising process that even the rigid lineaments of imitative desire are sidelined often. That is because the object of imitation is no longer a mere human rival but the god himself. *Cuckold* is about the education of one like ourselves – yet, at the same time, as a 16th century heir apparent to the throne, decidedly and explicitly not like ourselves – in the ways of that devotion to Krishna which is *bhakti*. As educations go, it is anything but boring; it involves a continuous un-learning of all the rivalrous modes of thought and behaviour that dominate the Maharaj Kumar's world. The main un-learning the Maharaj Kumar faces is that of transcending the jealous rage of the cuckold, the rivalrous relationship that gives the book its title. The object of rivalry, at least as the Maharaj Kumar feels it at first, is his very own wife, the bride of Krishna, and the beloved poet of verses addressed to the god. And the rival is the god himself. Or, is his true rival his wife? and the object Krishna himself? The Maharaj Kumar tries at times to wrest Krishna from his wife's grasp, and, failing in that, even goes so far at one point as to impersonate the god, covering himself in blue paint so that he might cuckold the cuckolder. Yet, Krishna, as the source of all desire, utterly thwarts all efforts to bend him into a rivalrous circularity. That is because he is the soul of play. "Dynamic" and "protean" are adjectives the Maharaj Kumar uses of him early in the novel, where he is explaining why Krishna attracted him far more than the other gods, relatively stable figures upholding closed meanings and *status quo*. To pursue Krishna is to find that all aspects of human behaviour, even the worst, the most violent, even scapegoating itself, are made beautiful in artfulness. Much more than coyness is implied here, rather the upliftment of the human spirit from its imprisonment in literalisms and circularities. Metaphor is its medium, and indirection its behavioural norm. One makes oneself known not through what one asserts but through what one withholds. Human relations, in so far as they mirror (or, "imitate") this playfulness, are transformed, made beautiful. (We think of the playfulness between the Maharaj Kumar and Leelawati in the novel's early pages, a playfulness later crushed by the Maharaj Kumar's half-brother's envious spite.) *Cuckold* poses the special problem, however, of how *bhakti*, the all-embracing and embraced love of Krishna, could become political. It asks, Could play transform the self-destructive rivalries of the political realm? *Cuckold* shows, on the one hand tragically, that it could not. The Maharaj Kumar's efforts to reform the kingdom (its manners, its sewer systems, its means of conducting warfare) come to nothing; all memory of him is lost, while the Rajput empire presided over by his father is overthrown by the Moghul warlord, Babur. Yet, the tragic result is depicted with so many ambiguities that it is impossible not to agree with the Maharaj Kumar's father, when he says to the Maharaj Kumar that he is a "prophet before his time." The father is speaking here primarily of the Maharaj Kumar's "success" – the success which led directly to the Maharaj Kumar's downfall – in overcoming, with a minimum of casualties, the army of Gujarat led by Malik Ayaz. These pages are a brilliant illustration of the costs involved in bringing *bhakti* into a world not yet ready for it. What becomes poetry of unequivocal greatness in the hands of the Little Saint becomes the Maharaj Kumar's self-acknowledged "treachery" in sending 10,000 of Malik Ayaz's men to an ignoble, pitiable death in a quagmire. The treachery is not only to those men. It is as well a treachery to the "chivalric" code governing the conduct of warfare and politics throughout the known world. And it is a treachery which completely overrides both the brilliance of the Maharaj Kumar's Krishna-like subterfuges (his "playing" with the enemy in guerrilla warfare; his defensive strategy of "absence," as opposed to aggressive, "heroic" modes) and his successful protection of his own men from slaughter in futile imitation of the enemy's "proven classical strategies." The Maharaj Kumar pauses in his account of the battle – he has just killed a defenceless enemy soldier to prevent a weakening in his army's resolve to pursue the new strategies-in order to reflect on the consequences of his attempt at political *bhakti*:

> Deception, diplomacy, intrigue, prestidigitation, machination, all these and many small and great things, the Flautist had taught me, were the tricks of a king's dharma and trade. But where had I inherited this wanton cruelty from? I remembered then how the great warrior Arjun and his mentor, the Flautist – mine too till a few years ago – had burnt the whole of the Khandava forest and all its inhabitants without cause or provocation. It was one of the strangest episodes in the *Mahabharata*, one that I could not understand, nor make sense of, try as I might. Perhaps this is the point the great epic is trying to make, that life is not explicable, nor does it pass the test of reason; that some, if not much of it, is meaningless. No amount of culture and civilization can subdue or hide the wanton violence in man. (232-33)

Rene Girard would say of the last line that culture cannot hope to "subdue the wanton violence" it continually produces, if it is to be culture as we know it at all. To believe that it could, would be like imagining that a process could turn itself inside out, become its own contradiction. The Gujaratis and everyone else "universally" need their pogroms and bloodlettings in order to free themselves of a mutual hatred so strong as to swallow up every living person in its vortex. It is expedient for them and for us that one man – or one army or one nation – should die for the people. So, yes, life is "meaningless." Or, at least "much of it" is: the part that isn't has been embraced by the god.

That embrace grows tighter the more one tries to escape it. That is why the Maharaj Kumar's claim to have dismissed his divine mentor "a few years ago" cannot be taken literally. Nothing can be taken literally by those caught up in *bhakti*. Krishna thrives in absence, in negation. He is never more present than when rejected. In terms of the novel, Krishna becomes ever more subtly involved in the Maharaj Kumar's fate as the latter's "failure" becomes clear: his rejection and near death at the hands of a mob as he approaches home, ostensibly in triumph; his subsequent trial for treason; his marginalisation at court; his loss of his father's always uncertain favour; his ineffectuality in influencing the course of events that lead to the eventual overthrow of the kingdom by the Moghul invader, Babur; his apparent abandonment by the Little Saint at the novel's end. The piling-up of these "failures" is accompanied, however, by an ever-deepening understanding of their causes. But what use that understanding, one might ask, when so little can be done, even with Krishna's help, to reverse them? We ask this question with greater urgency, knowing as we do the ultimate failure: the fact that the Maharaj Kumar is a historical cipher. As Nagarkar informs us in the novel's "Afterword," the Maharaj Kumar "is a person about whom we know nothing but the fact that he was born, married and died." What can allegiance to Krishna mean when the outcome is near total erasure from memory? Or, to put the matter in the Girardian terms we have been employing, what sort of "answer" to the problem of imitative desire is this, that the protagonist seems so clearly defeated by the cultural forces which his faithfulness to Krishna (a faithfulness not diminished by rejection and backsliding) was meant to overcome? And why assume that such an "answer" was proposed in the first place, since the Maharaj Kumar's entire struggle is merely a figment of the novelist's imagination?"Merely a figment of the novelist's imagination": if this novel (or any great novel) teaches us anything, it is to be very wary of such literalness, such naivete in assuming that "facts" can be disengaged from the imagining of them. For the "fact" is that the Maharaj Kumar does exist, in the novelist's mind first, and then – because we are talking about true art – in our own. The Epilogue to *Cuckold* brilliantly demonstrates this passing-on of imagined reality. Here, for the first time, we get what sounds like a certifiable outsider's voice, one that picks up the story after we hear the Maharaj Kumar for the last time, pursued by Prince Vikramaditya's assassins and mulling over his next move. As ever he is full of contradictory motives. Rush toward the waiting arms of Leelawati? Yes! No! "But there is only one woman for me, It is not Leelawati and it is not Kausalya. It is my wife. I will follow her to Brindaban, to Mathura, to the gates of hell, even to heaven if the gods will have me." After this burst of romantic bravura, the voice of the Epilogue enters to sort through the rumors of what did "actually" happen. Did he perish at the hands of his step-brother's (and rival's) henchmen? Did he betake himself to Leelawati after all? Or to the Little Saint? The reader may want to imagine it that way. But he or she needs to be careful!

"The fourth version seemed to suggest something more complicated." In this version, clearly the one we are teased into entertaining, the Maharaj Kumar makes good on a veiled threat voiced just previously, to "settle scores with someone in the temple." The "someone" is Krishna. In this fourth version, the Maharaj Kumar approaches the statue of the Flautist there, drawing his sword in order to hack off the statue's head. But he hears a voice: "How long will you nurse this enmity? How long will you fight this personal war? And to what purpose? Do you not know that you and I are one?" The Maharaj suspects Krishna of "equivocating," of saying (as usual) whatever it takes to get out of a tight spot. "Wasn't that one of the reasons the Maharaj Kumar had thought him one of the greatest statesmen of all time and hoped the people of Mewar would learn the art of diplomacy and war from him?" The Maharaj Kumar becomes of two minds himself. Believe what he has heard? Or, seek retribution?

We are back to the final scene in *Ravan & Eddie*. In

that novel, the two rivals, when confronting each other for the last time, do not hesitate to become locked in an endless spiral of imitative desire. But here the rivals are the god and the man. The man, true to his cultural conditioning, cannot sustain the weight of playful ambiguity and brings his sword down, determined to cut all doubleness in two. The god intervenes – or so the story goes! "Was his hand stayed in mid-air?" We are enticed to tell this part of the story ourselves, and thus to "disappear" into the tale. But we are given one further glimpse of "something more complicated." The Flautist embraces the Maharaj Kumar as the astonished assassins approach. "One minute the Maharaj Kumar was there, the next he had become invisible." Only a vestige is left: the end of the Maharaj Kumar's turban "showing from the left edge of the Flautist's chest." We can continue the story ourselves. It is what Krishna wants us to do. For this is why the Maharaj Kumar became "invisible," that he could become visible again in our imaginations. And as the Maharaj Kumar becomes visible, so does Krishna. Or perhaps it is Christ we see. Does not the fluttering turban recall the burial wrappings lying in Jesus' empty tomb? "He is not here," the angels say, in one telling of the story. In another telling, Mary Magdalene, having rushed to the tomb and found it empty, turns away, disconsolate. A man she takes to be the gardener asks why she is weeping and whom she is looking for. It is not the gardener. It is Jesus. Yes, it is dangerous to push parallels like these too far. But themes of deification, of disguise, and of the sheer openness to wonder in both the Gospel accounts and *Cuckold* are suggestively similar, to say the least. Nagarkar, of course, is not trying to proclaim a new religion, or even to revive an old one. He is trying to tell a story. But stories belong to their readers. And the story of *Cuckold*, if looked at through a Girardian prism, opens up hope for a transformation in the way we think about the besetting problem of imitative desire. No easy answer emerges from it all, any more than it does from the gospels. But *Cuckold* hints that despite the failure that seems to attend all efforts at political *bhakti*, we are still somehow surrounded by a divine music, one that sustains and lifts our hearts even when – perhaps especially when – we refuse to hear it. All that matters is that we engage, that we never allow ourselves to be ruled by the rote responses which are imitative desire's stock-in-trade. Suppleness, indirection, playfulness, infinite hope, infinite love: these are Krishna's gifts to a humanity otherwise entombed within its fixed rituals of sacrificial retaliation and exclusion. And so, thanks to Nagarkar, thanks to art, the Maharaj Kumar's very historical invisibility is not a nullity, not an absence, but a presence. It is a presence because it is a crucial and urgent question, not only for India, but also for us in the West, about our own violent stagnations as well as our own playful capacities to become partners of the god. Would that the question had less, much less, universality than it does.

Works Cited

Girard, Rene. *Deceit, Desire, and the Novel*. Baltimore: Johns Hopkins UP, 1976.

———. *Violence and the Sacred*. Baltimore: Johns Hopkins UP, 1979.

———. *Things Hidden Since the Foundation of the World*. Stanford: Stanford UP, 1994.

Notes on Contributors

ANIRUDH DESHPANDE is presently a Fellow at the Centre for Contemporary Studies, Nehru Memorial Museum and Library, Teen Murti Bhawan, New Delhi. He is currently researching audiovisual representations of Indian history in 20th century India. He holds a doctorate in modern history on British Military Policy in India, 1900-1945 from the Centre for Historical Studies (CHS), Jawaharlal Nehru University, New Delhi. He has co-edited with the late Professor Partha Sarathy Gupta in 2002 a volume of academic essays *The British Raj and its Indian Armed Forces, 1857-1939*. His monograph *Colonial Constraints and Declining Power: British Military Policy in India, 1900-1945* is shortly being brought out by Manohar. In the year 2000 as a national consultant historian for the United Nations Drug Control Programme (UNDCP) he wrote a scientific paper on opium production in India and its regulation by the colonial and post-colonial Indian state.

C. T. INDRA is Professor and Head, Department of English, University of Madras. She was a Fulbright Post-Doctoral Scholar at Harvard and the University of California at Santa Barbara. Her area of research is literary criticism and theory. Her publications include *Practical Criticism* (1990) (with Prof. V. S. Seturaman and T. Sriraman), *Exploring Deconstruction* (1998) (with Kathleen Wheeler), *Teaching Poetry* (1999) and *Post-Coloniality: Reading Literature* (2000) (with Meenakshi Shivraman). Her current interest is Translation Studies and her translation of the play *The Legend of Nandan* (by Indira Parthasarathy in Tamil) was published by Oxford University Press (2002).

GEORGE DARDESS is the Director of the Hispanic Institute for the Catholic Diocese of Rochester, New York. He has been writing widely on American literature. He is the co-editor of *Divine Inspiration: The Life of Jesus in World Poetry* (1997). Currently, he is under contract by Paraclete Press for a book to be entitled *Meeting Islam as a Christian.*

HIRA STEVEN taught English at Elphinstone College, Ruia College and Sophia College, Bombay, and Loreto College, Calcutta. She has been a visiting lecturer at the University of Mumbai since 1985, lecturing on the Postmodern novel.

JACQUELIN SINGH was born in Pasadena, California and educated at the University of California, Berkeley, where she received an M. A. in German literature and linguistics. She is the author of a collection of short stories, *Uncle's Concubine* (HarperCollins India, 1993) and two novels *Season* (Penguin Books India) and *Home to India* (Permanent Press, New York, 1997). For children, she has *Fat Gopal* (Harcourt Brace, San Diego, 1984) to her credit. *Dee Kay and the Laughing Nataraj* and *The Case of the Shady Sheikh* (1993) are collections for children published in India. A book reviewer and freelance writer, Jacquelin Singh lives and works in Chandigarh.

JANET GILTROW is Professor in the English Department of the University of British Columbia, in Vancouver, Canada. She is the editor of *Academic Reading: reading and writing in the disciplines*, 2nd ed. (2002), and the author of *Academic Writing: writing and reading in the disciplines*, 3rd ed. (2002). She has also written articles and book chapters in literary and non-literary stylistics, rhetorical theories of genre, and ideologies of language.

MAKARAND PARANJAPE is Professor of English at the Jawaharlal Nehru University and has taught at several American Universities. A well-known poet, novelist, critic, and columnist, he is the author of *The Serene Flame* (1991), *Playing the Dark God* (1992) and *Used Book* (2001) (poetry); *This Time I Promise It'll Be Different: Short Stories* (1994) and *The Narrator: A Novel* (1995) (fiction); and *Mysticism in Indian English Poetry* (1988), *Decolonization and Development: Hind Swaraj Revisited* (1993) and *Towards a Poetics of the Indian English Novel* (2000) (criticism). His edited works include *Sarojini Naidu: Selected Poetry and Prose* (1996), *The Best of Raja Rao* (1998), *The Penguin Sri Aurobindo Reader* (1999) and *In Diaspora: Theories, Histories, Texts* (2001).

MANJULA PADMANABHAN is a writer, painter, illustrator and cartoonist. Her books include *Hot Death, Cold Soup* (Kali for Women, 1996) a collection of short stories, and *Getting There* (Picador India, 1999) a travel memoir. *Harvest*, her fifth play, won the 1997 Onassis Prize for Theatre. It was published in India by Kali for Women in 1998 and subsequently in three separate international anthologies. She has illustrated 22 books for children including, most recently, her first novel for children, *Mouse Attack* (Macmillan Children's Books. UK, 2003). Her comic strips appeared regularly in The Sunday Observer (Bombay, 1982-86) and in The Pioneer (New Delhi, 1991-97). In 2000 she published a selection from the strips entitled *This is Suki!* (Duckfoot Press, 2000).

MARIA LUISA PARRA is affiliated to the National University of Mexico. She has worked mainly in the fields of literature and philosophy. She has just finished her thesis on the Freudian perspective on the hero-villain in the Gothic novel. She is presently working on Mikhail Bakhtin.

MEENAKSHI MUKHERJEE is a distinguished literary scholar. She has taught literature in several universities in India and abroad, the longest spell being at Jawaharlal Nehru

University, Delhi. She has written extensively on the novel. Her books include *The Twice Born Fiction: Themes and Techniques of the Indian novel in English* (1971), an anthology of critical essays entitled *Considerations: Twelve Studies of Indo-Anglian Writing* (1977), *Realism and Reality* (1984), *Rereading Jane Austen* (1991) and *The Perishable Empire* (2001).

PEGGY ROSENTHAL, an independent scholar, has many publications in language and semantics. A Ph.D. in English literature from Rutgers University, she has written *The Poet's Jesus* (2002) and *Praying Through Poetry: Hope For Violent Times* (2003).

SHOBHA VISWANATH is the creative director of The Karadi Tales Co. Pvt. Ltd. a children's publishing house based in Chennai. She scripts and edits stories for the audiobook series and since 1997 has produced 11 books for the series. She has also authored a picture book called *The Proud Story* for Scholastic India. She currently working on *A Skyfull of Stories* for Puffin India.

USHA HEMMADY taught English Sydenham College and Elphinstone College, Mumbai. She has numerous book reviews and articles in leading journals and newspapers. She is at present writing and reviewing and working as copy editor for various writers and publishers.

V. PADMA is a Senior Research Fellow in the Department of English, University of Madras working on A Critique of Literary-Cultural Ethos in India since 1980s. Her interests include Indian Literature, Indian mythology, film criticism and cultural studies. She has written on Namita Gokhale and Sunetra Gupta in the *Routledge Encyclopaedia of Post-Colonial Literatures*.

YASMEEN LUKMANI is Professor of English, and former Head of Department, University of Mumbai. She straddles the field of Applied Linguistics and Literature and has taken an active role in syllabus reform in English at the undergraduate and postgraduate levels. The syllabi she has spearheaded have become models followed in various parts of the country. She has conducted numerous teacher training programmes over the years, as part of a sustained campaign for improving English teaching methodology in the country. She has written widely in the field of applied English linguistics, in India and abroad, particularly in the areas of stylistics, testing, reading and writing. She has also produced two audio-cassettes, *Stories for English Language Learning* (2 vols) and *English Poetry from India*.